How to Live and Die

The Wisdom Culture Series

The Wisdom Culture Series is published by Wisdom Publications in association with the Foundation for the Preservation of the Mahayana Tradition (FPMT). Under the guidance of the late Lama Zopa Rinpoche, the series provides English-language readers with key works for the study and cultivation of the Mahayana Buddhist path, especially works of masters within the lineage of Lama Tsongkhapa and the Geluk school of Tibetan Buddhism. "Wisdom culture," an expression frequently used by Lama Yeshe, is a Dharma culture rooted in wisdom and compassion. The Wisdom Culture Series is intended to support this vision by transmitting the timeless wisdom of the Dharma through authoritative and accessible publications.

Volumes:

The Middle-Length Treatise on the Stages of the Path to Enlightenment, Tsongkhapa

The Power of Mantra, Lama Zopa Rinpoche

The Swift Path, Paṇchen Losang Yeshé

Perseverance, Lama Zopa Rinpoche

The Power of Meditation, Lama Zopa Rinpoche

More volumes to come!

• THE WISDOM CULTURE SERIES •

How to Live and Die

The Transformative Power of Meditating on Impermanence

Lama Zopa Rinpoche

Compiled and Edited by Gordon McDougall

Wisdom

Wisdom Publications
132 Perry Street
New York, NY 10014 USA
wisdom.org

Library of Congress Cataloging-in-Publication Data

Names: Thubten Zopa, Rinpoche, 1945– author. |
McDougall, Gordon, 1948– compiler, editor.
Title: How to live and die: the transformative power of meditating on impermanence / Lama Zopa Rinpoche; compiled and edited by Gordon McDougall.
Description: New York, NY, USA: Wisdom, [2025] | Series: The wisdom culture series | Includes bibliographical references and index.
Identifiers: LCCN 2024060631 (print) | LCCN 2024060632 (ebook) |
ISBN 9798890700018 (paperback) | ISBN 9798890700117 (ebook)
Subjects: LCSH: Impermanence (Buddhism) | Life—Religious aspects—Buddhism. |
Death—Religious aspects—Buddhism.
Classification: LCC BQ4261 .T58 2025 (print) | LCC BQ4261 (ebook) |
DDC 294.3/42—dc23/eng/20250521
LC record available at https://lccn.loc.gov/2024060631
LC ebook record available at https://lccn.loc.gov/2024060632

ISBN 979-8-89070-001-8 ebook ISBN 979-8-89070-011-7

29 28 27 26 25
5 4 3 2 1

Cover design by Gopa & Ted 2, Inc. Interior design by Tony Lulek.

Printed on acid-free paper that meets the guidelines for permanence and durability of the Production Guidelines for Book Longevity of the Council on Library Resources.

Printed in the United States of America.

MIX
Paper | Supporting responsible forestry
FSC® C005010
www.fsc.org

Please visit fscus.org.

PUBLISHER'S ACKNOWLEDGMENT

The publisher thanks the Lama Yeshe Wisdom Archive for sponsoring this book via a grant from Kasih Hospice, Malaysia.

CONTENTS

EDITOR'S PREFACE

RECENTLY, I REWATCHED Akira Kurosawa's *Ran*, the masterly retelling of *King Lear*, in which the old warlord is driven to madness by the betrayal of two of his sons after having refused to believe the grim warning of his third son. Shunning the words of honest people because their news is grim and embracing the flatterers pointedly reminded me of the argument between the climate scientists and the corporate denialists.

The world is a very different place now than it was when I previously watched *Ran* over a decade ago. The old world is rapidly fading, and it is very easy to be traumatized by the rapid changes taking place. It seems to me that our mental survival depends on embracing the changes at the deepest level. And we have a vital tool right here, in the traditional Buddhist subject of impermanence and death, one that will allow us to keep our mental well-being in the midst what is happening.

The Dharma is our real refuge in these difficult times and, as Lama Zopa Rinpoche says, quoting the Kadampa lamas, we simply cannot practice Dharma without a strong understanding of impermanence and death. We see the centrality of impermanence in the four seals—a set of four statements that outline the basic contours of authentic Buddhadharma, the first of which says, "All conditioned phenomena are impermanent." Indeed, without a good appreciation of death we will be forever bound up in short-term worldly concerns, unable to take action in a meaningful way.

The teachings on the perfect human rebirth found in the graduated path to enlightenment show us that our current human condition is precious and rare. Many of us are starting to appreciate the preciousness and fragility not just of our own life but of the planet's. The teachings on impermanence and death urgently tell us that we have not a moment to waste, that this precious and rare opportunity we now have can be snatched from us at any moment by death. As we will see with the nine-point death meditation that Rinpoche explains in detail, we not only need to practice the Dharma, but we need to practice the Dharma *now*.

The teachings on death provide us with the tool we need not only to face our own death without fear but also to become a better, more caring person. This is the gem that lies within this topic that Lama Zopa has taught on persistently over the last fifty years. Amazingly, rather than being morbid and depressing, there is a liberation in facing our own mortality rather than denying it. It can be both fascinating and transformative.

In general, quotations in this book have been taken from published texts and have been cited accordingly, but some are Rinpoche's own translations, which I have taken from the transcripts.

To compile this book, I have used teachings stored in the Lama Yeshe Wisdom Archive (LYWA), which have been lovingly recorded, transcribed, and checked by a vast number of people, all working to preserve the precious words of a great teacher. I would like to thank everybody who contributed to this book: those at LYWA, the audio team who recorded the teachings, and the team at Wisdom Publications, who are an inspiration to work with, especially Laura Cunningham.

I apologize for any errors found in this book; they are 100 percent mine. May this book be a tool to allow people to transform their life into the Dharma, where every thought and action is motivated to help others. May whatever merit gained from the creation of this book be dedicated to the long life and well-being of Kyabje Lama Zopa Rinpoche's reincarnation, and may he or she quickly be able to guide us again; to peace in this troubled world and an alleviation of the climate crisis; to the long life, well-being, and fulfillment of the wishes of all our holy teachers, especially His Holiness the Dalai Lama; and to the flourishing of the Foundation for the Preservation of the Mahayana Tradition and of the Dharma throughout the world.

Gordon McDougall
Bath, UK

1. REMEMBERING DEATH

The Most Important Education

A complete education about death is the most important education we can have. What death is, how we die, what minds we need at death, and what happens after death—only by knowing about death and rebirth can we actually fully understand what life is and so learn how to live fully.

In the West, such questions are generally not studied. What happens at the very beginning of this life and at the end are like two big black holes; there is no clarity. Even if there are some scientific explanations, these are based on hypotheses, not on personal experience. It seems that if scientists cannot verify something with their instruments, it doesn't exist for them. They can explain how, at death, the cells break down and the brain stops functioning, but they cannot go beyond that, and they can never address the real question of what happens to us at death.

While Buddhism might not talk about molecular structures or details such as that, on another level it has the whole answer, the complete education on life, death, and rebirth, especially when we study the subtle explanations given in the Vajrayana, the tantric teachings,[1] which explain about the gross, subtle, and very subtle bodies and minds.

Death is a reality, and to deny it, as many people do in the West, is very dangerous. Living with attachment and self-cherishing, our life becomes a hallucination. It is like we spend our whole life sleeping and don't see the reality of what is happening. And then, when death happens, it is a huge shock.

Suddenly, without any warning, death is there facing us. Life is gone, and there is nothing we can do about it. Our time to meditate, to develop our mind, has run out. Now, for the first time, we are facing the reality of life, and no matter how much fear we have, there is no time to do anything to remedy it.

When that happens, there is so much regret. When we die, it is said that we see our whole life clearly, like watching a documentary with everything we have ever done vividly played back to us—all the mistakes, all the selfishness, all the harm we have done to others. I have often heard that when people go through this, they die overwhelmed with great terror and regret. Even for somebody who rejects reincarnation, there is still great fear that something terrible is about to happen.

For worldly people, success has nothing to do with the mind. Their definition of success is being wealthy and famous. To have properties in many countries, to be able to make millions or billions of dollars in business; that is the definition of a successful life. Whoever can make the most money is regarded as the most successful—regardless of how stressful or berserk the life of that millionaire or billionaire actually is.

In fact, their inner life could be extremely unhappy, fragmented into pieces, with so much depression, sadness, dissatisfaction, and discontentment. Their life could be full of suffering—worse, even, than the poorest beggar, whose mind might be quite peaceful, with neither reputation nor wealth that could be lost. This happens because, relying on external things for happiness, their strong attachment has caused them to harm others (and themselves) to get what they want. They have no idea that true happiness only comes from developing a good heart.

Working solely for the comforts of this life is not what being a human is all about. Even animals do this. This is something even worms, rats, or ants can do, so the billionaire is no better than the worm in this. If we only work for material comfort, we will die with such regret. We need to go beyond this. We need to at least try to obtain a better rebirth. Then we will be able to die without fear, having the potential to continue to develop our Dharma practice in our next life.

Until we can fully understand our own life—how it is impermanent and how death is inevitable—it is very difficult to fully appreciate the unique opportunity we now have with this perfect human rebirth. Without that appreciation, the rest of the path to enlightenment will make little sense. That is why I say that understanding impermanence and death is the most important education we can have.

The teachings on impermanence and death come very early on in the Tibetan Buddhist system of study and practice known as *lamrim*, which means "graduated path." The lamrim was first explained by the great master Atisha[2] in his *Lamp for the Path to Enlightenment*. In the lamrim, the entire teachings of Guru Shakyamuni Buddha[3] are divided into a step-by-step approach, set up to lead us from where we are now all the way to enlightenment.

In traditional texts, such as Lama Tsongkhapa's *Great Treatise on the Stages of the Path to Enlightenment* (*Lamrim Chenmo*) and Pabongka Dechen Nyingpo's *Liberation in the Palm of Your Hand*,[4] we see that after discussing how to rely on the spiritual teacher, the lamrim begins with explaining the value and rarity of this precious human life, with its eight freedoms and ten richnesses,[5] followed by an extensive exploration of the reality of impermanence and death. These first steps on the path show us how we need to seize this life firmly and make the most of it.

The various subjects of the lamrim are divided into three levels of training known as the graduated path of the three capable beings, or the three scopes. They are the graduated path of the lower capable being, the graduated path of the middle capable being, and the graduated path of the higher capable being. These three correspond to the three motivations: the lower one of attaining a better rebirth, the middle one of attaining liberation, and the higher one of attaining enlightenment. The teachings on impermanence and death are part of the graduated path of the lower capable being and are designed to help us develop the aspiration for a positive, happy rebirth. We do this by clearly seeing the transitory quality of our present rebirth—how it can finish at any moment. We also come to understand what happens after our death—whether our next rebirth is one of happiness of suffering—depends on the positive or negative state of our mind. If we can fully realize even these very basic topics, we will be unable to bear *not* practicing Dharma; everything else will seem totally meaningless.

The teachings on impermanence and death offer explanations of what happens to us at death. Buddhism offers a complete picture of what death is. In the Abhidharma[6] texts there are detailed explanations of the nature of the mind and its continuity—that is, how it continues life after life. In the Vajrayana teachings, there are detailed and precise descriptions of how the extremely subtle mind moves beyond death to another life.

Being successful in worldly affairs, in obtaining the comforts of this life—food, clothing, reputation, and so forth—is not regarded as a capability in Buddhism; it is considered ordinary and without lasting meaning. Although the graduated path of the lower capable being is about securing a better rebirth, that is not the ultimate goal of our spiritual journey. By seeing how the whole of cyclic existence (samsara) is in the nature of suffering, we can determine to renounce samsara and attain the liberation of nirvana.[7] This is the goal of the middle capable being.

It is an amazing goal, but even that isn't the ultimate. We can take it even further by realizing that all sentient beings[8] are also suffering, and whereas we have the means to achieve true happiness, in their present states, they don't. And so we can develop great compassion for them and determine to achieve the exalted state of bodhichitta, the mind that determines to attain enlightenment in order to best benefit each and every sentient being. Enlightenment itself is the goal of the higher capable being.

The mind continues after death, taking a different body in a different realm. There are just two ways to go—we will be born either in the fortunate realms of the humans or gods or in the suffering realms of the animals, hungry ghosts, or hell beings. This is definite. Which rebirth we will take depends on karma, the karma we have created in this life and in previous lives.

Why Should We Be Scared of Death?

Why should we be scared of death? Life is full of problems, so if the consciousness or mind stopped at death—consciousness and mind are synonyms—all our problems would also cease at death. Therefore, wouldn't it be better to die as quickly as possible, rather than having to experience all of life's difficulties? Then, there would be no more problems; that would be the simplest thing. There would be no need to struggle to stay healthy and live as long as possible. There would be no need for meditation, for religion, for a spiritual path. There would be no need to build anything, no need to do anything!

It is not like that, however. When death happens, the mind does not stop with the physical body, like a candle flame finishing when the candle is extinguished. Just as the mind existed before this rebirth, even though the physical body ceases at death, the mind continues. And with it, all our problems.

The Delusion of Permanence

After attaining enlightenment over two and a half thousand years ago under the bodhi tree in Bodhgaya, India, Shakyamuni Buddha taught over 84,000 teachings and revealed the entire unmistaken path that can lead us to enlightenment. All these teachings can be summed up in one short four-line verse of the Buddha:

> Do not commit any unwholesome actions.
> Engage in perfect, wholesome actions.
> Subdue one's own mind.
> This is the teaching of the Buddha.[9]

This verse contains everything, including the four noble truths, the very first teaching the Buddha gave after his enlightenment. *Do not commit any unwholesome actions* contains the first two noble truths: the truth of suffering, which identifies suffering as a basic condition of life, and the truth of the cause of suffering, which identifies the actions and proclivities that cause all the problems we experience in our life. *Engage in perfect, wholesome actions* contains the third and fourth noble truths: the truth of the cessation of suffering—that there can be an end to this suffering—and the truth of the path that leads to the cessation of suffering.

These four noble truths constitute the entire Buddhist path, which is summarized in the third line: *Subdue one's own mind.* Why does this short line encapsulate the whole path to enlightenment? Because not one atom of suffering comes from outside. It is not created externally; there is no external agent that forces us to suffer. All suffering comes from within, from our own mind. In exactly the same way, happiness is not dependent on external factors but is a product of our own mind. Therefore, the method to destroy suffering and attain true happiness is to subdue our own mind. All of the Buddha's teachings lead us to this; hence the final line: *This is the teaching of the Buddha.*

All of the Buddha's teachings revolve around this central imperative of subduing one's own mind through avoiding nonvirtuous actions and performing only virtuous actions. This is the intent of all the teachings he gave, and because of that, everything within the Dharma—the teachings of the Buddha—exists to help beings overcome suffering and obtain happiness. In fact, that is the definition of Dharma: that which leads us away from suffering and toward true happiness.

By subduing our own mind, we achieve all happiness. The path that leads us to that is the fourth noble truth, the truth of the path. When we completely subdue our own mind, we achieve the cessation of suffering, which is either liberation as one pursuing individual liberation or enlightenment as a Mahayana practitioner.[10] With a fully subdued mind, we are a buddha. The Sanskrit term *buddha* means "fully awakened," and so we are a fully enlightened or awakened being, a being with a mind whose faults have been completely eliminated and whose good qualities—compassion, love, equanimity, the understanding of the nature of reality, and so forth—have been fully realized.

One of the fundamental problems that we encounter is our mistaken notion of permanence, our misapprehending phenomena that are, by nature, impermanent as permanent. All things—we ourselves, our own life, our body, our friends, our enemies, strangers, the sense objects, and so forth—are all naturally subject to change. They are all changing moment to moment and can perish at any moment. That is not how we apprehend them, however. We apprehend them as permanent, as unchanging. Our friends, our possessions, our life, and so forth, exist in this way now, and they will continue to exist like that. Although, rationally, we might know this is not true, we live our life with this concept of permanence. So long as we remain trapped in our concepts of permanence and true existence, there will be only problems and suffering.

If we could live our life with the right understanding that sees all phenomena as impermanent, we would see the reality of how things really exist; with no reason for ignorance, anger, attachment, or the other delusions to arise, there would be few problems in life. With no reason for dissatisfaction to arise, we would naturally have a contented mind. This way of seeing gives us freedom; the other way locks us into the prison of our delusions.

How the Concept of Permanence Creates Dissatisfaction

Clinging on to things as if they are permanent becomes the basis for the dissatisfied mind, causing disturbing emotions to arise. It becomes the basis for problems and pain in our life, such as relationship problems, loneliness, and so forth. A mind under the control of the concept of permanence is, itself, a disturbed mind, and that disturbed mind then creates more confusion and pain, bringing more of the disturbing thoughts that cause even more problems in our life.

At present, we hold on to and believe in this concept of permanence. A permanent object simply does not exist; and yet that is exactly how we see things: we see them in a way that is the complete opposite of how they actually exist. In our life, we see a permanent I, a permanent life, permanent people around us, permanent possessions, and so forth. We think these things are going to remain as they appear to us now, which is completely contradictory to reality. We fail to see that because they are under the control of causes and conditions, they are all changing with every second. They are conditioned phenomena—things that come into existence due to various causes and conditions. That is why change happens, that is why decay happens, that is why things perish.

As we get older, many friends that we thought of as permanent will die. We have probably all seen this within our own family: a family member becomes sick and dies, and the whole family feels so much pain, their eyes full of tears. Even passing a house where somebody has died, we can feel an unsettled atmosphere. When people talk about a friend who has died, they speak in a whisper, almost in disbelief. They cannot comprehend how this has happened.

Seeing this happening to other people, it is not difficult to know that this will definitely happen to us at some time as well. And when that time comes, we will probably be so upset, so fearful. When the out-breath is much stronger than the in-breath, we will start to really know that death is near, and we will think, "I am really dying. I, this person, me, *now* I am dying." And we will start to realize that we will soon be separated from our beloved family, our cherished possessions, and all the things that had seemed such a permanent part of our life.

We might look back on our life and wonder whether anything we have done has been worthwhile. We might see how our life has been completely empty, and thinking how we have wasted this precious life, we could feel such regret.

Death will definitely happen to us one day, possibly very soon. Unless we can learn to subdue our mind before then, we could experience great suffering. The Dharma is the only thing that can benefit us at death. Without the Dharma, there is no chance of escaping the lower realms. With the Dharma, we can be assured of a better future life, and we can even achieve ultimate happiness, attaining liberation or even enlightenment, through which we will be able to work solely for the well-being of all other sentient beings.

Being Aware of Death

We currently have a perfect human rebirth, this combination of body and mind that is so favorable to realizing our full potential. If it were to last three or four hundred years, there would be no hurry; we could possibly just have a rest. But the truth is that our perfect human rebirth could very well finish at any moment, and we are not free to choose our next rebirth. Only our karma can determine where we will be born, and if we find ourselves in the lower realms, we will have no chance at all to create any virtue and thus escape even more terrible suffering. Being born in the lower suffering realms is like being in a very dangerous place on a completely dark night, without moon or stars, surrounded by fog and totally unprotected. There is great suffering and always the chance of falling into even more suffering.

If we do not desire a sorrowful death and a terrible rebirth, we have to purify the negative karma we have accumulated and ensure we don't create any more negative karma; that is the essential preparation. That is why we must train ourselves to maintain a constant awareness of death, which is the basic method for preparing ourselves for the most crucial time in our life—the moment we die. Just as a car or a plane needs fuel to move, we need the fuel of remembering death, otherwise we won't have the incentive to renounce nonvirtue, we won't have the energy to turn our back on worldly concerns and concentrate only on practicing Dharma.

We need to take the Dharma firmly into our hearts. No matter how much Dharma we know, if that understanding is merely intellectual, it will be unable to transform our life. We can know thousands and thousands of Buddhist texts by heart; we can be a world authority in Buddhism lecturing at the great universities; we can defeat other scholars in the most esoteric debates. But none of that means anything if we have not made preparations for our own death. Without such preparation, when death comes, we will die in great terror, unable to control the arising of negative states of mind.

The truth is that we are racing toward death. From the moment we were conceived in our mother's womb, we have been rushing toward the Lord of Death. It is like we are in a police car with the sirens screaming, driving at high speed through the streets to our execution. We can arrive at any moment; we just don't know when.

Facing the Consequences

We are constantly changing—every month, every day, every hour, every minute, every second, we are changing. Even during the shortest possible period of time—counted in Tibetan Buddhism as one-sixty-fifth of the length of a snap of the fingers—we are changing. As each year passes, each month, each week, each day, each hour, each second, that much of our life finishes. As each second passes, our life gets shorter and shorter.

We don't want to think about this passing of time. In the West, it is not tactful to ask somebody their age. People color their hair as they get older or have plastic surgery to pull their skin this way or that. They try to deny impermanence, always grasping on to the fantasy of youth. We see this with pop stars, like Michael Jackson, who are constantly going into plastic surgeons to "fix" their faces, reshape their noses, or have their breasts pulled up! As they get older, they need more and more plastic surgery, but it still doesn't stop them facing the great suffering of getting older and dying.

Only when we understand the true nature of reality will we be able to move beyond suffering. Suffering is not created externally; it is the product of the deluded mind. And just as the mind creates suffering, with wisdom and compassion it can overcome suffering. We are ultimately in control of our own life; we are the ones who create our own suffering and happiness. All external factors are just conditions; the real cause is the state of our own mind.

As it is mentioned in the *Abhidharmakosha*,[11] the various worlds are all born from karma. We sentient beings who live on this earth have accumulated specific karma created in the past. This is why we were born in this particular time and place, although each of us experiences the world differently depending on our karma.

Even climate change has been created by our own mind. Besides the ongoing global problems of war and poverty that continue to beset us, there are now also more and more problems related to the weather, with ice melting and terrible storms becoming more frequent, even destroying whole cities. Some countries that used to be cold are now much warmer due to climate change. When I asked Khadro-la[12] about the likelihood of another destructive earthquake hitting San Francisco, she explained the greater danger is from rising sea levels.

Under the control of disturbing thoughts, our internal elements become unbalanced, causing problems for ourselves and collectively disturbing the external elements.[13] This internal imbalance affects the external environment, causing floods, droughts, hailstorms, famines, and the many other natural disasters that bring great harm to sentient beings. I think the world is getting nearer and nearer the time when, as it is said, the teachings of the Buddha will have finally set like the evening sun.

But while global problems may increase, at the same time, there will still be individual beings who are able to practice and become enlightened. We should never take for granted the opportunity we now have to transform our mind. Just as one individual's mind can cause incredible suffering—like Osama bin Laden's—one's individual's mind can also cause incredible happiness. We can use our mind not only to stop harming others but to benefit them, bringing happiness to all sentient beings.

At this moment, most beings are suffering in the three lower realms, especially in the hell realms. Their suffering has not been created by God or fixed by some other being. It is only a creation of those suffering beings' minds, just as, in a dream, we may sometimes suffer in a fire or from fierce demons attacking us. In the same way that these fearful dreams and visions are the creation of our deluded mind, so the sufferings and the realms of the hell beings are created by their own minds.

However, the hell realms are not the same as dreams; they are karmic creations of the ignorant mind. This is similar to the way that two different people can perceive the same place differently. To one person, the place might be a paradise; to another, it might be hellish. The classic example in Buddhist literature is of a container of liquid that is seen by a human as a glass of water, by a god as nectar, and by a hungry ghost as disgusting pus. Although the object is the same, the view varies according to the level of mind and the karma of the being experiencing it.

Each being's samsara is a creation of that mind. Similarly, each being's enlightenment is also brought about through their own mental activity.

Just as we are responsible for the karma that keeps us trapped in the cycle of suffering, so we are also responsible for, and capable of, lifting our mind *out* of that suffering. But caught up in ignorance, how can we ever change our mind from suffering to happiness? This is where the Dharma becomes a vital tool. As the Buddha said,

> The Great Ones do not wash away sin with water;
> they do not rid beings of suffering with their hands;
> they do not transfer realizations of suchness onto others.
> They liberate by teaching the truth of suchness.[14]

We are the only one who can rescue ourselves, but we need the Buddha's help to do that. We are like a person who has fallen down a deep well in which the walls are smooth and slippery and there is no way at all we can climb out. We are trapped and we will certainly die. But in the circle of sky above we see a face; a compassionate person has seen us fall and has come to help. They can't lift us out, but they can throw down a rope and hold onto the other end as we climb out. Unless we realize that the rope is our means of escape, there is no way out of the well. We need to grab the rope and pull ourselves up with it. If, on the other hand, we *like* being down the well, then of course we won't even think of escaping. We need to see the danger we are in and recognize the help that we need to escape that danger.

The infinite enlightened beings' only wish is that each and every sentient being is free from suffering. If they could accomplish this without the sentient beings working from their own side, this would have been done countless eons ago, and there would be no more samsara. But it is not like that. The buddhas can teach and guide, but we must climb the rope to freedom ourselves.

The more we practice Dharma by refraining from nonvirtuous actions and by purifying the delusions that plague our mind at present, the stronger our essential practice of Dharma will be. Whatever actions we do every day—studying, working in an office, working at home, raising children—if our actions serve to cleanse our mind of the stains of negativity that hold it back now, then we are practicing the Dharma. It does not depend on being a Buddhist. We could be Hindu, Muslim, Christian, Jewish, or no religion at all. As long as our actions are motivated by a virtuous mind and not a nonvirtuous one, we will slowly clear the delusions from our mindstream and cut the cause of suffering. This is something we can all do. For this, however, we need to know exactly what a virtuous action is, and that requires wisdom. Without wisdom, we may think that an action is a Dharma action while, really, it is only developing the negative mind.

If we are reborn in the lower realms in our next life, we will have to endure the most terrible suffering for many eons without being able to create any positive karma at all. We will remain continuously cycling in samsara, moving from one terrible environment to another, only extremely rarely finding a fortunate rebirth.

None of us wants to experience suffering, even for five minutes. Even the thought of being burned by a match or bitten by a flea frightens us, so how can we bear to think of all the sufferings of the lower realms that we must experience for such unimaginable lengths of time? When we decide that we must do whatever we can to avoid this, we will see that there is nothing whatsoever that can help us except the Dharma. And because death is definite and the time of our death is very uncertain—it can happen any moment—the time to start practicing Dharma is now.

Living for Others

To ensure a positive rebirth and the ability to continue our spiritual journey as purely as possible, we need to be fully prepared for death. There are many practices within Buddhism that can help us, such as accumulating extensive merit,[15] doing prostrations, reciting mantras, and so forth. Besides these specific purification practices, we need to have a good heart in our daily life and try to help others as much as possible.

Wherever we are, whatever we do, whoever we are with, if we always practice holding the welfare of all beings in our heart and remain aware that the purpose of our life is to help others, we will never create the causes of suffering, either for ourselves or others. Furthermore, we become the source of happiness for all sentient beings, and they, in turn, become the cause of our enlightenment.

Whenever we see an insect, we should think that we are here to give happiness to that insect; whenever we hear a bird, we should think that we are here to give happiness to that bird; whenever a friend phones, we should think that we are here to give happiness to that friend; whenever there is a difficult person at work, we should think that we are here to give happiness to that person. That is our job, to give happiness to all others.

With such a mindset, not only does practicing the Dharma become a joy but, because we are aware of its great importance, we are able to have the meaning of the Dharma in our heart instead of just studying the words dryly. This is the way to subdue our own mind, to make it softer, more patient, more tolerant, more compassionate, more loving, and more kind to others.

Having developed a more expansive mind that cherishes others, any serious problems that might occur in our life will no longer devastate us. Even if our business fails completely or we are diagnosed with cancer, since our focus is on the happiness of others, these problems will not hit us as hard. When somebody becomes angry with us, because we are deeply concerned about that person's happiness, we won't react back with anger or indignation; we will do whatever is necessary to help that person. Living with a good heart doesn't mean never having problems, but it means that we will be able to deal with those problems in an entirely different way, in a compassionate way that helps others and helps ourselves. Living for others allows us to remain happy when problems arise rather than becoming upset or depressed.

By experiencing problems that arise with compassion and care for other living beings—whether it is becoming sick, having relationship problems, losing our job, or whatever—the problem can even become enjoyable, like experiencing a pleasant sense object: delightful music for the ears, delicious food for the mouth, beautiful forms for the eye.

These very basic qualities of care and compassion for others give value to our human life, making the possession of this human body utterly meaningful. This is what brings real joy into our life.

2. THE SHORTCOMINGS OF NOT REMEMBERING DEATH

THE TRADITIONAL BUDDHIST TEACHINGS on impermanence and death talk about the shortcomings of not remembering death and the advantages of remembering death. Looking at these points, it becomes very clear that our Dharma practice can only really develop strongly when we take this topic seriously. Although, of course, there are many more, the six shortcomings of not remembering death are usually given as follows:

- We do not remember to practice the Dharma.
- We remember but we postpone our practice.
- We practice but we do so impurely.
- We practice purely but not continuously.
- We create nonvirtue.
- We die with much worry and fear.

If we fail to remember impermanence and death, we will be unable to remember to practice the Dharma. We may think we will die someday but not today. This misconception lasts until the day we die, and then it is too late to do anything worthwhile. This is one of the great disturbances to Dharma practice. In his *Lamrim Chenmo* Lama Tsongkhapa says,

> With each passing day people think, "I will not die today; I will not die today," clinging to this thought until the moment of death.[16]

Not remembering death means we can so easily become distracted. Being always under the control of distractions means that every day we think we need this and need that and then go about trying to obtain what we believe we need. And so our life is taken up in trying to obtain possessions and we have no time for anything meaningful.

With this conception of permanence, we get up in the morning, certain we will live for a long time, for another fifty or sixty years. When we go to bed, we still have this thought. With this misconception blocking us from practicing the Dharma, we are not motivated to do even a single practice. And then death comes—we experience the car accident or the heart attack where our life suddenly finishes—and we are still harboring this wrong conception.

We Do Not Remember to Practice the Dharma

If we fail to remember death, we will not remember the Dharma. When we feel that we definitely won't die today, today's concerns become more important than preparing for death. Wrapped up in working for our own selfish ends, we create negative karma, leaving no time to create any merit at all.

We become overwhelmed by worldly problems—money problems, health problems, mental problems, relationship problems. And when death comes, we see how we have wasted our life and what terrible suffering awaits us.

Every day, we plan things with the underlying assumption that we will complete them, that we not going to die. That sense of permanence, that instinctive feeling that we will live for a very long time, will betray us one day—because it is not true. Countless people who have started the day with the thought that they would not die have never finished the day.

Living with this sense of permanence, we are unable to truly practice Dharma. We might think we should practice, but we become lazy, putting it off, feeling that worldly activities are more important. Under the control of the eight worldly dharmas,[17] we are unprotected. At the time of death, all the hard work we have done clinging to this life, trying to enjoy the transient pleasures, all the nonvirtuous actions we have committed because of that—killing, stealing, sexual misconduct, lying, and so forth—all this is revealed as utterly meaningless.

Without remembering impermanence and death, nothing we do becomes Dharma, not even our Buddhist practices. Eating, sleeping, working, and shopping are all done with a sense of permanence and, hence, only act to reinforce our own selfish interests. This is also the case with prostrating, meditating, saying mantras, reading Dharma books, and so forth. Nothing becomes Dharma unless we remember death.

Not remembering death places us in great danger. Whenever somebody disturbs us, we are overwhelmed with delusions, like a tsunami sweeping away a whole city. When we are faced with difficulties, we become so filled with our own problems that we are totally unable to practice whatever Dharma we might have learned.

Even when life is going smoothly, if we don't remember impermanence and death, there will be great hindrances to our Dharma practice. We will find that we have no time or energy to meditate. We have plenty of time to sleep, watch television, eat, or look at the scenery, but reading a Dharma book or meditating seems too hard. People in the West often say they have no time to meditate because they are so busy. Usually, however, hindrances to practicing the Dharma come from the mind, not from external circumstances. If we had the correct attitude, it would be easy to practice the Dharma.

The Kadampa geshés[18] say that if we don't remember impermanence and death when our day begins in the morning, then nothing we do throughout the whole morning becomes Dharma; everything just becomes the worldly activities of this life. In the same way, if we don't remember impermanence and death at noon, then nothing we do in the afternoon becomes Dharma; it remains worldly dharma, the activities of this lifetime. And if we don't remember impermanence and death in the evening, then whatever we do in the evening and throughout the night will only be worldly dharma, which creates even more nonvirtue.

If we observe all the actions we do on a typical day, we will probably see that we do more selfish, nonvirtuous acts than selfless, virtuous ones. From the moment we rise and have that first cup of coffee, are we working selflessly for others or are we working for our own self-interest, trying to obtain a bit of sense pleasure and enjoyment? When we go to work, when we interact with colleagues at work, when we have lunch, when we go out at night, is it done with a bodhichitta motivation—to attain enlightenment in order to free all beings from suffering—or is it solely for our own comfort? If most of our daily actions are done out of self-interest, then that will surely also be so when we are about to die.

We Have a Hundred Thoughts but Not One Thought

There is a wonderful saying from the Kadampa geshés:

> You have a hundred thoughts, but the mistake is not having thought the one thought.

This was said for Tibetans but it is equally relevant for Westerners. Westerners have generally received a rich education. You know a lot and you are excellent at things like making money. You have "a hundred thoughts," billions of thoughts in fact, but the big mistake most of us make is not having the thought of impermanence and death.

Not reflecting on the nature of our life—that it is impermanent and will end in death—means that even though many of us met the Dharma a long time ago, we still haven't achieved any of the realizations of the lamrim—not even attaining the graduated path of the lower capable being that ensures us of a good future rebirth.

We are still a long way from realizing that one thought that understands death and impermanence. We are still bound up in the meaningless affairs of this life. We might know all the lamrim topics by heart—from guru devotion to emptiness—and be able to teach on them continuously. We may even call ourselves tantric practitioners. We might even earn money and fame lecturing on Buddhism, but our "hundred thoughts" don't lead us any nearer to happiness. Without a real understanding of impermanence and death—this "one thought"—all the other thoughts mean very little.

Reflecting on impermanence and death, we naturally let go of attachment, and our problems dissolve. Where there was a mountain of problems, now there is only more and more genuine peace and happiness in our heart—all from this one thought, the thought of impermanence and death.

Reflecting on impermanence and death is the start of our Dharma path. It gives us the bravery to do whatever is needed in order to develop on the path, to overcome the hindrances we find in our way. It gives us the courage to turn away from the meaningless activities that ensnare worldly beings, those activities that create samsara. Because it gives us the courage to never again engage in negative actions, it destroys the cause of the lower realms. Having developed a strong sense of the reality of impermanence and death, every action we do becomes virtuous.

We Remember but We Postpone Our Practice

Even if we are able to remember the Dharma, unless we reflect on impermanence and death, we will be unable to practice properly. Although we may see that practicing Dharma is worthwhile and that we need it in order to be happy, the work of worldly concerns still somehow gets in the way. This life's affairs must be dealt with before we can think about anything else.

For example, imagine you have traveled abroad for a meditation course and upon returning home you have resolved to continue to meditate and study the Dharma. First, though, you will need to get a good job. Then, you determine to practice the Dharma as soon as you have bought a new apartment. Then, you decide to work for several years so you can have enough money to go into retreat. You will practice the Dharma when you have dealt with the problems you have. Soon, you have a partner and children and you must consider looking after the family and the children's education, so it is still not the time to focus on meditation. But you resolve that as soon as the children have grown up, you will find the time to go to a quiet place to meditate and practice the Dharma.

Somehow, there is always the work of this life to take care of before we can practice the Dharma. Months go by, years go by. The wish to practice is there, but the thought of the eight worldly dharmas is stronger. And so, through not remembering impermanence and death, the Dharma is postponed. And then, before we actually get around to it, we die.

Until our desire to practice the holy Dharma is stronger than our desire to pursue worldly dharma, this is how it will be. Only when we remember impermanence and death, will we gain the deeper motivation needed to practice Dharma. Until then, there will always be a thousand good excuses why we must postpone our Dharma practice.

Even though we know how beneficial it is to recite even one mala[19] of a mantra, somehow it does not get done; we are too busy doing worldly activities. We put off the retreat until later, when we think the conditions will be better. Waiting for better conditions that never come, waiting for free time that never happens, we somehow never do anything worthwhile.

We might have the intention of studying the Dharma, but that intention by itself, while very worthwhile, will not bring us any benefit. The time to practice the Dharma is now, when we have time. Soon it will be too late.

If we could continuously reflect on impermanence and death, we would find that we have plenty of time to practice Dharma, and even our everyday work would become meaningful, even while living in the city without changing jobs or partners. Our external life would be the same, but our mind would be completely changed. Everything we do would become pure Dharma.

We Practice but We Do It Impurely

Having no sense that we might die prevents our Dharma practice from becoming pure. Perhaps we can overcome our reluctance to meditate and no longer postpone our practice, but somehow the energy is not there to make our practice effective. When we sit down to meditate, our mind is sluggish or distracted, running off to other more exciting things. We know the value of prostrations and other practices for collecting merit, but it seems so hard to actually do them.

We try to meditate, but we don't have a strong motivation. Underneath the wish to practice is the wish to have comfort in this life. The lack of awareness of death is robbing us of the pure motivation that would cause us to work only for the goals of liberation and enlightenment.

Although we may perform Dharma actions, in our heart there is still self-interest. For example, we may make offerings because we want people to respect us and think we are a very religious person. They see that even though we live in the West, we still meditate every morning, sitting in a perfect meditation posture! Without checking our motivation carefully, this mixing of a Dharma and worldly attitude can easily happen. It's like delicious food that has been poisoned.

We need to get to the stage when our daily Dharma practice is as important for us as our breakfast. In fact, it needs to be as important as our breakfast, lunch, dinner, and all the snacks we have during the day! If, for some reason, we have to miss out on lunch, it can often feel as if our world is collapsing! Do we feel like that when we miss out on doing some part of our daily Dharma practice?

And even if we start to practice Dharma purely, it will falter unless we continually remember the reality of death. Losing our pure motivation, small troubles preoccupy us and cause us to lose the energy to meditate. That is what will happen if we do not continually remember death.

We know logically that we might die at any moment, but this realization rarely sinks in deeply because, in our heart, we have a deep belief in our own permanence. Until the knowledge of death truly penetrates, we will get very little done. We need to get to the stage where we discard the need for the comforts of this life like we discard used toilet paper. Lama Tsongkhapa said that we should wake up with the complete acceptance that we will die today. Instead of rejecting death, we should see it as a very real and definite possibility.

We Practice Purely but Not Continuously

Without a deep sense of impermanence and death, even if our Dharma practice is strong, it will not be consistent or continuous. Our very last thought before our death is the key to our next rebirth. It is so important to be able to control this last moment.

There is the story of a man who felt that he had achieved a high enough level of practice that he told his wife and friends that he was ready to die. He knew that his next rebirth would be in the pure land of Padmasambhava,[20] and that he could go any time he pleased. However, even though he still asserted that he had the power to choose whatever rebirth he wished, he told his family that he preferred to stay with them rather than go to a pure land. Because he had not, in fact, freed himself from his attachment, he had no choice; he was still tied to samsara.

Holding the thought for a few days that we might die today and then forgetting it is not enough. To be able to continuously and purely practice the Dharma, it is necessary to hold this thought continuously. It is quite common to push too hard when beginning a new Dharma practice—for example, we may be enthusiastic about going to the mountains and meditating, while having very little understanding of Dharma. We may meditate intensely for a month or two but then let go and return to our previous routines, basically back to the same position that we were in before.

Sometimes we squeeze too tightly, and when it becomes too much, we let it all go and overdo the relaxation, losing whatever progress we have made. We often don't really know what we need to do in order to continue to practice and progress. We may fool ourselves, thinking that we are learning a lot about Buddhism, yet fail to see how vital it is in our life. We know the words, but they fail to become the medicine that we need to cure us. And because we feel that we are not getting better, we lose the energy to continue.

We have to be free from attachment before we die, and knowing that we can die at any time, we see we cannot waste a moment—we need to start to develop renunciation now. Life is full of the conditions that cause death. Right now, we have all the conditions for developing our mind to its ultimate, but those conditions will not last long.

We Create Nonvirtue

Of the traditional list of six disadvantages of not remembering death, the last two have to do with the suffering we experience through creating nonvirtuous actions. The Seventh Dalai Lama says,

> After birth, you don't have the freedom to rest a moment
> In the race you run toward Yama, the Lord of Death.[21]

When we are at the moment of death, we will think, "I am really dying now," understanding that we are leaving our relatives, possessions, and body. We will look back on our life and see all the things we will never experience again, causing great attachment to arise. In a strict meditation retreat, we might feel incredibly isolated and miss our normal comfortable lifestyle terribly, but this is nothing to how we will feel at the time of death, when we are about to lose everything.

We know nothing of karma—or rather, we act as if we know nothing. Karma, by its nature, expands. The karma of killing a mosquito, if not purified, expands within a couple of weeks to become as powerful as the karma from killing a human being, and it keeps expanding. Every negative action we do has this potential, sitting in our mindstream as a karmic imprint, ready to ripen as suffering when the conditions come together. Within one hour we create countless tiny negative actions, all capable of bringing huge suffering unless we can purify them in some way.

Unmindful of this, we thoughtlessly commit nonvirtuous actions, which the Buddha listed as ten:

- killing
- stealing
- sexual misconduct

- lying
- slander
- harsh words
- idle gossip
- covetousness
- ill will
- heresy[22]

In a single day, we can very easily commit all ten nonvirtuous actions, all through our attachment and clinging to this life.

The definition of *nonvirtue* is that which brings suffering. It describes any action motivated by one of the three poisons of attachment, anger, and ignorance, but it is mostly attachment and clinging to this life that is the source of our suffering. Anger and the other negative states of mind stem from this desire for samsaric life. Attachment to the happiness of *future* lives, conversely, is not considered nonvirtue, because such desire encourages us to engage in virtuous actions, such as acts of devotion, generosity, and so forth.

Nonvirtuous actions can be the result of any negative state of mind. Usually, killing is the result of hatred, but it can also result from ignorance. Mao Zedong, the Communist Chinese leader, was responsible for the terrible destruction of holy objects in Tibet as well as the deaths of so many Tibetan and Chinese people. In his meeting with His Holiness the Dalai Lama in 1955, he told His Holiness that he thought religion was poison,[23] so, for him, the destruction of monasteries and holy objects and the deaths of so many monks, nuns, and laypeople in Tibet was justified. This is ignorance—specifically, the ignorance of not understanding karma.

If we could see the consequences of our actions, we would be a lot more careful. Instead, we generally live our life heedless of the motivation for our actions, ruled by the mindset of clinging to the happiness of this life. The eight worldly dharmas are our boss and we obey them completely. We pursue fame, reputation, comfort, possessions—whatever we mistakenly see as the cause of happiness—regardless of the consequences.

Wrapped up in mundane concerns, we believe that *my* wishes are more important than *yours*. It is like a family in which everyone wants something different for dinner. One wants steak, one wants turkey or fish, one is a vegetarian. Whatever is chosen, the others are unhappy because their wishes were disregarded, not even tasting the food offered. On a larger scale, this self-cherishing attitude results in wars and the destruction of whole nations.

Unless we remember death and become aware of the karmic effects of our actions, we will continue to be ruled by our greed, anger, and ignorance, like a cat who can't stop chasing after mice. Under the sway of such negative emotions, we see whoever gets in the way of our attachments as an enemy to be harmed without a second thought. So, what can we do to reverse this negative spiral that keeps us trapped in the suffering of samsara?

We Are Trapped in Samsara

We should begin by recognizing that this life of freedom and richness that we now enjoy is unbelievably rare. It is more precious and rarer than a universe filled with wish-granting jewels.[24] Even to have a human body without the attributes of the perfect human rebirth is an extremely rare gift.

Shantideva[25] shows this at the start of his wonderful text *A Guide to the Bodhisattva's Way of Life*, where he says,

> This unique opportunity, so difficult to obtain,
> once it has been obtained can bring to realization all human aspirations.
> If then one does not set the mind on what is beneficial,
> how will this opportunity come again?[26]

We have worked so hard to create the conditions to have this opportunity and we must continue to work hard so it is not lost, to ensure we have another perfect human rebirth. Pure morality, great generosity, and the fervent wish to have such a body are the three things we must develop the most if we are to succeed.

If, on the other hand, we squander this precious opportunity, then how can we possibly expect to have it again? Why would we waste this amazing potential and risk untold suffering for ourselves in future lives? It's like having a winning lottery ticket and not bothering to cash it in. This perfect human rebirth is like fertile ground, and to waste its potential is like planting worthless seeds in the ground and getting no return from the rich soil.

Chöden Rinpoché[27] describes samsara as the continuity of the contaminated aggregates. These contaminated aggregates are both caused *by* karma and delusions and are, themselves, the cause *of* further karma and delusions that arise. This viscous cycle thus traps us in a never-ending cycle of suffering. In *A Hymn of Experience*, Lama Tsongkhapa says,

> If you do not put effort into contemplating true sufferings—the faults of samsara—
> You will not develop the wish for liberation.
> If you do not contemplate true origins—the steps for entering samsara—
> You will not understand how to cut the roots of samsara.
> Therefore, rely on weariness, definite emergence from samsara;
> And cherish the knowledge of what binds you to samsara.
> You, the perfect guru, practiced in this way.
> I, who am seeking liberation, will also practice in this way.[28]

Samsara is not a physical place but a state of mind. It is not a country, a city, a prison, a swamp. Our body is not samsara; our hair is not samsara. Some people see monks and nuns and mistakenly think, "If I shave my head, I will be free from samsara." They think that putting on robes frees them from samsara. There is the story of a lama's attendant who had such a wrong concept. He thought that laypeople were in samsara and the sangha weren't, and that simply by changing his clothes he could be free. When a lama saw him in robes, he asked what practice he was doing. The attendant replied, "I have *just* given up samsara." When the lama asked how, he replied, "I have taken off my pants!"

As long as we are not free from karma and delusions, we are not free from suffering and we are not free from samsara. Samsara is the suffering state that we live in continuously, without choice. As long as we have this imperfect body with this deluded mind, we must suffer. Geshé Sopa in *Steps on the Path to Enlightenment* says,

> When you are forced to wander helplessly in cyclic existence, constantly assaulted by innumerable types of suffering, completely under the power of karma and afflictions, you cannot even do anything to help yourself, so how could you possibly do anything that would benefit others? This helpless entrapment is the door through which all the troubles of all beings arrive.[29]

Samsara goes around and around like this, always circling, with karma ripening and karma being created, ceaselessly tying us to this wheel that turns and turns without end, pushing us higher then lower, higher then lower, from the fortunate upper rebirths to the various terrible sufferings of the lower realms, from the tip of samsara to the lowest hell realm. We are never free from the burden of the karmic imprints. We will never be free from this cyclic existence until we can overcome our delusions.

At present, we are carrying the burden of a human existence, caused by karma and delusions. When we die, we will take another bundle of aggregates—the mental and physical constituents that are the sum total of what we are—and continue to carry this samsaric burden. Whether we are reborn as a cat, a dog, a bird, or a worm, we continue to carry this samsaric burden, although now in the aggregates of an animal. Whatever manifestation we are born into, the cause is karma and delusions. The suffering might be greater than our previous life or it might be less, but it is still suffering.

Worldly work is not only ultimately unimportant, but it is also unending. Like the ripples on a lake that just keep coming over and over again, samsaric life is an endless repetition of meaningless, frustrating actions. As long as we remain trapped in samsara, the work we must do will never end and it will never bring any satisfaction. That is the very nature of samsara. We have been doing samsaric work since beginningless time, and we have still not finished it. There is no way to complete it—how can there be? We do it to gain some satisfaction, and yet it is incapable of satisfying us, so we must just keep on doing it, like a rat on a treadmill.

In contrast, practicing Dharma can be finished very quickly, depending on how skillful and how determined we are. It is said that to attain enlightenment by the sutra method requires three countless great eons—a very long time indeed! But we can also do it within two countless great eons, or within sixteen lifetimes, or within three lifetimes, within one life, or even within twelve years. It's possible. The great yogi Gyalwa Ensapa,[30] using Vajrayana techniques, achieved enlightenment within twelve years without much effort.

If being unmindful of impermanence and death is like a huge mountain of obstacles that brings untold problems—so huge and solid it seems unassailable—remembering impermanence and death is like an atomic bomb that can level that mountain in one second. It is so powerful. Guns and stones can't do anything to the mountain, but the atomic bomb of remembering impermanence and death easily can, subduing the mind and controlling anger and attachment and all the other deluded minds. By remembering impermanence and death, we see our deluded minds as the nonsense they are and wonder how we were ever so crazy. Our petty attachments and animosities seem so childish. Then, when somebody has the potential to harm us and make us angry, we see the danger and we can easily avert it.

We Die with Much Worry and Fear

Even people who reject reincarnation and karma can experience a lot of fear at the time of their death, terrified about what will happen after they die. Some people die happily and peacefully, others in great fear. Whether there is happiness or fear at the time of death is normally related to the way a person has lived; it is the result of their past attitudes and actions.

Everybody knows about Elvis Presley. He was possibly the most famous man in the world for a while, especially to young people. They wanted to emulate him, to look and act just like him. He was the most successful entertainer in the world, but the year he was going to die, maybe while he was singing the last song, he was crying, his tears flowing out. And the audience were crying too. It was very, very sad. Even though he had achieved the best reputation in the world and had so much money and so many friends, there was still such sadness and depression in his heart when he saw he was going to die without having achieved satisfaction. All this is due to the attachment and clinging to this life.

The richest businessperson or the most important world leader may seem beyond worries, but they can die feeling totally terrified, crying like a child. Surrounded by friends and servants, surrounded by the richest possessions and total comfort, they can be far more afraid than the poorest beggar. As they near death, they can see all the negative actions they have done in their life in order to have all their wealth and power and know that none of this will help them at all now.

This can be our death too. We can die in real terror, deeply upset at losing the things and people we love and are attached to and horrified at what awaits us. We are unable to face the fact that there is absolutely no choice, that everything that we cherished in this life must be left behind, even this body that we have nurtured and taken such care of since we were very small. We have no control; we have no choice; everything will cease to exist for us at the moment of death. For many people, this thought is too awful, and they break down and weep uncontrollably.

If we have not learned to let go of our attachment by the time we die, that attachment will cause us the most horrible death. It is quite possible that, due to our negativities, when we die, we will experience karmic visions, terrifying experiences that are a portent of our next life.

The life we know will fade, and the future life will appear before us, and it can be unbelievably horrifying, with fearful animals, humans, and maras[31] with weapons attacking us, terrible sounds ringing in our ears—so many different things tormenting us. Those around us cannot see these things, but they will be very real to us.

The imprints left by a person's past negative actions produce terrifying hallucinations. Just as we cannot see the dreams of other people, even of someone sleeping next to us, we cannot see the hallucinations of a dying person. Such fearful appearances are the result of negative karma and a sign that the person will be reborn in one of the lower realms.

This happened in Tibet to a leader who had tortured many people. All the people he had tormented while he was a leader came to him as he was dying and attacked him and pressed down on him. He screamed to his friends and servants that he was being attacked, flailing his arms in the air in terror, but they could neither see what he was seeing nor help him. His past victims—not actual people, but projections of his own mind—were taking revenge for the terrible things he had done to them.

Once, a great meditator called Geshé Jampa Wangdu[32] helped a dying neighbor who lived near his meditation cave near Dharamsala.[33] The man was screaming and opening his mouth as if he was drowning. His face was distorted and fearful as he kept trying to ward off invisible enemies—a great many sheep, who were digging into his body with their sharp horns, attacking him and trying to gore him to death. It seems that he had been a butcher and these were the kind of sheep that he regularly killed. He had never thought that there was anything wrong with his occupation, and so had had no thoughts of needing to purify his mind. But now as he was dying, these visions were manifesting. Even before his consciousness left that human body, it was already creating the hell realm it was going to inhabit for eons.

If there were no future lives, if we just ceased to exist when this body dies, then why should such fear arise at the thought of the life to come? Talking to some students at Vajrapani Institute in California who worked in hospitals, I asked them which kind of people had more fear at the time of death. They replied that, in their experience, alcoholics did. If there were no past or future lives, why should fear arise, whether a person is an alcoholic or not? The fact that they become afraid shows that, as they were dying, there were signs of what awaited them after death.

These visions of their next rebirth are more than just fantasies of a deluded mind; they are karmically created visions of what the future will definitely be. Perhaps, for somebody who enjoyed fishing, even if they are not aware that there was anything wrong with killing the fish and worms, because the karma of killing is nevertheless on their consciousness, they may suffer terrifying visions of being attacked, causing them to die with so much fear.

Studying people who are dying like this can be such an important lesson for us. When we see a person dying in fear like this, it is good to look back on the kind of life they led and see what might have caused that fear to manifest.

If we haven't made any preparations for death, we will have no remedy at the time of the death for any problems that arise from our attachment, anger, and so forth. Without having already overcome these delusions, our strong clinging to things will cause us great terror as we die. It is too late at death; no remedy can be found. That is what makes it so hard to die. Instead of thinking that what follows after death will be another, better life, one with more freedom to practice the Dharma and benefit others, we are overwhelmed with fear that everything we cherish, especially our own life, is finishing.

We Go to the Lower Realms

If our very last thought is a nonvirtuous one, even though we might have tried to practice some Dharma in our life, our death becomes nonvirtuous and that becomes the cause of rebirth in the suffering lower realms. If we die with an angry mind, or an attached mind, or with any delusion—jealousy, miserliness, and so forth—we assure ourselves of an unfortunate rebirth. That is why it is extremely important to maintain a virtuous mind as we die.

Death is the transition from one state of samsara to another. Once, when Lama Atisha's disciple Dromtönpa[34] asked him to explain the results of actions done with attachment, Atisha answered,

> Ask me what the results are of actions done desirous of the happiness, fame, and respect of this life and I will tell you: they are only the results of this life. Ask me what will happen in your next lives and I will tell you: you will be a hell being, a hungry ghost, or an animal.[35]

The positive or negative state of our mind when we die will decide where we will be reborn. Whether our attitude is a positive or negative one can be seen by how we lead our life, each hour, each day, each month, each year, from birth until now. We can see where we will be reborn by examining our mind. We don't need a fortune teller.

If our life ended at this moment, it's almost certain that we would be reborn in one of the three lower suffering realms. If we look at the karma we create in just one day and see whether it is positive or negative, we can easily see that we create more negative karma than positive karma. We might try to do virtuous actions, but because we usually have either no real motivation or a very weak one, these actions are often incomplete. And if we do manage to have a good motivation, we often spoil it by allowing pride or miserliness to arise. Somehow, our virtuous actions are always weaker than our nonvirtuous ones. And this is just talking about one day from this life—we have been accumulating negative karma for countless lifetimes.

As we die, whichever thought we are most habituated to will be the one manifesting and directing our next rebirth. Can we be completely sure it will be a virtuous one? Until we remember death and change our attitude to one of virtue, we are right to fear the lower realms.

I have taught on the lower realms many times—it's one of my favorite subjects—so I won't go into detail here, but I urge you to read as much as you can about the lower realms.[36] The more you are convinced such places exist and the more you understand how close you are to being there, the more determination you will have to never create negative karma again. Understanding the lower realms is a very powerful tool to ensure we avoid future suffering.

There are three lower realms: the realms of the animals, of the hungry ghosts, and of the hell beings. Each is unimaginably terrible; each has more suffering than the one above it.

The first time I was in Australia, I met a monk who denied the existence of the hell realms, his reasoning being that this was an ancient teaching that is not relevant to this modern world. Even though there are whole sutras devoted to describing and explaining the lower realms, and even though many of the teachings on karma make little sense unless we can see how our actions link to past and future lives, this monk felt that the hell realms were no longer pertinent. Just because these teachings are not comfortable for us does not mean we should deny them. If we reject this most vital aspect of the Buddha's teachings, our misunderstandings about the Dharma can easily grow deeper and deeper. The Buddha, the great yogis that followed him, and the learned monastic scholars of both past and present all explain the lower realms clearly and from their own clairvoyance. They have seen such realms and they know they exist. To say that we know better than the Buddha and those who followed him is both arrogant and very silly.

If we are afraid of even the temporal physical sufferings that we sometimes experience, why shouldn't we fear the greater sufferings that exist in the lower realms? The only reason we are not afraid is because, due to our clouded, deluded mind, we do not remember the beginningless times we have suffered in those realms. We have even forgotten the sufferings from the earlier parts of *this* life.

The hell realm exists, the hungry ghost realm exists, and nobody here now, no matter how many books that person has read, can disprove that. The burning iron house of one of the hells seems inconceivable to us, but can we guarantee that we will never have to experience it?

If we have created the cause, we will definitely experience the result. That is the immutable law of karma. And if we have created the cause for the lower realms, we will definitely be reborn there. We need to know this.

The animal realm, the realm we can see, has the least suffering of the three lower realms, although if we examine the lives of the various animals, we will see just how miserable and hopeless they are. The main cause of being reborn as an animal is ignorance, and an animal's problems often come from its stupidity. Its main suffering is being eaten and hurt by other animals (including, of course, humans, who eat and exploit animals terribly). The carnivores have no choice but to kill, creating terrible karma and future suffering, and the herbivores have no choice but to be killed. Even the most pampered pet is trapped in ignorance, unable to understand anything other than how to manipulate its owners. It certainly cannot understand the Dharma and how to create the causes of happiness.

Imagine how terrible it would be if you suddenly became an animal. Your face starts to grow fur, your body contracts and you have to go down on four legs, you grow a tail. Or maybe you suddenly become a bird. Perhaps you think it would be wonderful to fly, but for a bird, flight is just a means of killing insects or escaping predators; there is no joy there at all. Imagine desperately digging the ground for worms while always worried about the hawks hovering overhead. Becoming an animal, the lower realm being with the least suffering, is still a truly awful rebirth.

The second of the lower realms is that of the hungry ghosts (*preta*). The main cause of rebirth in this realm is attachment, and the hungry ghost's main suffering is hunger and thirst. Because of attachment, these beings are unable to find what they are most attached to: food and drink. A hungry ghost's body is the perfect instrument of suffering, with a huge belly and a tiny throat. Even if it can find food, there is no way it can swallow it. But usually, hungry ghosts must wander for hundreds of years, desperately looking for even a scrap of food and never being able to find it.

Remember, if you can, a time when you had no food to eat for a day or two for some reason or other. Remember how obsessed with food you became. I'm sure you wouldn't have been able to practice the Dharma at such a time. Life as a hungry ghost is not just for a few days but for hundreds of years. The hungry ghosts do not die of hunger, but their desperation for food and drink never lessens either. If we were to be reborn as a hungry ghost, we would not be able to bear it for a second, and yet we would have to endure year after year, without respite, for hundreds and even thousands of years.

Even so, the hungry ghost realm is infinitely preferable to the lowest of the lower realms, the hell realm (*narak*). The main cause of being reborn as a hell being is anger, and the main suffering is extreme heat and cold. It is impossible as a human being to have any idea what degree of heat or cold a hell being has to experience. It is said that the heat of the "coolest" of the hot hells is much hotter than the fire that consumes the universe at the end of the last great eon, which, in turn, is seventy times hotter than the hottest fire that exists in our world system. And each of the succeeding hells—there are eight hot hells—doubles in heat and doubles in suffering. Hell beings are as huge as a mountain, and their skin is as sensitive as a baby's such that even touching it with a soft cloth would be agony. And yet, the hell being must live in states where its body is in constant contact with a ground of red-hot iron.

Even the least of the hot hells, the *hell of being born again and again*, is unimaginable to us. Born in a place of red-hot iron mountains and terrible winds, the being must continuously fight enemies and is constantly being cut into pieces but unable to die. This goes on over and over again, until its karma to be in this hell is finished, which is said to be billions of years.

Then, with each succeeding hell, the duration and the suffering double. In one, the being is cut with red-hot wires along its body; in another, it is crushed to a pulp between two great mountains, usually in the shape of the beings it killed in its previous life. In the *hell of crying* the being finds itself in a burning iron house without windows or doors. The heat of these flames and suffocating air is doubled in the next hell, where the being is trapped in *two* burning iron houses, one inside the other. The *inexhaustible hot hell* is the worst suffering there is in samsara, where the being has no body as such; it is like the butter of a butter lamp that has melted to become one with the flame. The only way the hell being can be distinguished is by the screams that it emits.

In the same way, the cold hells are colder than we can imagine, and there are also eight, each much colder than the one before. There are also *surrounding hells*, like the suburbs that surround a city, and *occasional hells* where the beings must endure terrible suffering, but not constantly. For example, there is a story of a butcher who took precepts but could only abide by them at night because of his job. Because of that, in his next life, he enjoyed incredible luxury and sense pleasure in a luxurious mansion with beautiful goddesses at night, but during the day, the house turned into a burning prison, and the women into fierce dogs who ripped him apart.

We need to understand that if we have created the negative karma, we could soon be exchanging this body for the body of a hell being. Hell beings create their own world from the heavy negative actions they have done in previous lives. This is why in *A Guide to the Bodhisattva's Way of Life* Shantideva says,

> Who fashioned so carefully the swords of hell, the pavement of red-hot iron?
> The Sage has explained that all and each of these arise from sinful thoughts.
> Therefore, in the three worlds there is nothing more frightful than mind itself.[37]

Similarly, Shakyamuni Buddha said,

> No one has arranged the thousands of ways of suffering but your own evil mind.

When we read accounts of the hell and hungry ghost realms, we are afraid. We might even be so terrified that we reject the descriptions, denying them completely. We, who cannot even bear the slightest pain, will be unable to bear the heat or cold of the hell realm or the hunger and thirst of the hungry ghost realm, and yet we will be forced to endure those sufferings for thousands and thousands of years—for thousands of eons—without the slightest respite.

The protection from such a rebirth is refuge in the Buddha, Dharma, and Sangha. If we can die with refuge in our heart, if we can remember prayers like *The Heart Sutra* or mantras such as Chenrezig's, it is impossible to be reborn in the lower realms. Even having faith in an ordained member of the sangha, let alone all the Three Rare Sublime Ones,[38] will save us from the lower realms. Refuge—real refuge—is so powerful. Nothing in Western science or medicine can stop us from experiencing the unbearable suffering of the lower realms. Nothing in modern education or in self-help books can help, only refuge.

At present, we are just the reflection of a Dharma practitioner because, as Pabongka Dechen Nyingpo said, we practice the eight worldly dharmas as our heart meditation. But, by remembering impermanence and death, we can renounce this life and free ourselves from the fear of the lower realms.

3. THE ADVANTAGES OF REMEMBERING DEATH

IMAGINE THAT YOU ARE an archer standing in a field and drawing back your bow, ready to loose an arrow. But as you are about to shoot, you realize that you don't know where the target is or what you should be shooting at. In this situation, no matter how skilled an archer you are, you are not going to have much success if you don't know what your target is—and may even cause harm! Similarly, unless we know the purpose for meditating on impermanence and death, we will likely become confused and not make much progress. Instead of our meditations being the medicine to cure our delusions, we could simply become terrified at losing what we so cherish. Therefore, we need to be clear that *the purpose of meditating on impermanence and death is to destroy our delusions*. That is the whole point.

If we live next to a river that is rising and just about to flood, we shouldn't wait until the water is pouring into our house to do something to escape. We need to see the danger and to take precautions before it's too late. In the same way, we need to prepare now so we can die with a virtuous mind and be assured of a positive rebirth.

We all need to remember impermanence and death all the time. For those of us who don't yet practice the Dharma, we should start by realizing our predicament, which will motivate us to seek out the Dharma and practice it. If we already practice the Dharma, it is useful to constantly reflect on impermanence and death, to keep in mind the changes that are always occurring and the brevity of this human life. If we do this, the distractions that hinder our Dharma practice will fall away. Even advanced meditators who are committed to long retreats in order to attain high realizations need the energy and determination brought by the meditation on impermanence and death, without which their advanced practices would be impossible.

If we wanted to go to India from Europe we could walk—that is theoretically possible—or we could ride a bike or drive a car, but these methods would take a long time and we might very easily lose heart before we get there. It is so much easier to fly, which allows us to get there quickly and without much effort. Remembering impermanence and death is like flying to India rather than walking there; it gets us to our destination quickly and easily.

Remembering impermanence and death is a key component of all levels of Dharma practice. If our goal is to attain a better human rebirth, it allows us to easily do that; if our goal is full enlightenment—to become a buddha ourselves—it enables us to do that as well. Remembering impermanence and death can also bring us so much happiness in this and future lives.

The six benefits of remembering impermanence and death mentioned in the traditional texts are important to know:

- We avoid the lower realms and attain a perfect human rebirth.
- We attain great power to destroy the negative mind.
- We gain great benefit at the beginning of our practice.
- We gain great benefit in the middle of our practice.
- We gain great benefit at the end of our practice.
- We have no fear at the time of death.

We Avoid the Lower Realms and Attain a Perfect Human Rebirth

No matter how much we might suffer as a human being, it is nothing compared to the suffering we will have to endure if we end up in the lower realms. No matter how little freedom we have, we are infinitely free in comparison.

The reasons we practice the Dharma are the same reasons that we do anything at all: to have happiness and to avoid suffering. The huge difference between the Dharma and worldly activities is that the Dharma leads to lasting happiness, while worldly activities lead to suffering. It is as simple as that. We need the Dharma even more than we need hospitals or doctors because without eliminating the principal cause of suffering, no problem can really be cured. We might be able to stop some forms of suffering using worldly methods, but unless we eliminate the main cause, these problems will just recur. Our whole life is spent fixing problems with temporary, ultimately unsatisfactory solutions, only to have them, or others like them, recur again and again. If we want to truly destroy the suffering that plagues us, we must transform the mind by practicing the Dharma.

We human beings have so much intelligence and potential. But just being able to understand things doesn't mean that we are always able to keep our mind virtuous. We still find it very difficult to control our mind, to stop dissatisfaction, anger, jealousy, and other negative thoughts from arising constantly, to have a pure attitude without self-cherishing and without desire.

We must make the most of our human potential. What if we were reborn as an animal? As a human being, we can fight for our human rights, but an animal can't fight for its animal rights. When an animal has a problem, it can't go to its union and go on strike. It can't come out into the streets waving a placard. There is no way to make an animal understand what virtue means, what the cause of happiness or the cause of suffering means. Even though a parrot can be trained to recite the mantra OM MANI PADME HUM, it is just imitating the words; it cannot understand the meaning. As a human, we can understand so easily.

So, the first benefit of remembering impermanence and death is that doing so has the power to prevent us from being reborn in the lower realms. When things go wrong in our life—when a relationship goes very wrong, when a valuable possession is stolen, when we lose our job—things that would have caused us to completely lose our mind in anger, worry, and despair, if we remember impermanence and death, we will see that there is no point in being attached. The situation will still be there, but the suffering comes from the deluded mind of attachment or anger that arises in reaction to that situation, and it is this delusion that is the cause for a rebirth in the lower realms. Remembering impermanence and death, and seeing how silly we have been, enables us to destroy any negative states of mind that would have normally arisen in such circumstances.

With this simple practice, we are saved from the lower realms. Even if we do no other form of Dharma practice in this life, if we can gain a deep understanding of impermanence and death we will be saved from the lower realms. This thought has the power to save us. How amazing! It has unbelievable benefit.

We Attain Another Perfect Human Rebirth

The minute we change our attitude to one of concern for others, we find true peace, true happiness in our life. We might still work in the same job, but now we find it less stressful and more satisfying. Before, we worked purely for the happiness of this life; now, our efforts are dedicated purely to the happiness of future lives and to helping others.

In *A Hymn of Experience*, Lama Tsongkhapa says,

> This body of leisure, more precious than a wish-fulfilling jewel,
> Is found but once. Though difficult to obtain again,
> It finishes as quickly as lightning in the sky.
> Having reflected in this way, realizing that all worldly activities
> Are like winnowed chaff,
> You must take its essence day and night.
> You, the perfect guru, practiced in this way.
> I, who am seeking liberation, will also practice in this way.[39]

These wonderful lines really show how vital taking the essence of this perfect human rebirth is. There are two main points we need to realize: (1) that this life is like a flash of lightning, ending so quickly, and (2) that our worldly activities are utterly without essence, like empty husks of grain, and must be discarded so we can focus our efforts on the very essence of this life, the Dharma.

Only now are the conditions perfect. This life we have allows us to do anything we want, but it can be snatched away from us at any moment. Therefore, we must take hold of its essence *now*, in this very moment.

When death comes, whatever we have experienced during this life, even moments of incredible happiness or incredible suffering, will seem fleeting and insubstantial, like a flash of lightning in the sky. At death, this life, which is so short, just dissolves, like a dream upon awaking. What, then, is the point of getting attached to anything or getting angry with anybody? Lama Tsongkhapa tells us to take the essence of this human existence day and night.

If we were moving to New York tomorrow, we wouldn't be concerned about redecorating our current apartment to make it more comfortable, knowing we will never see it again. Our mind would be concerned only with the move and what we will do when we get to New York. In the same way, if we have a good understanding of impermanence and death, we will be concerned with the preparations for death and what happens beyond that.

But as long as we are under the delusion of permanence, where impermanent things appear to us as permanent, we will definitely suffer, and liberation will be impossible. The only result we can expect is more samsara. On the other hand, having a good understanding of impermanence makes a huge difference, as big as the difference between the sky and the earth. Realizing impermanence and death leads to the end of suffering.

With this realization, even when difficulties arise, we will face them with a new mind. Just as the pain of an antivenom injection would seem like nothing if we had been bitten by a poisonous snake, when we realize impermanence and death, whatever problems might arise will seem like nothing compared with the great suffering of dying with a negative mind.

Remembering death is like medicine for whatever problems we are experiencing. When anger begins to arise, the thought of our imminent death bursts it like a pin popping a balloon. It is like pouring cold water into a pot of boiling water, cooling and settling it: when our mind boils and bubbles with all the agitation that we experience, rather than letting it boil over and cause more and more suffering, we can bring the cool water of remembering impermanence and death and immediately calm the agitation.

By a miracle, it seems, we have attained a perfect human rebirth. It is as Nagarjuna says in *Friendly Letter*:

> With all its many risks, this life endures
> No more than windblown bubbles in a stream.
> How marvelous to breathe in and out again,
> To fall asleep and then awake refreshed.[40]

It's incredible to have had the opportunity to wake up this morning, to be alive, to not have died in the night. When we wake up, we should think, "I wasn't one of those who died last night. This is so unbelievable. How fortunate I am." Then, we should think how precious each second of having this perfect human body is, like a whole sky filled with wish-granting jewels.

What is most surprising for me is how we have left the body of a hell being or a hungry ghost or an animal and somehow attained this human body. While in that lower realm, it is virtually impossible to create any positive karma at all, and to attain a human rebirth we need to have created so much positive karma. And yet we have made it. That is quite extraordinary!

Attaining a perfect human rebirth is like pushing a huge boulder up a steep mountain. It has been incredibly hard work, but we have made it to the peak. And now we must not falter. If we create nonvirtuous actions, we could easily be reborn in the lower realms; it would be like letting the boulder slip and plummet back to the bottom of the mountain. Once we become lost again in the lower realms, it would be so difficult to start the long climb back up. We can see how even animals, the beings of the one lower realm visible to us, find it next to impossible to create positive karma. If we were an animal—or worse, a hungry ghost or a hell being—we wouldn't even hear the phrase "human rebirth" let alone have the ability to create the karma to be reborn as a human being.

But we have found this perfect human rebirth. How amazing! Not only have we attained a human body but we have this perfect human rebirth where we have met the teachings of the Buddha and where we have the possibility to progress all the way to enlightenment. If we don't do everything we can to ensure another human rebirth after this one, that is completely foolish. To squander this life and end up in our next life with a body with thousands of legs or as a dog or chicken, there is nothing more foolish this this; there is nothing crazier than this.

We must seize this unique chance. Reflecting on impermanence and death makes us brave. But it is not the kind of bravery that gives us the courage to get angry and harm our enemies or to develop attachment to desirable objects; it is not the courage to do samsaric activities; it is *real* courage, the courage to happily persevere in doing what is virtuous. This is the courage that will enable us to achieve happiness in all future lives to come, to actualize the path that leads to freedom from suffering, to actualize the five Mahayana paths and the ten *bhumis*.[41] This is the courage to collect merit for three countless great eons, practicing the six perfections to complete the merit of wisdom and merit of method and achieve the two kayas, the *rupakaya* and the *dharmakaya*.[42]

Reflecting on impermanence and death gives us the courage to become like Milarepa, who bore great hardships to practice the Dharma and achieve enlightenment in a single lifetime. Milarepa initially faced unbelievable hardships to practice the Dharma, but he persevered, practicing Dharma in a cold and isolated cave, with nothing in the way of possessions or comforts. What gave him the courage to do this was his realization of impermanence and death.

We need to not just consider *our own* impermanence. The impermanence of other sentient beings is there to see every day. On television, in the papers, every time we hear an ambulance's siren, we are reminded of the many sentient beings around us who have just died. They are giving us the best lesson on impermanence and death. Whenever we hear somebody has died, we should think that that could easily have been us, that we could die this year, this month, today. But when we see others suffering like this, it also becomes a teaching on compassion. Every being is suffering, and so every being equally deserves our compassion. We must develop bodhichitta for them, to help free them from suffering and lead them to enlightenment.

The purpose of our life is to benefit others. Otherwise, even if we were to stay healthy for thousands of years, with no cancer, dementia, or arthritis, if our life is not useful in bringing happiness to other sentient beings and freeing them from suffering, it would be an empty, meaningless life.

The purpose of our life is not to be healthy and live long, nor is it to be wealthy or to have a good education. It is not even to ensure that we have a happy rebirth. The ultimate goal of our life, whether we are rich or poor, healthy or unhealthy, is to be of benefit to other sentient beings.

We Attain Great Power to Destroy the Negative Mind

Not Concerned with the Guesthouse of the Body

In his text *The Thirty-Seven Practices of the Bodhisattva*, the great bodhisattva Thokmé Sangpo[43] explains,

> Loved ones who have long kept company will part.
> Wealth created with difficulty will be left behind.
> Consciousness, the guest, will leave the guesthouse of the body.
> Let go of this life—
> This is the practice of bodhisattvas.[44]

Thokmé Sangpo calls the body a "guesthouse" and the mind a "guest." That's how it is. The mind is just a temporary guest staying a few nights in the guesthouse of the body. And yet we spend our whole life working to support this impermanent body, which we will only have to leave with great sorrow. In that vein, the great yogi Phadampa Sangyé[45] gave the following advice to people of the village where he settled:

> Families are as fleeting as a crowd on market day;
> People of Tingri, don't bicker or fight.
> Wealth and poverty, like a magic show, just seduce and deceive;
> People of Tingri, don't let the knot of avarice bind you.[46]

Our spouse, our family, our children, our friends and relations: all seem permanent, but they are actually very transient. We should, therefore, regard them all as temporary guests just passing through our life. We might remain together until death—their deaths or ours—but, still, the relationship is impermanent, not something that continues forever. In the larger sweep of our many lifetimes, it's like being together for a few hours, a few minutes. At the moment, we do not think this way, but at the time of death we will see our whole life as being like a flash of lightning, so short. Therefore, there is no reason to become attached to others, and no reason to fight with them and wish them harm. That does not mean we should immediately distance ourselves from those we love, just that we should work to overcome our attachment to them.

With no understanding of karma and reincarnation, we might come to see how short life is, and even how we might die at any time, but this might only cause us to cling *more* tightly to our friends and possessions. It may make us feel that we must enjoy all the things of this life even more, because they will soon be gone forever. Thinking in this way, we fail to understand the cause of happiness and suffering, and trying to attain worldly happiness, we end up creating even more nonvirtuous karma. In short, we jump into the fire of samsara with no idea why we must endure so many problems, so much suffering.

Just as we should see family and friends as temporary guests—like a crowd in a market that will soon disperse—we should see all our possessions, including our body, as temporary things that we have just borrowed for the time being. When we die, whatever we own will be gone, even though, momentarily, they are ours for this short time. We should think about possessions as temporary loans, like books from a library. That way, attachment and miserliness will not arise, and when we separate from our friends and possessions, there will be no unhappiness or regret.

Our body was given to us by our parents, and we will soon lose it. Therefore, we should also see it as just on temporary loan. This body is made entirely from the three elements of the mother and the three of the father;[47] it is a sack of dirty things, of impurities, and yet this is the thing we are most attached to. Why be attached to our body when very soon our body is going to become a corpse? When we spend so much money and effort clothing and feeding our body, we should remember impermanence and death and remind ourselves that we are only clothing and feeding a corpse. When we go to sleep, we should feel that the blanket covering us is a funeral shroud covering a dead body.

In the same way, we should see our possessions as just things we have borrowed from other people and which will soon be the property of others again; why, then, should we feel such painful attachment to them? We may currently have such attachment for the house we live in, feeling that it is permanently ours. But our house will soon belong to somebody else. In a very short time, our new house could be a grave, a box in the ground with a stone on top engraved with our name. Our bones might still be there in our new house, but our consciousness will have moved on.

The great yogis often use human skullcaps and thigh bones in their practice to remind themselves of the impermanence of life and of death and to remind themselves not to become caught up in attachment to this life. When they hold a skull that had once definitely belonged to somebody who once lived and breathed, they are reminded that now only the skull remains and that, very soon, it will be the same for them.

Nobody can tell from external appearances who has renounced this life and who hasn't. Renunciation is a state of mind, and the number of possessions we have is no indication at all. Renouncing this life is a mental action, not a physical action. If it were only a question of not having any possessions, all the animals and insects who have no possessions, living in holes, without food to eat, should be regarded as highly renounced beings. At Lawudo Retreat Center near Mount Everest, there are many caves that used to be the homes of great yogis. When I went to see them, the caves had been used by yaks for sleeping, probably because the caves were warm. If the definition of a yogi is somebody who lives in a cave, perhaps we should consider the yaks in that area great yogis!

Tomorrow or the Next Life?

Attachment can arise so easily before we have a chance to realize it. Like a rat seeing poisoned meat in a trap and unthinkingly running to it and eating it, often when we see an object of attachment, the thought of wanting to possess it explodes in us and we are helpless. When this happens, there is no peace at all. Meditating on impermanence and death keeps us constantly conscious of the trap of attachment. Just as the rat will avoid the trap if it knows that the meat is poisoned, when we see the poison in attachment, we will be able to avoid it.

A popular quote says,

> You cannot be sure which will come first:
> Tomorrow or the next life.
> Therefore, do not put effort into tomorrow's plans,
> But instead it is worthwhile to attend to the next life.[48]

Are we really sure that our next life won't begin before tomorrow does? We should ask ourselves this. How sure are we that we will still exist tomorrow, that tomorrow will come for us? Even if we are doubtful that there will be a next life, it is still very worthwhile to make arrangements just in case.

Worldly people actively prepare for many things. If we live in a place that could flood, it is wise to build a dam or a levee in advance to protect ourselves. In the same way, it is wise to prepare for death well before it comes, rather than only thinking as it is happening that we should have prepared.

Reflecting on impermanence and death, we see that clinging is pointless; we are like a prisoner in a cell, awaiting execution, utterly uninterested in our previous life—the beautiful possessions, the luxurious home, the expensive clothes. At death's door, the condemned person has no concern for the things that seemed so important before.

In the same way, when we have realized impermanence and death, we will find no attraction in temporal things, not really caring whether some object is cheap or valuable, good or bad. We might be given delicious food, but its taste will not seem important. Countless holy beings have lived without the need for possessions, friends, and material comforts, achieving incredible happiness without them.

Milarepa lived in the most austere conditions possible, eating only nettle soup, but because his happiness was based on internal realizations and not external sense pleasures, he was blissfully happy. This happiness didn't happen immediately or instinctively. He had to turn his back on worldly pleasures, and in doing so, he made his life so simple, so beneficial, so happy. By contrast, most people spend their lives chasing meaningless activities, and their lives are complicated and unhappy. The life of a yogi and the life of a worldly person are complete opposites. Yogis get rich in merit, realizations, and happiness; we get rich in possessions, confusion, and misery.

A Sense of Impermanence Overcomes Anger and Ignorance

Just as remembering impermanence and death is crucial in overcoming the mind of attachment, it will also overcome anger. Anger is the most frightening state of mind. One instant of anger can destroy eons of positive karma, and if we are angry as we die, we will have to endure an unimaginable length of time in the terrible suffering of the hell realm. Because this is the worst possible thing that could happen to us, we need to fear the mind of anger.

Anger comes from attachment, from not getting what we want. That frustration leads to hatred and violence. Whether it's one person, one family, a hundred people, a whole city, or an entire country, being unable to control the mind of anger leads to so many problems. We can easily see how wars start from the dissatisfied mind of attachment always wanting more—more power, more wealth, more property, more respect.

Think of all the effort that it takes to create a city: all the buildings, the bridges and roads, the businesses, schools, hospitals, and so forth that are built to make the people comfortable. All this can be destroyed in an hour by hatred and anger.

When we are angry, we are unhappy and disturbed. With our confusion, we feel more and more suffocated, bringing on more and more problems. Unable to think straight, we blame others for our condition and strike out. No matter how much somebody may have harmed us, what is the point of getting angry? The harm that person did is finished; the harm we are continuing to do ourselves with our anger goes on; and if we die with an angry mind, the harm will be incalculable. By continuing to be angry, we are only cheating ourselves.

If we were to die with a mind full of anger, we would definitely be reborn in the lower realms, and almost definitely in the hell realm. We should visualize what that would be like—the red-hot iron ground, the black-line hell, and so forth—and see that it is our anger that is driving us there. Because we obviously do not want to experience this, we must determine never to create its cause.

When we are overwhelmed by anger and are in danger of greatly harming another being, if we can remember that death can happen at any time, suddenly we will find our anger is ridiculous. Harming others does not serve any purpose and it harms us greatly. Remembering impermanence and death has the power to destroy anger.

Furthermore, remembering impermanence and death has the power to cut *all* deluded states of mind. It cuts off not only uncontrollable anger, but also uncontrollable pride and ill will. By remembering impermanence and death, we will no longer be under the sway of our delusions, no longer driven to creating negative karma. We become very calm and relaxed, very peaceful.

With a mind free from anger, attachment, and the other strong delusions, we are able to overcome the most fundamental delusion, ignorance. Because we can focus much more easily, we will be able to realize the absolute nature of the self, investigating emptiness without the distractions of an agitated mind.

We have to be strongly focused to effectively meditate on emptiness. This cannot happen if our mind is polluted with attachment, controlled by anger, or overwhelmed by ignorance. It is like trying to hold a candle flame in a strong wind: the flame might be bright, but we need it to also be steady to see what we are looking at. If it is flickering in the wind, we will never be able to see the object. In meditation, we must not only *understand* the object of meditation; we must also be able to hold the object clearly and steadily.

Remembering Death Conquers Laziness

If we were walking through a forest where a tiger was known to roam, our eyes would be wide open all the time. We wouldn't daydream at all. All we would think about would be the tiger, watching and listening for it, fearful of every movement or noise. The tiger in the forest is our death, which can pounce at any moment. If we could see this, we would always be so mindful. We would have no problem with concentration.

Instead of always thinking the opposite—that we will not die—we need to reverse our attitude and live with the knowledge that we could die at any moment. We should deliberately think, "I will definitely die tonight, in the next hour, at this time." With that thought, we will have the energy to make any action pure and perfect. There will be no hindrance, no distraction. Protected from hindrances, our concentration will naturally last much longer.

Thus, in *Four Hundred Stanzas*, Aryadeva says,

> Whoever has the firm conviction,
> "I am going to die,"
> Has completely relinquished attachment.
> So why would he fear even the Lord of Death?[49]

Remembering death conquers laziness. There are three types of laziness that we need to look out for. The first is the laziness that finds excuses for not doing things because we feel they are beyond our capabilities. The second is the laziness that prefers negative actions to positive ones, seeing only short-term pleasure as important. The third type is the laziness that destroys our energy to practice Dharma and makes us postpone it. This is the laziness that seeks distractions when we want to concentrate or that makes our mind dull when we are trying to understand something.

Because we do not remember our past sufferings and do not know those that lie ahead, we work motivated largely by ignorance and greed. Being driven by attachment, spending all day and all night working for samsaric comforts, is considered laziness from a Dharma point of view. We can overcome attachments, such as our attachment to another person, by meditating on death. Doing this does not mean that we must leave this other person. This meditation has nothing to do with the physical body; it is only a mental action. We are trying to overcome our attachment to them, not our love for them.

I remember when the US attacked Iraq; they had missiles that could fly hundreds of miles and hit exactly the right spot, destroying the enemy. People were so happy that the American military had this amazing technology that they forgot that people were being killed. Here, we are killing the real enemy—the lazy mind of attachment that seeks only the pleasure of this life—with the missile of remembering impermanence and death. If we can do that, it would be a real reason for happiness.

Because attachment brings hundreds of thousands of thoughts—what we want, what we don't want, how to get this, how to avoid that, why this person has something that we don't, and on and on—the mind cannot help but be distracted and confused by it. But by thinking that we will definitely die today, those irrelevant thoughts will be destroyed, like being hit by a nuclear missile.

In *The Foundation of All Good Qualities*, Lama Tsongkhapa says,

> When I have discovered that the precious freedom of this rebirth
> is found only once,
> Is extremely difficult to find again, and is greatly meaningful,

> Please bless me to unceasingly generate the mind,
> Taking its essence, day and night.[50]

By thinking of our imminent death, nothing will appear meaningful except the Dharma, and so we will have no time for anything else. For example, if you have seen somebody you are close to dying, at home or in a hospital, you will know that, at that moment, nothing makes sense except the Dharma. Even seeing a dead person, we see that Dharma is the only refuge, the only source of lasting happiness.

When we actually have the deep realization of impermanence and death, we will never do anything meaningless again. To illustrate this point, there is the story of Geshé Kharag, who was a highly renounced yogi who spent his life meditating in a cave in Tibet. Always mindful of death, he was always aware when he started a meditation session that he may not finish it. When he left the cave for a pipi, it was always with the mind that he might die and never return. There was a thorn bush that grew by the entrance of his cave, and sometimes when he went out of the cave, his robe would catch and tear on the thorns. But, somehow, he never managed to cut back the bush; he thought it far more meaningful to return to meditation than to do this mundane activity. In that way, always mindful of death, he never wasted a second of his life.

There is also the story of a monk who lived in Bodhgaya many years ago, who went to see a doctor after a heart attack. The doctor told him that the heart attack had been a serious one and that he might die at any moment. The monk was deeply shocked, and when he returned to the monastery, he began to prepare for his death. He gave away everything he had, and although he didn't have much money, he made vast offerings to the monastery and the high lamas—including the tutor of His Holiness the Dalai Lama—sponsoring them to give lamrim and Vajrayana teachings and to pray for him. Thousands of people came to the teachings that he sponsored. Every day he did whatever he could to make the most extensive merit possible for his next life. As it turned out, the monk did not die but lived for many years, all the time continuing to do practice and generate merit in preparation for his death. Perhaps the doctor was incompetent and misdiagnosed him, but in fact I think the doctor was actually extremely kind to this monk, making him stop his normal life (I think he was a bit lazy before) and devote all his energy to preparing for death.

We Attain Great Power

Remembering death has great purpose and great power. Whatever nonvirtuous actions we have created in this life and in previous lives can definitely be purified, but it requires incredible determination. Pabongka Rinpoché said that remembering impermanence and death is like a hammer that can destroy all our delusions in one stroke.[51]

There are many inspiring stories about yogis who transformed their minds from grossly negative ones to highly realized ones in one lifetime. Some even attained liberation or enlightenment. A clear illustration of this is the story of Angulimala, who lived in India during the Buddha's time. Angulimala's guru told him to kill one thousand people and give him a mala made of one finger from each person. *Angulimala* actually means "Mala of Fingers." Trusting this false teacher, Angulimala killed 999 people. He was about to kill the thousandth person, his own mother, when the Buddha appeared and told him to come to him. Even though the Buddha was walking very slowly, no matter how hard Angulimala tried, he could not catch him because of the Buddha's psychic power. In that way, the Buddha was able to help Angulimala subdue his mind. Thereupon, Angulimala was ordained by the Buddha and went from being a figure of terror for everybody to a figure of great respect, and people greeted him and bowed to him wherever he went.

Milarepa is perhaps the most famous yogi in Tibetan history, but he did not start out as a great practitioner. In fact, he was a murderer in his early life. Through black magic, he made the house of his uncle and aunt collapse on top of them and their family, killing many people and animals. His mother was very pleased and placed a pair of trousers on top of the house as a banner, saying, "May my son conquer." And yet, through strong regret and incredible determination, Milarepa was able to totally transform his mind and actually attained enlightenment in one lifetime. How could he do that? He did it through remembering death. Even though he had created so much negative karma, by remembering the inevitability and imminence of death, he was able to generate the energy to lead an ascetic life and practice purely, and to eventually attain enlightenment. That such a heavy collection of negative karma can be purified in this life shows the great strength and power that can arise from the remembrance of death.

We Gain Great Benefit at the Beginning, Middle, and End

As it is said in *The Sayings of the Kadam Masters*,

> Once the spiritual mentor Potowa was asked by an upasaka,[52] "To engage in a single-pointed practice of Dharma, what is most important?" Potowa replied, "To engage in a single-pointed practice of Dharma, the contemplation on impermanence is most important. For if you contemplate death and impermanence, *in the beginning* it will cause you to enter the Dharma. *In the middle*, it will act as an impetus to engage in virtuous actions. *Finally*, it will act as a complement to realizing perfect equanimity of the ultimate nature of reality.
>
> "Again, if you contemplate impermanence, *first* it will act as a cause for enabling you to let go of attachment to this life. *In the middle*, it will act as a condition for averting clinging to all aspects of cyclic existence. *Finally*, it will act as a complementary factor for entering the path of nirvana."[53]

Fear of death motivates us to meditate on the path and to have realizations of each of the graduated paths of the three capable beings: the lower capable being, the middle capable being, and the higher capable being. It spurs us to develop our compassion, our bodhichitta, and to enter into the practices of the bodhisattva, the six perfections. It is the spur to practice highest yoga tantra with its two stages. Remembering death stops laziness; it cuts desire and makes the mind free.

At the beginning of our spiritual journey, it is vital to remember impermanence and death because it gives us the energy to practice Dharma without difficulty. The start of our Dharma practice is when we start to see beyond the happiness of this life and start to prepare for our future lives. This is the graduated path of the lower capable being, where we do everything we possibly can to avoid the lower realms and to attain another human birth—hopefully one with the eight freedoms and ten richnesses of a perfect human rebirth, providing the optimal conditions for practicing the Dharma. This level of the path includes the basic lamrim meditations on such topics as karma, perfect human rebirth, and of course, impermanence and death. These meditations, and the insights they impart, are the fuel that propels our plane, the butter that burns in the butter lamp. Without this fuel there can be no journey, no light.

As we have seen, we first of all need to transcend the mindset that is entrapped in the thought of the eight worldly dharmas, the attachment to the pleasure of this life alone. But it is not the case that we *first* renounce the mind attached to the eight worldly dharmas and *then* realize impermanence and death. It must be the other way around. It is our realization of impermanence and death that will lead us to renounce the thought of the eight worldly dharmas. It is this realization that closes the door on the lower realms.

When this happens, we can say we have attained this level of practice, and we can face death without fear. This is a great achievement! With this attainment, we will not be worried about leaving this life and going to another, because we are sure that the next life will be a better one. Even though we have no clairvoyance and no way of knowing what sort of rebirth we will have, we will know that we have avoided the lower realms and we are certain that we will be able to continue our Dharma practice in our next life.

Beyond the graduated path of the lower capable being is the graduated path of the middle capable being, the path that leads us out of samsara altogether. Although at this level, the mind is much more advanced than the one that we currently have, there are still obstacles to practice due to the ripening of negative karmic imprints on the mind. Because we could still easily slip back, we have to continue practicing diligently at this level; we need to observe our karma and purify our mind as much as possible. Our Dharma practice still requires effort, and if we are not careful and falter in our determination, we can lose what we have achieved. That is why realizing impermanence and death is still vital even at this fairly advanced stage. We still need the spur of knowing that we may die at any moment to keep our Dharma practice strong.

Remembering impermanence and death gives us the strength to overcome the three poisons of attachment, anger, and ignorance. And when that happens, we will have guaranteed that we will not be controlled by karma and delusions in our future births and will be well on the way to overcoming death itself. Even before we become an *arhat* or a bodhisattva, one who has realized emptiness directly, our life will be incredibly meaningful, our death so blissful, and we will only ever reborn into ever more favorable states. And when we reach the stage where we realize emptiness directly, we will be free from death.

And so, as a middle level practitioner, we will die with great peace, completely confident that the next life—either as another human being or in a pure land—will be even more blissful and provide us with an even better opportunity to progress quickly on the path.

It is important to remember impermanence and death even at the culmination of our Dharma practice, during the graduated path of the higher capable being, because doing so helps us manifest how we die and where we are reborn. The higher realizations that fall like rain when we are near the end of our practice are strengthened by this understanding.

There are five paths that we pass through from the time we enter the Mahayana path until we realize the complete cessation of suffering, attain liberation, and finally enter into enlightenment. These five paths are the path of merit, the path of preparation, the path of right seeing, the path of meditation, and the path of no more learning.

In the Hinayana teachings, when we have attained the final path of no more learning, we have overcome all suffering and become an arhat. At this point, there is no more old age or sickness, no more death, and no more rebirth. In the Mahayana, all of these are overcome by attaining the third path, the path of right seeing. By attaining this third path, the arya bodhisattva completely overcomes these sufferings. So, according to the Mahayana, this happens well before achieving enlightenment.

In the highest yoga tantra there are two stages, the generation stage and the completion stage, and the completion stage itself has various stages: the isolation of body, the isolation of speech, the isolation of mind, clear light, the illusory body, and the union of clear light and illusory body. Not until we attain the fourth stage of highest yoga tantra, clear light, can we be considered a yogi. Before that, we might have the external appearance of a yogi but not the necessary level of realization. From that time on, the yogi has no worry about death. This stage corresponds to the Mahayana path of right seeing, the third of the five paths. At that stage, the fear of death is overcome, and we have complete control over our death and rebirth.

Until we reach the third path, death is still a concern. Even though our practice might be very advanced, the outcome is still not guaranteed due to the lingering presence of delusions in our mindstream. And as long as even subtle delusions remain, there is still the chance of those delusions ripening and causing us to create more negative karma, starting a downward spiral leading to rebirth in the lower realms. Once we have attained the path of right seeing, however, we can truly be said to be self-supporting.

To be self-supporting means to be able to look after ourselves. In some ways, the spiritual meaning of this term mirrors its worldly meaning. When we are young, we rely entirely on our parents for our food and shelter, for our school fees and clothes, and so on. But when we become an adult, we leave home and earn our own money, therefore becoming "self-supporting." For a Dharma practitioner, we become self-supporting when we can manage our own death, which means being completely free from the three poisons. How do we achieve this? His Holiness the Dalai Lama says,

> The real definition of being self-supporting is to die with bodhichitta, the mind cherishing others. This is the best way to die.

Of the unending qualities of bodhichitta, Shantideva says,

> Truly, all other goods perish after bearing fruit,
> like a plantain tree;
> but the tree of the thought of awakening never perishes after
> bearing its fruit,
> and remains fruitful thereafter.[54]

Many of the great Buddhist masters were known to have demonstrated great equanimity at the time of death. Pabongka Dechen Nyingpo said toward the end of his life that even if he died at that moment, because he had studied the Dharma well, he would have no worry at all. Lama Yeshe, the founder of the Foundation for the Preseveration of the Mahayana Tradition (FPMT) and my great and kind guru who is kinder than the buddhas of the three times, showed this clearly when he died. When the time of death came, he was able to do the crucial practices on his own in order to be assured of the best possible rebirth. Before being flown to the United States for an operation, Lama was in hospital in Delhi on oxygen and with wires coming out all over his body. At that time, he said that even if the operation was not successful, it didn't matter because he had dedicated his life to serving others, and that is all that mattered. If he died during the operation, there would be no regrets. In that, he was showing a real bodhisattva's attitude.

Being happy to die, and even wanting to die if it is more beneficial, is very different from a worldly being committing suicide. The wish to commit suicide is the product of a deluded mind; although it arises from the wish to end one's suffering, that deluded and unskillful act only creates far more. On the other hand, when the great practitioners wish to die, this arises from their selfless attitude, from their wish to benefit others. Their choice is so simple: if it is more beneficial for them to live, then they wish to live; if it is more beneficial for them to die, then they wish to die. Death holds no fear for them. They control death, not the other way around.

Even if an advanced Dharma practitioner has not attained full enlightenment by the time of death, they still have great control over their future life. They can direct their mindstream to be reborn in a pure land, or if they have taken the bodhisattva path and attained a high level, they can direct their next rebirth to whatever situation will be most beneficial to others. This is what happens with the reincarnated lamas (*tulkus*), whom we call *rinpoché* ("precious one").[55]

Great bodhisattvas will even choose to be reborn in a difficult environment rather than a place like a pure land. They can progress quickly in a pure land, but a difficult environment provides more opportunities to benefit other sentient beings here in samsara. Some even pray to be reborn in the hells, where they would be able to benefit those sentient beings suffering the most. This is explicitly discussed within the *lojong* (thought transformation) practices. There is another practice, called *chöd* (slaying the ego), where the practitioner sits in a charnel ground and imagines disembodying themselves and offering all the parts to all the sentient beings. It takes an incredibly brave mind to have such a wish. The bodhisattva is the bravest of the brave.

Lama Yeshe and many high lamas, geshés, and meditators—not only monks but also laypeople—actualized the three principal aspects of the path—renunciation, bodhichitta, and emptiness—and then used the mind of bodhichitta to attain the generation stage and then the completion stage of the highest yoga tantra practices. With completion-stage practices such as the six yogas of Naropa,[56] all the gross consciousnesses are absorbed, and what is called *the union of clear light and illusory body*, the mind that immediately precedes enlightenment, is attained.

Once we have this realization, there is no need for further effort. What a wonderful moment that will be. At present, we are exactly the opposite; we need so much effort to even think about the fact we might die, whereas the realizations of attachment, anger, or ignorance are constantly, strongly there. We don't have to meditate to generate attachment; there is no need to put special effort into it at all. Attachment intuitively arises while we are eating food, while we are sleeping, while we are walking. When hunger comes, we instinctively feel the need to eat, without one second of analysis. To make eating part of the path to enlightenment, on the other hand, doesn't arise spontaneously. *That*, we need to work on.

We Can Attain a Pure Land

Another outcome of doing extended and strong Dharma practice is to be reborn in a pure land, so called because the beings living there have far less delusion than in other realms, allowing them to progress much more quickly. Pure lands are created by specific buddhas who have aspired to relieve sentient beings from suffering more quickly. But the pure land we are born into is our creation, and the objects of enjoyment that we see are creations of our mind. The pure land that we inhabit exists due to our prayers and devotion, but also due to our strong purification and accumulation of merit. The fuel that will take us to the pure land is the desire to be born there, just as other cravings at the time of death will take us to one of the other realms. In the Chinese tradition, there are many people who continuously and strongly pray to be reborn in the pure land of Amitabha. Being born in a pure land is one of the quickest ways to attain enlightenment because we develop realizations more quickly there and because there is the chance to receive teachings from the buddha of that particular pure land.

There is a story of an old monk in Tibet who practiced so hard in order to be reborn in Tushita,[57] the pure land of Maitreya, the next buddha of this world system. He had practiced hard all his life, and in his last months he had been doing a special practice called *powa*,[58] which would enable him to transfer his consciousness into the pure land just before he died. For some reason, he was experiencing obstacles to successfully doing this practice, and neither he nor his teacher could see why. One of the most important conditions needed to attain a pure land is for the practitioner to completely let go of attachment. The old monk, who seemed to live so austerely, seemed to have fulfilled this requirement. However, when his teacher, who was in another monastery, checked carefully with his psychic powers, he noticed that the monk was still attached to one thing: his butter tea, especially to the thin film of butter that floats on the surface of the tea and is left over at the bottom of the bowl when the tea is drunk. Things are very basic in Tibet; there are very few indulgences, and the rich, salty butter tea is sort of like chocolate or ice cream to many Tibetans. And so the teacher sent a young monk with a message to the old monk saying that there is better butter tea in Tushita. As soon as the young monk whispered the message, the old monk was able to let go of this one last thing, and his mind was immediately released and was reborn in the pure land of Tushita.

We Have No Fear at the Time of Death

The final benefit of remembering impermanence and death, as related in the traditional teachings, is that we will have no fear at the time of death. As we will see, there are two kinds of fear: (1) the ignorant fear that a worldly person experiences when faced with death, and (2) the wise, healthy fear of death that somebody aware of impermanence and death has when they see how they have created much negative karma and are likely to fall into the lower realms after death. This second kind of fear is a positive fear, but it is also one we transcend as we progress in our Dharma practice. The short-term goal of Dharma practice is to die happily and to attain a favorable rebirth so we can continue on the path to enlightenment. This sixth benefit tells us that this will definitely happen if we constantly remember impermanence and death and practice Dharma diligently because of that.

If we practice Dharma sincerely from the heart as much as we can and do service for other sentient beings out of compassion and loving-kindness—if we can see this is our life, of course there will be great joy when we die. Even if we aren't as accomplished as Milarepa, we will still have great confidence that we will not be reborn in the lower realms and can continue our spiritual journey in our next life. This is the cause for so much joy. Rather than wondering whether we will have four, six, or a thousand legs in our next life, we can look forward to progressing further and faster on the path.

I remember listening to a long radio chat show in Adelaide, Australia, that was conducted by one of my students. One of the topics was the lack of space in the cemeteries, and somehow, during the interview with the cemetery manager, the interviewer let some Dharma slip out, mentioning the importance of acknowledging death and the help meditation gives. The cemetery manager was silent when she had finished; I don't think he knew what to say. During the show, an old lady phoned in and said how she was so happy with her life. She said she had led a good life and she was perfectly content because she knew where she was going. I think she meant that she knew what would happen to her after death. It made me think that when we have a good heart, we have no reason to fear death.

Dying happily has a big impact on those around us too. We become a great source of inspiration when people can see that it is possible to have a happy death. Instead of having a terrified face and screaming in terror, instead of clinging desperately to what we are about to lose, by being extremely calm and peaceful and completely without any sense of unhappiness at our imminent death, we can profoundly influence others for the better. Not only can we help make their grief at losing us so much less, we can even make them feel happy, even as we are dying. We can be a great object lesson to them on nonattachment and the importance of having a good heart. We can show others how vital it is to always remember impermanence and death.

For the most advanced Dharma practitioner, death is like returning home or going for a picnic. It is like going to the beach when the sun is shining and the waves are very high. The mind is extremely happy to be going to such a beautiful place for a holiday. Such people feel great joy as they are dying. This is the best way to die. Less accomplished practitioners are happy and comfortable at the time of death and are fully confident that they will have a happy rebirth. And even the least accomplished practitioners die without worry or fear. Enjoyment of death, as well as fear of death, is created by the mind; it does not exist from its own side.

4. OVERCOMING THE FEAR OF DEATH

Death is usually not a popular subject, especially in Western culture. People do not seem to want to hear about it. Just asking somebody how old they are can be seen as somehow threatening or insensitive. If somebody tries to talk about death, people's minds go into retreat! People do not even want to hear the word *death* because they have a great fear of it. This aversion stems from suppression, not freedom. To turn our minds away from death out of fear is to deny something that is totally natural.

Although people generally block out any thoughts of death, it still seems to be on most people's minds, judging by how much effort people expend on protecting themselves from death, like the Americans in the last century who built bomb shelters to be safe from the atomic bombs they feared would be dropped by the USSR. These were places to escape death. Even worldly people recognize that protecting oneself from future danger is important. We might be doubtful about future lives, but it is still beneficial to prepare for death—not for the possibility of nuclear annihilation, but for the inevitable death we must all face.

Death Is Not Frightening from Its Own Side

There is nothing to be afraid of in death. There is nothing difficult about death. Death is nothing more than the consciousness leaving this body. That's all. The connection with this body finishes, and the mindstream leaves the body and finds another one. It is not death itself that is frightening; it is the mind's projections about death that make us frightened. It is our own mind that creates the fear, not death itself.

Death is the mind separating from the body under the control of karma and delusions. As long as the consciousness is associated with the body, there is life. The association of mind and body is life; the disassociation of mind from body is death.

In other words, what is called "death" is created by our mind. Death is merely a label that our mind creates to describe the process of the consciousness leaving the body. When that separation occurs, the mind imputes "death." There is no real death that exists inherently, from its own side. It is merely a convenient label, ultimately unreal. Therefore, not only is there no such thing as a frightening death, there is also no such thing as *death*, in reality. The real death that we so fear—that real independent death—is merely labeled by the mind.

The concept of a fearful death has been created by the mind that clings to the "permanent" things of this world, things that it sees it will lose when death happens: our body, friends, possessions, and so forth. Because the mind is not able to let go of this life and the things of this life, death becomes terrifying. The unsubdued mind that is controlled by attachment to worldly pleasure creates this fear; it is not death itself that creates it. And yet, even though this imputed idea is nothing but a hallucination, we believe in this wrong concept of an independent frightening death. The great master Naropa[59] said,

> When we are born, the concept is born; when we are sick, the concept is sick; and even when we are dying, the concept is dying.

In other words, everything is a concept. When we logically analyze what death really is, we find that the way that it appears to us and the way we apprehend it to exist is false.

The great yogi Saraha said that without the concept, there are no external enemies; there are no vicious tigers, no poisonous snakes. If we have anger, we find external enemies; if we have no anger, we won't be able to find external enemies. If we have the concept of an enemy, we see an enemy; if we have no concept of an enemy, we don't see an enemy.

If we have no anger and no concept of an enemy, we will be completely unable to find an enemy, even if everyone around us is angry with us, criticizes us, or even kills us.

Whether or not death is a problem depends on the mind. Death itself is not terrifying, but our concept of death can be terrifying. When we change our clothes, we leave our old clothes behind and put on new ones. Like that, the mind leaves this body and takes another one, all dependent on causes and conditions. The mind labels this phenomenon of mind separating from body as "death," incorrectly seeing it as permanent and inherent.

There is no reason to fear death, and yet many great yogis say that we need to have a healthy fear of death. Is this a contradiction? In a text called *Realizing Past, Present, and Future*, the First Karmapa,[60] Düsum Kyenpa, says,

> Why should I be afraid of death? Because when the Lord of Death comes, it is difficult for the mind to be happy.

If the whole of Buddhism is focused on making us truly happy, why then is it skillful to be frightened of death? Surely not worrying about death is the Buddhist way, because the Buddha wants us to be happy.

There are two kinds of people who do not worry about death: the highly realized beings who have transcended their delusions and who have no need to fear death, and the ignorant, worldly people who are blind to what will happen to them at death. Somebody can claim to be a highly realized meditator and yet die with great fear. That is a sign that they have not pacified their mind properly. On the other hand, a very normal-looking person can die with real joy, which shows that their mind has been pacified.

A worldly person can also seem to have no fear of death, but this lack of fear is completely the opposite from that of an advanced meditator. The worldly person believes in just this life—that there is no reincarnation. They believe that because there is no karma, their actions have no consequences beyond this life. They are always so busy, filling their life with so many things. They ignore the thought of death, denying it or putting it off as much as possible. Then, when death suddenly happens, they are filled with unbelievable terror. This comes from never having thought about death during their lifetime.

This kind of fearless person is like a baby who reaches for a flame because it's bright and warm, heedless of the danger and with no idea of the consequences of the action. If a responsible person is not around, the baby will likely be badly burned. The baby in this example is fearless but also ignorant, whereas the baby's parents have learned that lesson and would never think of putting their hands in the fire.

A person with no Dharma understanding chases wrong concepts, going after what will harm them while thinking that these things are the source of happiness. Such a person is like a moth drawn toward a flame; enchanted by the brightness of the flame, the moth fails to see the danger and flies right into the flame and is incinerated. It is not that the moth craves suffering and death, but the attraction of the flame is too strong. Likewise, the person denying death does not want to die—indeed, they simply want to avoid suffering. But they are driven there by wrong conceptions, thinking that only this moment's sense pleasures are important.

One day, death will become real to them and they will have made no preparations. At that time, confronting death, they are frozen with fear, but this is not a skillful fear; it serves no purpose at all. This is the fear that an animal has when it knows it is about to die. A dog facing death won't immediately apply some method to overcome its fear; it has no capacity to practice Dharma, or even to recite OM MANI PADME HUM and take refuge in the Buddha, Dharma, and Sangha.

We worldly people put all our effort into making this life as comfortable and enjoyable as we can and have no thought of anything more. But no matter how successful we are in our worldly endeavors, we cannot stop death. When death happens, it is a huge shock. We see that we have wasted our entire life, and there is now nothing we can do about it.

Although we work so hard for this life, almost everything we do is concerned with external changes. We jog miles every day in the hot sun until the sweat pours out; we spend hours on exercise machines or doing push-ups and lifting heavy weights. We do all sorts of workouts and routines to improve our fitness and physical appearance. And yet nothing can stop us from dying. Because we never think about either karma or impermanence and death, we tend to ignore the things are truly important. And when we finally come face to face with death, we are paralyzed with terror.

This fear of death is totally different from the fear of death that a Dharma practitioner has. Rather than being paralyzed by fear, Dharma practitioners use their natural fear of death to awaken a sense of deeper purpose within themselves. Unless we harness our fear of death, face up to its inevitability, and use this awareness to change our life so we will die well, then it is completely useless.

A Healthy Fear of Death

The fear of death we need is the fear of what will happen to us if we fail to transform our mind and stop creating nonvirtuous actions. This kind of fear can provide us with boundless energy to do whatever is needed. Milarepa once said,

> I fled to the mountains because I feared death.
> I have realized emptiness, the mind's primordial state.
> Were I to die now, I have no fear.[61]

Milarepa was motivated by a deep fear of the terrible death that awaited him because of his misdeeds, having killed his uncle's family by black magic. That fear sent him to find the Dharma and to practice it in the mountains, where he realized the absolute nature of the mind and lost that fear. This is the way it works. First, we need a healthy fear of death, the kind that motivates us into action and turns our life around. Then, through the purifying power of Dharma practice, we get to the stage of spiritual development where we know that we will have a good death and a happy rebirth, and thus, we lose the fear of death. Reflecting constantly on impermanence and death is what brings about this incredible transformation.

We have everything that Milarepa had—many of us, in fact, are even better endowed in terms of health and resources than he was. Milarepa's body was known to be skinny and emaciated from living on nothing but nettles, like it could be blown away in the lightest breeze. Except for a torn rag he went naked, and his skin was a kind of blue-green color from his nettle diet. His holy body wasn't like our body, very fat and strong and shiny, like it is polished. All he had in his cave was a seat made of grass, to aid his meditation posture, and a pot to cook the nettles. Outwardly he was not very impressive, so we cannot argue that he had the right body for enlightenment but we don't.

Nor can we argue that when he started he had a wonderful, pure mind, whereas we haven't. He had killed many people and so his mindstream was burdened by very heavy negative karma. No wonder he was scared of death. His advantage—and the reason for his success—was not in possessing a superior body and mind but in his superior determination and courage, which kept him going until he attained complete realization. Before he turned to the Dharma, death had controlled him; afterward, he controlled death, and so he felt no fear at all about dying.

Milarepa was not unique in this; all the great meditators have defeated their delusions and so overcome their fear of death. Another Tibetan yogi, Longdrol Lama Rinpoché, who wrote many texts and was in constant communication with the female buddha Tara, also meditated on impermanence and death, attaining many realizations and eventually overcoming his fear of death. He says,

> I am not afraid of being impermanent.
> I will be an old monk in the morning and get the body of a god that night.[62]

His perfect confidence destroyed his fear of death completely.

Why, then, should *we* be afraid of death? Why can't we be like the great meditators and be happy, knowing that whatever happens after death will only be wonderful? The reason is because we simply do not really *know* that things will be good after death, and if we are honest, we will accept that we have not reached the stage where we can safely face death without fear. Along with an understanding of impermanence and death—knowing that we will definitely die and that the time of that death is uncertain—we also need to have an understanding of karma. In particular, we need to understand and accept we have created a lot of very negative actions in the past that still sit on our mindstream as imprints, and that we are still incapable of creating only virtuous actions because of our past habituation.

Lama Tsongkhapa explained that unless we overcome our attachment to this life and attain the happiness of future lives, not only will liberation be impossible but we will be reborn in the lower realms in our next life. This shows us the kind of fear of death we need. The worldly person's fear of death—the fear of separation from all the objects of desire—is due to attachment and is a great hindrance at death. The fear of being thrown into the lower suffering realms, however, is the best possible antidote for attachment. This fear is extremely useful to have now, while we have the time to do something about it.

Up to now, we have failed to recognize the cause of suffering. But now we can see that all of the problems in life come from nonvirtuous actions, and that nonvirtuous actions will continue to cause great suffering in our next life. If fear comes from this thought, that is good—it should. That is a positive fear. Before, we were ignorant of the source of our suffering, but now we know its source, and because of that, we can do something about it.

Even though we may regularly perform virtuous actions, we usually create more nonvirtue than virtue in any given day. Unless we are able to purify our mindstream of the negative imprints of this nonvirtue, we will have to experience the negative results of this karma that we are constantly creating. Nobody can experience the results of our negative karma on our behalf. We can't pay somebody to experience them for us. If it were possible for someone else to experience the effects of our nonvirtue for us, we could ask the buddhas to take on our negative karma, and because the buddhas are solely directed toward alleviating the suffering of every living being, they would do so, and nobody would ever have to experience suffering again. There would be no sentient beings left in samsara; there would be no samsara. Unfortunately, it is not like that. We create our own karma and must, alone, experience the result of it.

So what can we do about the nonvirtue that we create? The most vital thing we can do is gain an understanding of karma. By understanding what creates the cause for rebirth in the lower realms, we can avoid creating that cause. Then, we will no longer feel that creating only a small nonvirtue doesn't matter; every bit of nonvirtue matters.

It is like a farmer erecting an electric fence around a field that borders on a high cliff in order to protect the cows. If a cow wanders toward the cliff, it will touch the fence and receive a shock, making it move away from the cliff. The shock is not pleasant, but fear of the wire stops the cow straying and falling over the cliff. The fear of death is our electric fence. Without this healthy fear—fear that comes from wisdom—we can get careless and not care about our karma, leading us to create nonvirtuous actions that will tip us over the karmic cliff into the lower realms. Fear is a natural reaction to the presence of danger; it is very useful.

Perhaps we might think that if we dwell incessantly on our imminent death, this thought might consume us and we would lose interest in other things like eating, going to the toilet, reciting mantras, and so forth. We might be worried that when we have convinced ourselves that we are going to die in the next moment, we will just sit there waiting for it, everything else becoming totally meaningless. Of course, it's not like that. By facing the reality of death and impermanence, life does not become meaningless. Rather, the reality of death will serve to naturally turn our mind to what *is* meaningful. If we knew that we were definitely going to die today, wouldn't we want to make the last hours as meaningful as we can? We wouldn't freeze and be unable to do anything. His Holiness the Dalai Lama lives each day with a profound realization of impermanence and death, and nobody can accuse him of doing nothing.

The fear of death is a powerful trigger that can rapidly turn our mind toward the Dharma and jumpstart our spiritual practice. It can bring a deep sense of nonattachment, peace, and satisfaction. When we encounter a fear such as this, we look to what will save us, which is principally refuge in the Three Rare Sublime Ones, the Buddha, Dharma, and Sangha. The fear of death, and of rebirth in the lower realms, leads to an attitude of renunciation toward worldly attachments to this life. This, in turn, leads to the renunciation of our attachment to the whole of samsara, which leads us to the path of the higher capable being, the development of compassion and bodhichitta, and the wish to attain enlightenment in order to benefit all sentient beings.

When there is no longer the possibility of experiencing a suffering rebirth, the fear of death will naturally drop away. Through the fear of death, knowing we are going to die, we become motivated to practice Dharma with such energy that we renounce the whole of samsara, and thus, we not only transcend the fear of death, we transcend death itself. In *The Great Nirvana Sutra*, the Buddha says,

> Among all the reapings, the autumn harvest is supreme. Among all the tracks, the track of the elephant is supreme. Among all the ideas, the idea of impermanence and death is supreme because with it you eliminate all the attachment, ignorance, and pride of the three realms.[63]

Like the Buddha says here, the fear of death is founded on wisdom and not ignorance. It is a very healthy fear. We all need this fear. I wish I had more fear! But, as I have said, fear is only good when it comes from wisdom and not ignorance, so I would not be so happy about having ignorant fear. The fear of losing the things that we cling to—the "me" and "mine"—is the kind of fear that arises from ignorance. The wise fear that the Buddha describes above is completely different. Instead allowing our delusions to make us afraid, we develop a health fear of our delusions, which encourages us to do whatever we can to overcome them. Seeing ourselves and the world as permanent, we trap ourselves in the prison of samsara; understanding impermanence and death, we liberate ourselves from that prison.

By reminding ourselves that we might die at any time, we will naturally be very careful in our actions and have great energy to practice virtuous actions and abandon nonvirtuous actions.

The Buddha's Two Great Lessons on Impermanence

At the time of the Buddha's birth as Prince Siddhartha, four other kings in India also welcomed new sons, and at that time the whole earth was filled with brilliant white light. Each king thought that this incredibly auspicious sign was because of his own son, but a very wise brahmin who could foretell the future saw that it was the birth of Siddhartha, the son of the king of the Shakyas, who had caused the light. The brahmin saw that Prince Siddhartha would become a buddha, with the thirty-two major and eighty minor signs of a buddha[64] and that he would be a great spiritual leader known throughout the world. When he told the king and queen this he was crying. When they asked him why he was crying, he explained that by the time the prince became enlightened and started teaching, he himself would be dead and so would be unable to see this future buddha.

Despite the sage's prophesy, the king determined that his son would be the next king of the Shakyas rather than a teacher and, in preparation for this, he only let his son know the luxuries of the palace. Even though his father tried to shield him from all suffering, there came a time when Siddhartha saw four things in quick succession, one at each of the four gates of the palace. First, he saw an old person, very thin and bent over with age, and he realized for the first time that we all have to age. Next, he saw a sick person, something he had never seen before. Then, he saw a dead body and he knew that death comes to all of us. This was a terrible revelation for a young man who had never seen the slightest suffering. At the fourth gate, he saw a poor meditating monk, a person who had none of the luxuries that Siddhartha had but nonetheless seemed incredibly calm and happy.

These four sights were like a light going on in a dark place for the prince. He saw his life in the palace for the empty, trivial thing it was and realized that samsaric happiness was meaningless, that it only ever led to old age, sickness, and death. By seeing the monk, he saw the way out of this trap and decided to become a renunciate, leaving his worldly life and worldly interests behind. This was the start of his spiritual quest.

He chose the life of an ascetic, practicing for six years with hardly any food in the most trying circumstances, before he realized that extreme austerity is as harmful as indulgence. This led to that amazing night when he sat beneath the bodhi tree and attained full enlightenment.

And so you see, Siddhartha's encounter with impermanence and death was the key that opened up his life of meditation. It gave him the determination to pursue the truth, no matter how difficult, and to finally attain enlightenment. He then taught for over forty years without a single error. It is due to Prince Siddhartha's—Shakyamuni Buddha's—kindness that we have the Buddhadharma now. As such, that encounter with impermanence and death at the four gates is the cause of the whole of Buddhism.

In the Mahayana version of the Buddha's lifestory, the Buddha is already enlightened and his first deed is his descent from the pure land of Tushita in order to be born to Queen Maya. The life he led is an object lesson to us. He lived eighty years and then he manifested passing away in order to teach impermanence to all sentient beings. This is the only reason. His entire life—including his death—was only an example, done for our sakes. From Shakyamuni Buddha's side, there was no reason to take birth as a prince, grow up in a palace, get married, give it all up to seek the truth, make a life of retreat and teaching, and finally pass away. The Buddha manifested passing away in order to teach us impermanence. When it was time to die, he took off his robes, lay down, and said to his disciples,

> All causative phenomena are impermanent.
> Work out your salvation with diligence.
> This is the last teaching of the tathagata.[65]

In that short verse, he summarized all the teachings on impermanence and how we alone can liberate ourselves from this mundane world of suffering. This is the most important lesson the Buddha could leave us before he passed away and entered *parinirvana.*

Stories of Highly Realized Beings at Death

When we ordinary people die, our karma propels us into whatever our next life will be, but very advanced practitioners can control how they die and where they are reborn. There have been many great meditators who have died in a state of meditation. They are a great inspiration to us. Many stay in the full meditation position for days, even weeks, after the heart has stopped beating. Whereas a normal corpse would soon start rotting and smelling very foul, their holy bodies do not rot but look radiant and actually emit a pleasant perfumed odor. The room that the body is in often has such a blissful and radiant energy that people want to be there to experience it. And when the consciousness finally leaves the body and the body is cremated, there are often tiny pearl-shaped objects, called *riksel* in Tibetan, left behind in the ashes, which is a sign of their incredible bodhichitta.

One of these great lamas was Geshé Lama Konchog (d. 2001), who was a great yogi who meditated in retreat for over twenty years in extremely difficult conditions in Nepal. Although he had the appearance of a very normal person, always laughing and joking with the monks and nuns and the Western students at Kopan Monastery, where he lived, he was actually a highly realized being. One of the teachers at Kopan said that a few days before he passed away, in October 2001, Geshé Lama Konchog said that he was experiencing the mirage-like and smoke-like visions that come just before death, showing that he was able to recognize the signs of death—the clear light and all those other things—and on the basis of that he was able to engage in the appropriate highest-yoga-tantra meditations during his death.

After his breathing stopped, he remained in a meditation state for about a week. I sent guidance about what to do with the body because we had gone through a similar process when Lama Yeshe passed away in 1984. When Geshé Lama Konchog's consciousness had finally left his body, his body was taken to be cremated. Lama Lhundrup, the abbot of Kopan, told me that when the holy body was offered to the fire, relics jumped out. The texts explain that such relics, usually in the form of tiny pearl-shaped objects, come from the holy body if the completion-stage realization of clear light has been reached. Geshé Lama Konchog's incarnation was subsequently identified in Tsum, the region in Nepal where Geshé-la himself was born.[66]

When Lama Yeshe died he also left many relics. He was cremated at Vajrapani Institute in California. When fire was put to the holy body, the smoke that first came out was white, which Kyabjé Zong Rinpoché interpreted as meaning that Lama was somebody who was able to fully actualize the tantric path by uniting the clear light and illusory body. In the "common view" of us ordinary people, Lama Yeshe achieved this unification at the moment of death, but according to the "uncommon view," he was already an enlightened being.

The great yogi Milarepa had a very ordinary-looking body, but as he was dying, his body changed appearance, manifesting as many different bodies. This allowed him to be simultaneously at a benefactor's house, with people in a village, in his cave meditating, and so forth. At each location, the people there thought that they alone were with Milarepa when he died, whereas, in fact, there were people present with him in many places with his various manifested bodies. As he died his holy body in its various manifestations dissolved into light.

Because of Milarepa's bad deeds earlier in his life, many people only remembered him as a murderer and refused to believe that he was a great meditator. But the miracles that occurred when he died completely wiped these ideas from these people's minds, replaced by great faith and devotion. When Milarepa's disciples started to offer his holy body to the fire, the fire did not take at first because Milarepa was waiting for one of his disciples called Rechung to arrive. And as soon as Rechung arrived, the flame was accepted, and the body was cremated. It is also said that while his body was burning Milarepa came out of meditation on the dharmakaya and stopped the flames in order to give some instructions to his disciples.

Marpa, the great yogi and guru of Milarepa, was also said to have had complete control over delusion when he died, even though he appeared perfectly ordinary to the worldly people, who saw him as a simple farmer with a wife and family. As Marpa was dying, dakinis came and invited him to a pure land. His secret wife, Dagmema,[67] was absorbed into his heart, and he followed the dakinis to the pure land in procession, like a king entering a city. When Marpa's corpse was cremated, there were many auspicious signs, such as beautifully colored rainbows and colored clouds appearing in the clear blue sky. When the fire died down, the people found mantras on the bones and the skull that remained.

Some Dharma practitioners build their funeral pyre themselves before they die. This not only reminds them of impermanence and death but is also very practical. For example, there was an accomplished meditator called Gomchen-la[68] from the Solu Khumbu region in Nepal who lived an interesting life. His guru sent him to build bridges and he spent many years doing this, often with great difficulty. Many times there were simply no stones with which to build the bridges. Later, based on directions from his guru, he meditated for many years in a cave that had been used by Milarepa. Often having only a tiny tent, a cooking pot, and a big *damaru*,[69] he practiced chöd in the mountains. Through such Vajrayana practices, he attained very high realizations, especially of emptiness. Later in his life, his niece, an elderly nun, served as his attendant, but her frailty meant that she could hardly do anything at all. Gomchen-la thought that while he was healthy, he had better build his own pyre so that, when he died, she would only have to drag his body out to the pre-made pyre and set it alight.

It is quite normal for Dharma practitioners—not only high lamas but ordinary monks and nuns and laypeople—to prepare everything before they die. They make sure not only that their room is clean but also that all their possessions, such as their altar and Dharma texts, are clean and tidy. They try to give away most of their few possessions, offering them to monasteries and the high lamas that they have been devoted to. Very often, they send relatives and disciples away, wanting to have peace as they die.

Through signs and omens, many of the great meditators know that their death is coming days before they actually die. Before each of the Karmapas died, they wrote on a piece of paper which family they would be reincarnated into. I heard that before His Holiness Trijang Rinpoché[70] died, he wrote everything about his death, mentioning exactly how long he was going to stay in meditation, what should be done with the body, the details of his reincarnation, and so forth. When it was time for him to pass away, he told his attendant, "If you don't believe me, look in my autobiography."

There was a time in the 1980s when so many lamas died of cancer. These amazing lamas still had had the ability to follow the whole death procedure, to experience all the absorptions with a completely focused mind. They were thus able to use the actual process of death as a path to enlightenment, a way to achieve enlightenment quickly by applying the experience of the completion stage, the union of clear light and illusory body.

Laypeople without a strong meditation practice can also die well. My own mother is a very good example of that. She had no education at all and very little Dharma knowledge, but she had the biggest heart, filled with loving-kindness and compassion for her family, her friends, the people she knew, and the animals she tended. Despite her extreme poverty, she was incredibly generous. She would offer whatever food she had with such a warm heart to any being who was hungry. She would constantly recite the Chenrezig mantra, OM MANI PADME HUM, morning and night. When she died she was so peaceful.

I remember many years ago the mother of one of our benefactors died. She was a very simple, kind person, with nothing outwardly special about her, but she had a special deity whose mantra she recited all the time. One day, knowing her time of death was approaching, she simply thanked her son for helping her, sat down on a chair, and asked for a glass of water, and before she had finished the water, she died peacefully, passing away in meditation.

We usually try to emulate those worldly beings whom we look up to—athletes, business tycoons, the rich and famous—wanting to look like them and to have the same material things that they have. But trying to copy other worldly people usually only causes confusion. Instead, we should try to follow the good examples of the holy beings and yogis who have transformed their minds through the power of Dharma. We should try to study, to practice, and to act more like them. This would, indeed, be a great accomplishment.

Remember the Real Enemy

At present, we are the complete opposite of the great meditators. Remembering that we might die, that things are impermanent—these thoughts don't come naturally to us. On the other hand, thoughts of attachment, anger, and ignorance are there all the time, while we are walking, eating, working, even sleeping. We need to overcome our disturbing emotions, our unsubdued mind. While the unsubdued mind dwells in our heart, we can never relax.

The unsubdued mind is not eternal; it is not an integral aspect of the mind. Rather, it is like dirt that has entered clear water and made it muddy. Just as dirt can be removed from water, we need to eliminate delusions from our mind. We need to persevere in this, even if progress is slow; it's just a matter of trying.

We can look to the example of the eleventh-century Kadampa geshé Ben Gungyal,[71] who would always end his day by thinking back on all the actions he did over the course of the day. The area around his meditation hut was filled with black and white stones. For each negative action that he remembered doing, he would place a black stone in one pile, and for each positive action that he remembered doing, he would place a white stone in another pile. At first, he accumulated a large pile of black stones but hardly any white ones. But over the years as he advanced in his practice, the piles began to grow even, and soon there were more white stones than black ones. Eventually his pile of white stones towered over the small pile of black stones. It would be very beneficial if we all would do something like this, reminding ourselves to constantly watch our mind.

Our mind has become familiar with delusions over countless lifetimes, meaning they have great strength. Therefore, we need to exert continuous effort over a very long time in order to control and overcome these delusions. To do this, we need to put in the work. If we study the Dharma but never actually practice it, then the Dharma will have very little transformative effect on our mind. As Shantideva says,

> Having made this resolution, I will make effort
> to put into practice the precepts exactly as they have been taught.
> Medicine can cure him, but how will the patient recover
> if he does not follow the physician's instructions?[72]

We can buy the most expensive medicine in the world from the world's most famous doctor, but we will never get better unless we actually *take* the medicine as instructed. Likewise, the Dharma is something we need to actualize in our own life. We can read many books on mind transformation and never transform our mind. The Dharma is the root of all happiness, but we need it planted in our heart. Then, our life will be radically transformed.

5. THE FIRST ROOT TRUTH: DEATH IS CERTAIN

OVER THE NEXT FEW CHAPTERS we will look at a linked set of meditations on death that have long been used throughout the Tibetan Buddhist tradition as means to radically transform the mind. These meditations are grounded in three fundamental truths about death: (1) that death is certain, (2) that the time of death is uncertain, and (3) that nothing can help us at death but the Dharma.[73] These three "root truths" are elaborated upon by a series of nine points—three for each truth (nine in total)—which give rise to a series of three conclusions that follow from these three truths and instruct us what we must do in light of these truths. The outline of this meditation is as follows:

First Root Truth: Death is certain.

- No being has ever escaped death.
- Our lifespan is constantly decreasing.
- There is very little time to practice Dharma.

Conclusion: We must practice Dharma.

Second Root Truth: The time of death is uncertain.

- The lifespan of human beings is not fixed.
- More factors endanger life than support it.
- Our body is extremely fragile.

Conclusion: We must practice Dharma *now.*

Third Root Truth: Nothing can help at the time of death except Dharma practice.

- Wealth and possessions cannot help.
- Friends and relatives cannot help.

• Our body cannot help.

Conclusion: We must practice Dharma *purely*.

In this chapter, we will look at the first root truth—that death is certain.

Considering our situation honestly, we can see that the only thing we can be sure of at all is that we will die. Death is definite. Whether or not we will complete the plans we have for tomorrow is uncertain; that we will be alive tomorrow is uncertain; but the fact that we will die at some point is certain.

The *time* of our death, however, is uncertain. We cannot be sure that we will live for so many years or months. When we get up in the morning, it would be a misconception to think that we will definitely still be alive that same evening, just as it is a misconception to think that we will definitely live to a certain number of years. Even on the actual day of our death, we assume we will be alive tomorrow; this misconception stays with us until the time we do actually die.

This denial of death, this trust in an imagined state of permanence is the greatest cheat. For innumerable lives since beginningless time we have relied on the illusion of permanence, and if we continue to do so in this life, we will continue to squander our potential, never getting around to practicing Dharma purely. The nine-point meditation provides three points to consider in relation to this first truth that death is certain: (1) no being has ever escaped death, (2) our lifespan is constantly decreasing, and (3) there is very little time to practice the Dharma.

No Being Has Ever Escaped Death

As soon as we are born, we start aging and we begin rushing toward death. No samsaric being in the history of this world or any world system has ever escaped death. When we consider the twelve links of dependent origination, we can see how death is inevitable, and when we understand that, we can understand how preparing for our death is of paramount importance.

This cycle we need to break completely from, samsara, is summed up with the drawing of the Wheel of Life. At the center of the wheel is the hub, with the whole of samsara revolving around it. In the hub there are three animals: a pig, a rooster, and a snake, which represent the three poisons of ignorance, attachment, and anger, respectively. In most depictions of the Wheel of Life, the rooster's tail is shown in the pig's mouth and the snake's tail is in the rooster's. This shows that attachment comes from ignorance, and anger is usually a result of attachment, although this is not always the way the animals are depicted.

The next level around the hub shows the six types of sentient beings. On the right, depicted against a black background are an animal, a hungry ghost, and a hell being, each falling downward. On the left side of this ring, on a white background, are a human being, a demigod, and a god, each rising up.

Moving outward, we next have a larger ring that is divided into six panels depicting the realms themselves. Around the rim of the wheel are twelve drawings depicting the twelve links of dependent origination, the mechanism keeping us in samsara.

Beings in the lower three realms are overwhelmed with extremely acute and heavy sufferings, which the Buddha described in the four noble truths as the suffering of pain. The upper realms' beings can also experience the suffering of pain, especially we humans. Even the gods experience such suffering in the form of the five signs of death that occur days before they die,[74] which is said to be as terrible for them as experiencing hell. But the suffering experienced by the beings of the upper realms is mainly the other two types described by the Buddha: the suffering of change and pervasive compounded suffering.[75] The temporary samsaric pleasures we feel, which we incorrectly see as happiness, serve to create the suffering of change. Whenever the sense consciousnesses—seeing, hearing, and so forth—make contact with a sense object, attachment or aversion generally arises. This compels us either to cling to the object or to push it away and to mistakenly perceive this clinging or aversion as a permanent characteristic of the object itself. Because this habitual response misperceives impermanent phenomena as being permanent, it will inevitably only lead to us to disappointment and suffering. This is the suffering of change, the suffering that arises when things that we are attached to change. The simple fact is that pleasure does not last. It cannot. Unfortunately, we are attached to it, and so we suffer when it ends. Only when we understand this can we start to understand that samsaric pleasure *is* suffering.

The Twelve Links of Dependent Origination

The Buddha's teaching on the twelve links of dependent origination explains how cyclic existence works. It provides us with a causal blueprint that shows us how we become trapped in samsara and how we can liberate ourselves from it. The twelve links are (1) ignorance, (2) compounding action, (3) consciousness, (4) name and form (5) sense bases, (6) contact, (7) feeling, (8) craving, (9) grasping, (10) becoming, (11) birth, (12) and aging and death. This twelfth link then links back to first link, creating the chain of samsara that leads us around, link by link, in an unbroken circle of cause and effect, dragging us continuously from one suffering rebirth to another. Understanding this sequence, this chain of causality, gives us the key to unlock that chain and to break the power that is has to keep us bound in samsara.

In the twelve links of dependent origination, birth is the eleventh link, and aging and death is the twelfth link. In the Buddhist tradition, birth is defined as the joining of the mental aggregates with the form aggregate under the control of karma and delusions. Like everything else, this is a dependent arising; mind joins with form, and birth occurs dependent upon that. Being born depends on all these factors coming together.

Similarly, aging is understood as the decay of the body aggregates due to their being under the control of karma and delusions. The conditions that created the body's form are the same conditions that ensure its decay. From the moment we are conceived in our mother's womb, the conditions for its decay are ripening; thus, even as the body is developing, it is decaying. As soon as we are born, we may not be *old*, but we are *aging*, becoming older every day, every second. We consider old age to have arrived when we become aware of how far along this continual decay has gone. When the decay reaches the stage where the body no longer functions, then death occurs and the mind separates. Again, this is a dependent arising; due to the decaying of the form aggregate, we age.

Death, too, is a dependent arising. Death occurs when the mind separates from the body under the control of karma and delusions. As long as the mind is joined with the form aggregate, we are alive; as soon as the mind separates from the form aggregate and there is no life, we are dead.

There are three ways that we can study the twelve links. The first way is to go through them sequentially from one to twelve, showing how each link leads to the next, locking us into cyclic existence. We can also study them in reverse order so we can understand how to undo the causal chain and break this never-ending cycle: if we don't want death, we must eliminate birth, and for that, we must eliminate becoming, and craving, and grasping, and so forth.

We can also study the twelve links by focusing on the way that different bundles of links operate over multiple lifetimes. In *Heart of Dependent Arising*, Nagarjuna says,

> The first, eighth, and ninth are delusions.
> The second and tenth are karma.
> The remaining seven are sufferings.[76]

Ignorance, craving, and grasping (the first, eighth, and ninth links) are the delusions that create karma, which consists of compounding action and becoming (the second and tenth links). These are the links that propel us into our next rebirth. The other links—(3) consciousness, (4) name and form, (5) the six sense bases, (6) contact, (7) feeling, (11) birth, and (12) aging and death—are the "sufferings" that result from karma and delusions. It is interesting to note that the seventh link, feeling, is described as a "result," but it also *causes* craving and grasping, which cause becoming, the link that makes us grasp a physical form and, thus, propels us into the next life. If there were no craving and grasping, there would be no rebirth, and no aging and death. In this way, we can see that we generally do not complete the full set of twelve links in one life but, rather, over the course of two or even three lives—and not necessarily consecutive lives.

Our current human body exists due to our attachment to having a physical form, and this attachment to form is due to ignorance, the first link. In our previous life, that ignorance led to us craving and then grasping on to a physical form as we were dying. This grasping on to form at the time of death led to the next link, becoming, which gave rise to our current rebirth in this physical body. We took birth in the *human* realm, rather than in the lower realms, because we kept extremely good morality, practiced generosity, and made aspirations to be reborn as a human. Without pure morality and great charity, we would have been unable to attain an ordinary human body, let alone the kind of "perfect" human rebirth that we now enjoy, which affords us the rare and precious opportunity to encounter and practice Dharma. But even if we were to be incredibly generous, accumulating much merit, but did not keep pure morality, we not be reborn as human but would probably take birth as some other kind of transmigratory being, such as a wealthy *naga*.[77]

The links of ignorance and compounding action that produced this life were completed in the previous life, as were the links of craving and grasping that were the immediate cause of becoming, taking this body, which finished with the link of birth. Unfortunately, that does not mean that craving and grasping are finished. Although we passed through specific instances of craving and grasping in our previous life, the wheel continues to turn, leading us through another set of the twelve links. There are countless sets of the twelve links ripening and being created all the time. This is samsara.

The craving and grasping that arise at death cause our consciousness to connect to the coming together of sperm and egg in our future mother's womb. That triggers the formation of the fetus with its sense bases. Contact comes through those sense bases and that leads to feelings based on that contact. In that way, the whole cycle of a new life commences.

This is how one set of twelve links finishes within two lives; this is how we are tied to samsara life after life. It can also take three lifetimes. In the first lifetime ignorance and compounding action are completed; in the second, craving, grasping, and becoming are completed; in the third, the other seven are completed. Between the second and third lifetimes there can be billions of years. After an interminable period in the lower realms, the craving and grasping to be a human can somehow ripen at the time of death, being stronger than other karmic imprints, and we get reborn as a human.

Just as ignorance is always there until we are liberated, so the other links of the chain are there; this means that birth, aging, and death are always there.

Nobody Escapes Death

We will die. Our loved ones will die. Our enemies will die. Nobody escapes death. Every second, we are getting closer to death. Our consciousness is beginningless; it existed before this human existence and it will continue to exist after the destruction of this body. We had a body before this one and we will have a body after this one. When the body dies, the consciousness has to go somewhere; and it could well go to an existence far worse than this one.

Every being has to die and be reborn again and again. How that happens depends on how that being has spent their life. The beggar who dies in poverty on the street and the king who dies surrounded by luxury in a bejeweled palace filled with servants both face death with the same fear. There is something very magnificent and permanent-looking about a great king, but when he dies he might die in misery, terrified of what will happen to him. Even his body, so pampered and fine, could look shriveled and pitiful as he dies.

The Buddha explained that the sun, the moon, the seven oceans, and even Mount Meru—the great axis of the world, which holds the realm of the gods and demigods—will all be burned in the great conflagration at the end of this world system, leaving not even a tiny particle of dust. If even this whole universe will one day be completely nonexistent, how can we expect this fragile body to exist forever?

The truth is that nobody escapes death. The life of the Buddha was an object lesson in this. He was born, he became enlightened and taught for over forty years, but even he had to die. He had taken on a physical body, which is inherently subject to decay and death. Dying was the Buddha's last great lesson to us on impermanence, showing us that death is an inevitable part of life.

The great arhats have to die, the bodhisattvas have to die, the holy beings who have shown us the Dharma in this very lifetime have to die. After death, only their names remain, only our memory of them. Why, then, do we think that we can escape this?

We are so fortunate to still have many great teachers among us to explain the Dharma to us. But they, too, will die. Since the time of the Buddha, countless great yogis have studied, meditated, and explained the Dharma to others, but they are not around now to guide us. The Buddha's two heart disciples, Shariputra and Maudgalyayana, and all those amazing scholars who attained high realizations and wrote the incredible teachings that clarified the Buddha's teachings—the teachers called the Two Sublime Ones, Gunaprabha and Shakyaprabha, and the Six Ornaments, Nagarjuna, Asanga, Aryadeva, Vasubandhu, Dignaga, and Dharmakirti—all these great beings are no longer here. We cannot meet them, no matter how much money we pay or how much we pray. All that is left are their holy names and the texts they left behind.

Similarly, the great yogis of Tibet, like Naropa, Tilopa, and Saraha, all the inspiring teachers of the four traditions—Marpa, Milarepa, Sakya Pandita, Padmasambhava, Lama Tsongkhapa, and so forth—not one of these precious ones who completed the path and benefited so many sentient beings is alive today. We can see their texts, we can visit the caves and monasteries where they lived, but we can't see them.

Even so many of the great teachers that introduced Tibetan Buddhism to the West have died: His Holiness Ling Rinpoché, His Holiness Trijang Rinpoché, His Holiness Zong Rinpoché, Kirti Tsenshab Rinpoché, Geshé Lama Konchog, and of course, Lama Yeshe, whose kindness in helping to bring Buddhadharma to the West is beyond words, who is kinder than the buddhas of the three times. We are so fortunate that many have been swiftly reborn, but that is not at all certain when a great master dies.

For so many Western students, Lama Yeshe was like a father. He gave teachings in a way that totally turned people's minds away from nonvirtue and toward pure virtue. He advised and looked after his students, solving their problems and showing them the way out of suffering. His Western students found it so easy to take refuge fully in him and never thought that it would ever be any different. And yet, when he died, so many of us were like a ship without a rudder, floating aimlessly and confused.

If these great teachers have to die, then there is no question that we, too, have to die. In the sutra *The Sayings of the Buddha on Impermanence*, the Buddha says,

> If all—even the buddhas, pratyekabuddhas,
> And shravaka disciples of the buddhas—
> Abandon their bodily remains,
> Need I speak of ordinary beings![78]

Considering the inevitability of death within our own family is a very effective way to better appreciate the impermanence of our own life. Besides talking about our past ancestors, whom we may know about but have never met, there are also the people, relatives and parents, that we have known in our life who have since died. All of them are only names now, existing only in the memories of those who still live. Even among our family members who are still alive, some might be quite old, and so we assume they will die before we do. We just don't know. We may dream of the inheritance we will get when an old aunt dies, but that is deluded thinking. Just because we may be young and healthy does not mean that we will outlive our older relatives. Anybody can die at any moment. There is always the possibility that we will be the next in our family to die.

The world is full of proof that people die every day—even though they, like us, probably never thought that they would—and yet we still ignore this evidence that is all around us. So many people have died *today* for so many reasons and in so many situations: an illness such as a sudden heart attack or stroke, a traffic accident or plane crash, while they were traveling, or working, or resting at home. Every second of the day people die, most confident that they would not die. Many of these are people who were younger and fitter than we are; maybe they were going to work, dancing in a club, enjoying a coffee, getting a haircut, shopping in a supermarket, all of them sure that they would not die today. All the projects that filled their lives will now never be finished. They were dancing a few hours ago, and now they lie in a morgue, immobile like a log or a pile of stones.

We have evidence of this everywhere. Whenever we read a newspaper or watch the television news, the stories are full of reminders of impermanence and death. Modern media constantly give us very effective meditations on death, as if impermanence and death is knocking on our door and saying hello, telling us that our life is exactly like this, completely in the nature of impermanence. These stories tell us that death is certain, and therefore we must hurry and not be lazy, that we have to work now to ensure the happiness of our future lives.

People that we know—people that we see often and think of as being permanent entities—suddenly die in the middle of their "permanent" life, popping like a bubble on the surface of the water. When we see bubbles on the surface of water, we may have no way of knowing which bubble will burst first—we just can't tell—but we can be assured that each one will pop sooner or later. When we look around, we can see how people can die at any age and for any reason. The richest person can die despite having a team of top doctors attending them. No one, no matter how wealthy or powerful, is immune to impermanence.

Nobody can escape death. If it were possible to be free from death, then there should be somebody alive today who is proof of that, but that is not so. We cannot point out anybody who was here when the earth began, or who has been alive for a thousand years, or even for two hundred years. Every being, sooner or later, has to leave the body behind and take a new one. For humans, that rarely means living even a hundred years.

Even the most famous person in the world cannot use their fame to buy their way out of death. Elvis, who was loved by millions, still died; Mao Zedong, who controlled the most populous nation in the world and had incredible power, still died. The most famous public figures, movie stars, and pop stars all still die sooner or later. Think of the people who were the most famous when you were a child; some are still alive, but most are probably dead. Some even became famous *because* they died!

Even if a person is very powerful, very strong, they cannot avoid death. A person as strong as an elephant will die as surely as the weakest person. Generally, when powerful people arrive at the moment of death, their demeanor completely changes. They might have been quite arrogant and pompous, but in the face of death they may become like a terrified, pleading child. There are often even physical changes that occur when death is near, such as the face becoming drawn and the body and hands shrinking.

The most powerful general cannot stop death. He can deploy all his army and fire all his missiles. He can even destroy the whole world with atomic bombs in an attempt to prevent himself from dying, but it will not work. The most ruthless dictator can train thousands of bodyguards to protect him day and night, and yet death will still sneak in and take him, all the bodyguards in the world being powerless to stop it.

When the time has come for us to die, we must die. It's as simple as that. We cannot cheat karma. There is a story of the Buddha that exemplifies this: Prince Virudhaka, the son of a powerful rival of the Buddha's natal clan, the Shakyas, decided to slaughter the entire Shakya clan because they had repeatedly insulted him and his family. Some of Shakya men and women ran to the Buddha and begged his help, so the Buddha used his miraculous powers to hide them in a begging bowl (whether he shrank them or expanded the bowl, I don't know). Although none of the enemy discovered them in the begging bowl, they still died because, as the Buddha explained, they had accumulated the karma to die on that day like the rest of the Shakyas. Maudgalyayana, one of the Buddha's two heart disciples, hid some people on a distant planet,[79] but they too died.

In *A Guide to the Bodhisattva's Way of Life*, Shantideva says,

> Day and night, without respite, my life is spent,
> with no possibility of restitution.
> How could it be
> that I would not die?[80]

Nobody escapes death, and there is nowhere in the world or beyond the world where we can go where we can escape death. Not even Disneyland! We can go to Disneyland to stay young forever and we will still die. We can build the deepest, thickest fallout shelter to protect ourselves from the nuclear bombs that could destroy us, but we can't escape death. We can bury ourselves in the middle of a huge mountain made of diamonds, something so solid and indestructible, but that will not stop death. There is no sanctuary that will hide us from death.

Even if we could leave the earth, we cannot leave death behind. We could buy a ticket on a space shuttle that would take us to other planets and even out of the solar system, maybe even to another galaxy. But when we got there, death would be waiting for us.

Understanding this cycle of life, death, and rebirth is the most important education we can have. Modern science, no matter how developed, is unable to teach us this. Many of us live in a wealthy country, where people have access to every convenience and live in a state of comfort that earlier generations could barely dream of. Whenever there is the slightest problem or discomfort, scientists discover ways to overcome it. But no matter how advanced and wonderful these scientific discoveries are, they will never be able to overcome death. Even leaving aside the problem of death itself, science is unable to stop even the suffering associated with death: that of aging, of sickness, of leaving behind all we love.

Friends Who Have Died

It is very useful to remember family and friends who have died and to reflect on how each of them was a part of our life and now is gone. In my own lifetime, many people that I have known have died: gurus, family members, monks, nuns, lay students, benefactors, and all sorts of people who were my friends. During the month-long retreats at our centers, we often read out the list of people who have died that I have been asked to pray for. Sometimes the list is very long.

Just think of your own family and consider all your ancestors that have lived throughout the past generations. You might be lucky and have a grandparent who is still alive but, beyond that, all those from the earlier generations have long since died. My own grandparents are no longer alive; even my parents have already died. I know it must be the same for many of you.

As a small child, I didn't know my grandfather at all; I only remember my grandmother, very old with gray hair, always carrying a mala and usually sitting next to the kitchen fire. Although I was born in Solu Khumbu, which is in northeastern Nepal very near Mount Everest, I was sent to Tibet to study for a few years. When I returned, my grandmother had become sick, then blind, and soon she couldn't do anything. A few years later she died. My uncle cared for her for many years, bringing her food and taking care of her daily needs. For a long time, he offered service to his mother in this way, even though he was not well himself.

Eventually my uncle couldn't eat and was in so much pain. He went to many doctors in Tibet and around Solu Khumbu, but the medicine they prescribed didn't help him. He eventually went to consult with a lama who lived near the cave at Lawudo, where I was born. I was very little at the time and I liked this lama a lot. He was kind and played with me. He told my uncle that his sickness was due to a karmic obscuration that could only be cured by purification. My uncle was very poor, but there was a family with a married lama who helped him with his temporal needs and food, and with their help he was able to build a little room where he could do his prostrations and look after his mother. I think he did about a hundred thousand prostrations a year for about seven years, and afterward he was completely cured and was never sick after that. His mother (my grandmother) died soon after this.

I never met my father in my life. About the time I was due to be born, he had already passed away to his future rebirth. The only thing of him that I remember is that when we children slept together at night, our blanket was our father's coat, what Tibetans call a *chuba*, made of animal skin with the fur on the inside and with long sleeves. Sometimes we would tell each other, "This belonged to Dad."

Two of my siblings died young. I had a brother who was born with a double head and died soon after he was born, and I also had an older sister who died in childhood.

My mother, who everybody called Amala, used to chant Chenrezig's mantra OM MANI PADME HUM fifty thousand times every day. She told me this one day in 1991 when we were sitting on the roof of Kopan Monastery, but she said she wasn't able to do that many anymore. Just then, an eagle landed on her head, which I later discovered from a text by Nagarjuna is a sign that a person is going to die soon.

That year, although she had some sickness, she still came all the way from Lawudo to Varanasi to attend a Kalachakra initiation that we had requested His Holiness the Dalai Lama to confer. She was almost blind by this time, so I'm not sure if she was able to see His Holiness, but she was able to meet His Holiness and received blessings directly from him. Later that same night, she passed away.

It is said that when those who have done great purification and are going to reborn in a pure land are dying, they see many holy beings. As my almost-blind mother was dying, this is what she said she saw, and when I later checked with somebody who can see such things, it seems she had been reborn in Chenrezig's pure land. Considering how unbelievably compassionate she was all her life, I was not surprised to hear this.

Sometime later, she took rebirth again in a family who lived close to where she had lived in Lawudo. When this reincarnation was four, he was enthroned at Kopan Monastery, but although it was my idea to educate him at Kopan, his parents had a divination done that said he should be educated in India at Penor Rinpoché's monastery, and they took that advice. He had only been there for fifteen days when a heavy storm started when he was playing outside. As he ran inside, he tripped and knocked his head on some stone steps and broke his skull. After some treatment in a small hospital, he was sent to Bangalore, where he was operated on by a surgeon who was a friend of my brother's wife. The operation seemed to go well, and Amala's reincarnation seemed to be recovering. Unfortunately, a piece of bone was left inside the wound, and the boy died. It was very sad that he didn't live long, but he has been reincarnated in Potala, Chenrezig's pure land, once again.

Then, there is the story of my first Western pen pal that I had when I was first in India as a young student, an old Jewish lady living in London called Rachel Levi. At that time, my schoolteacher was a Western woman who had become a Buddhist nun, Mrs. Freda Bedi; I think she must have been one of the first Western nuns. One of the ways she helped the monks was by finding them pen pals in the West, and the pen pal she found for me was Mrs. Levi. Once we started corresponding, she often sent photos of herself, some from when she was young and others as she was then, which was very old. I was confused because I was quite young and didn't realize the pictures were of the same person, so I didn't know which one was her. I thought she was sending me pictures of two different people. My understanding of aging and impermanence was so tiny at that age!

She was a very interesting person; she was supposed to have written some books and was very popular because of her very pleasant personality. She wrote me a letter a week for seven years. My room was full of her letters, strewn all over the place, but I didn't reply very often. She was in her late eighties and had so much interest in the Dharma, but my English was so limited so I couldn't really help much.

Then her flood of letters stopped, and I became worried. It seems that she had undergone an operation, and although she tried to write again, she couldn't even finish the letter she was writing. After that, I had a dream that somebody gave me a white letter at a place near to where I was living. The next day, I received a letter exactly like that from a friend of my pen pal explaining that she had died. I arranged for more than one thousand monks and high lamas who lived there to offer prayers for her to find a better rebirth.

My contact with Western people was very limited, but later, after Lama Yeshe and I had moved to India in the late 1960s, we met somebody who was to become our first Western student: Zina Rachevshy. People sometimes called her a princess because her father was somehow connected with the deposed Russian royal family, but before she went to India she had spent most of her life in America and France. She had a son and a daughter from different fathers and had lived many different lives ranging from rich to poor, upper class to peasant. There was almost nothing she had not tried and almost no kind of life she had not lived.

She was very important figure in the transmission of Tibetan Buddhism to the West. In 1968, she took ordination as a Buddhist nun and later helped us start Kopan Monastery, near Boudha outside Kathmandu in the early 1970s. In 1973, she went into a long retreat at Lawudo in the foothills of the Nepali Himalayas. After a few months, she sent a letter to Lama Yeshe and me in Dharamsala saying she had finished her retreat and would be coming to Dharamsala to take teachings from the great teachers that were there at that time. She was the sort of person who wrote lots of letters, but this one was written hurriedly in pencil, and she didn't even have time to sign it. Just after we received her letter, we received a telegram saying that she had died.

This was right after her long retreat, and she had received many initiations from the lama who was at the Lawudo Gompa. It seems from what the others said that she was very interested in the death process, having read lots of books on it, and she had some control throughout her death, so it wasn't bad that she died when she did. Even so, her death was totally unexpected.

According to the other people who lived there, she got sick two or three days before her death. But just before she died, she began to feel a little better and she sat up with her mala in her hand. Her daughter, Rea, who was there, looked her in the face and cried, "Mummy, please don't die!" I heard that her daughter was upset, but after three or four days she was playing with her toys again because she knew her mother was happy.

Even though Zina's illness progressed quickly, she had a little time to prepare for her death. She had many plans for things she wanted to do in the future, but all of a sudden, before she had time to do all these things, she was facing the end of her life. It had been her constant wish to help other people, but she was always worried that she was incapable of doing so. Still, she was very lucky that she could die as a nun.

Although Zina died in a very simple, tiny room far away from most of her family and friends, she had spent most of the previous year in retreat and was ready for death. In these ways, I think she was far luckier than somebody who dies in a luxury apartment in the West, surrounded by top doctors and a loving family. Later, it was confirmed by His Holiness the Sakya Trizin that a young French child had been recognized as Zina's reincarnation. Rea had trouble accepting the fact that her mother had reincarnated.

Another story is that of Lama Pasang, who was one of Lama Yeshe's students in Tibet, who served Lama Yeshe while he lived in Buxa Duar in India[81] and then later in Nepal. Later, when we founded Kopan Monastery, he took responsibility for the construction and equipping of the monastery. Lama Pasang was tall with a very strong body. He always looked so solid, so permanent. He was a constant presence around Kopan; every day we would see him busy shopping or looking after his workers. Serving Lama Yeshe by taking care of Kopan Monastery was his first priority and he offered his service to Lama from his heart for many years.

Observing Lama Pasang's skills and dedication, I asked him to be responsible for building a kitchen at the new nunnery that we had built nearby. Soon after, I went to Lawudo, on the trail that leads to Tibet, to consecrate the stupa built near there for my mother to accumulate merit. Upon my return to Kathmandu, as I got into the car at the airport, Venerable Roger told me that Lama Pasang had died the day before.

There was a well outside the nuns' kitchen, which Lama Pasang had covered, wanting to keep the water clean of construction debris. A young incarnate lama, Geleg Gyatso, however, advised him against it, worrying that covering the well would allow noxious gas to build up. Lama Pasang just laughed him off, saying he was the elder of the two.

One morning, a local worker went to the bottom of the well to fix something and was overcome by the gas and disappeared under the water. Lama Pasang always had a lot of compassion for his workers and, as soon as he saw this, he rushed down into the well, but because of the gas, he also collapsed. After that, another local worker also rushed into the well to try and rescue Lama Pasang. Both of the local workers, being quite small and weak, disappeared under the water. But Lama Pasang was tall and strong, and so I think his head remained above the water, although he could not speak because of the effects of the gas.

The nuns then tied a rope around the Kopan driver, Lobsang Rabgaye, and he started down into the well to try and rescue the men, but after only a few steps he also started to stumble and grow weak, crying out, "Now I'm dead!" The nuns then pulled him up with the rope, but the gas had made him delirious. The nuns burned the hair and pieces of robe of a high lama near his nose and gave him some sacred pills, which helped. The next day he had completely recovered, but Lama Pasang had died. So, even Lama Pasang, who always looked very strong and permanent, has gone. Now he doesn't exist.

Our Lifespan Is Constantly Decreasing

The second point to consider is that although though there are many factors that can bring us a premature death, nothing can add to our lifespan. We only have so many years in this body, and every second brings us closer and closer to death. Karma has determined we have this human body with these attributes, and one of those attributes is the lifespan. As soon as we are conceived in the womb that lifespan starts running out, like sand in an hourglass.

Maybe our lifespan is five years, maybe ten, maybe fifty, we just don't know. We do know it's not two hundred. Whatever our lifespan is, it is only a certain number of years, a certain number of days, and certain number of seconds. Just so many in-breaths and out-breaths. It is said that every day we take something like twenty thousand breaths. One day there will simply be an out-breath without the next in-breath. Dying does not involve a lot of hard work, it's just not breathing in after an exhalation. It's as simple as that.

Despite the brevity of life, because we cling to a false sense of permanence, we never feel that time is running out. In fact, the time left to us is constantly decreasing, and there's nothing we can do that can add to it. Certain practices, such as long-life initiations or sparing the lives of animals, can stop hindrances that cause us to die *prematurely* but can do nothing to *add* to our life at all. As we will see, there are so many more conditions that contribute toward death than toward life, so even though we might have a natural lifespan of, say, seventy years, there are many, many things that can cause our death well before we reach seventy. A serious life hindrance might mean that we could die at twenty, whereas if we do some animal liberation practice, we could clear that hindrance and then live our full lifespan.

Perhaps our lifespan is a million years. That is a very long time, too long to think about death, surely. A million years seems so long that it feels permanent. But a million years is nothing more than a collection of millennia, which in turn is a collection of centuries, which is a collection of years, which is a collection of months, which is a collection of days, which is a collection of hours, which is a collection of minutes, which is a collection of seconds. And we can even break seconds up into split-seconds and nanoseconds.

When we take a picture with a camera, the shutter may only open for a thousandth of a second. It is very good to relate this to how quickly our life finishes. In that thousandth of a second, we are that much closer to death. Our life consists of so many thousandths of seconds, ticking away constantly. So, a million years is nothing more than split-seconds, ticking away. From the moment our million-year lifespan starts, each second is a second closer to death.

Each tick of the clock reminds us that we are moving away from birth and toward death. The second hand of a clock moves around very quickly, marking off one more minute gone from our life. Soon a whole morning is gone, never to be recovered, and then a whole day. Sometimes it seems like we blink and we are a whole year older, and then fifty years has gone in a flash.

Think of what your lifespan will probably be if something else doesn't shorten it. Seventy years? Eighty years maybe? How many of the seventy years have already disappeared, never to be reclaimed? How quickly have you gone from that little baby to the person you now are? How much longer do you have? Say it's thirty years. Each year is so many days, so many hours, so many minutes, so many seconds. And those seconds are going, going, going.

A useful meditation that I recommend is to simply look at a watch. A watch can serve as a complete teaching on impermanence. As you listen to the watch ticking—not the loud ticking of a big clock but the soft ticking of a watch—be aware that with each tick there are only a certain number of these clicks left until you die. Think, "How quickly it finishes; how quickly it finishes." If the watch has a second hand, just observe how quickly that second hand goes around, marking off the seconds, each second, each minute never to be repeated, leaving us always that much closer to death.

We are powerless against death. It is like we are running as fast as we can toward a precipice, and nothing can stop us when we reach it. We have no brakes. Or imagine a stone falling from a high building toward the ground, or rocks tumbling down a mountain in an avalanche, never stopping for a moment. We are rushing toward death like that. From the moment we were conceived in our mother's womb until our eventual death, we are hurtling toward death without pausing for even a second. If we were actually aware that our life was like this, we would realize that we have no time to waste indulging in samsaric pleasure. Thinking like this is a very effective way of training the mind.

The sun rises in the morning, it gets higher in the sky, and before we know it, it descends and sinks below the horizon, another day gone so quickly. We light a stick of incense, and before we can think, it is nothing but ash. We plant a seed and watch the shoot break the surface, and then it is a bud and then a flower, and before we can really appreciate it, the flower is wilted and dead. The leaves on the trees come out in spring, turn red in the fall, and then die. Nothing is fixed; nothing is permanent.

It is like a mouse stealing just one grain at a time from a huge pile of rice. It might seem that the mouse will be working forever. But as each grain is taken, that is one less grain, and even though the pile is like a mountain, and even though the mouse takes only one grain each time, suddenly the pile is gone.

Atisha uses the example of a river to show impermanence. Something that seems permanent is nothing more than drops of water always moving past, never stopping even for an instant. We see this with a waterfall, which seems to be one stable thing but it is actually constantly changing, constantly flowing past our eyes. Like a river, like a waterfall, our life is flowing forward constantly. It can never be reversed.

We are moving closer and closer to our death and our next rebirth, which could well be in the suffering lower realms. It's far better to face that now while we can do something about it than to deny this truth and have to suffer so terribly in our next life. Being afraid of the prospect of being reborn in the lower realms is billions of times better than having to actually experience them. As Shantideva says,

> Wouldn't it be fortunate if a man condemned to death
> were freed after only having his hand cut [off]?
> Would it not be equally fortunate if one were to suffer pain
> in this life instead of ending up in hell?[82]

When we are tied up, waiting to be executed, it is better to have our hand cut off, no matter how painful it is, rather than submit to death.

People want to hang onto their youth forever, but it can't be done. So many people try to find artificial ways to stay young, wearing the new fashions, coloring their hair, having plastic surgery, and so forth. But nothing can stop us from aging. We can paint ourselves to pretend that we are not aging, but it is like painting rotting fruit. An old piece of fruit can be painted so it looks fresh and beautiful on the outside; but inside, it is still decaying, shriveling up, and becoming sour and inedible.

When a person is dying, there are obvious signs of death: they lose the ability to speak, their eyes roll up, their tongue becomes shorter and thicker, their mouth dries out, and there arises from them the smell of death. We don't have those signs of near death, and so we feel confident that we are fully living and not dying. But even so, there are signs that we don't see that indicate we are approaching death. Our body is changing year by year, day by day, minute by minute. Our body is aging, our breathing is weakening, our health is declining; we are slowly winding down like an old-fashioned wind-up watch.

Although it may be troubling to think about our approaching death in this way, doing so can be incredibly useful and valuable. Facing the reality of the inevitable exhaustion of the hours of our life can be wonderfully transformative. With such a mindset, we would have no time for idleness, for wasting what time we have; there would be nothing else to do but practice the Dharma.

Like a Criminal Led to Execution

The Fifth Dalai Lama once said that we are running toward the Lord of Death, so even though we call ourselves alive, we are actually like a dead person walking, like a condemned criminal being taken to the gallows. It is like we are in custody, being taken to where we will be executed for our crimes. The sentence has been passed and the judgment is final; there will be no reprieve. As we are being conducted to the place of execution, the streets might be lined with friends and loved ones, all begging the guards to spare us, but nothing can change our fate. They are weeping, crying, pleading with us not to die, but there is nothing they or we can do. They try to give us things that they think might make our last minutes happier: money, beautiful clothes, delicious food and drinks. But none of these things bring us any pleasure at all, the sight of them just making us more miserable, knowing we will never be able to enjoy them again.

We are in this situation because we have been overwhelmed with attachment to sense pleasure throughout our life, and now the sight of the objects of our desire brings us such misery. These things promised us happiness and now they have condemned us to this terrible death. The closer we get to the place of our execution, the more we realize how these objects of desire have deceived us. We think that each building we pass might be the jail where we will be executed. Even if the building is very beautiful and grand, it looks awful to us.

Perhaps if we could repent our crime the police would let us go, but we are too habituated to the mind of desire, and now that we are losing our most precious object, our body, we cling to it even more tightly. The evil thought of the eight worldly dharmas has us firmly in its hold. We cry out because now it's too late.

In reality, however, there is still time. If we can see where we will be led by the mind entrapped in this deceit and develop a strong determination not to follow this mind, we can start to practice Dharma purely and to transform our mindset from one of self-cherishing to one that cherishes others. This is why it is so beneficial to think like this. If we were rowing a boat on a beautiful lake, with all the time in the world, we wouldn't have the energy to do what we must do. But we are not; we are in a police car on our way to our execution, and things couldn't be more urgent.

When we see animals being led to slaughter, we can think that we are like those animals. Maybe this is something you generally don't see if you live in a country where meat is cut and wrapped and put into supermarket freezers before you buy it, but it's a common sight in Asia. There, it's common to see a goat tethered and pulled out of the yard where it has lived with its family and dragged down the road toward the butcher's place. Each step is a step closer to the cleaver that is waiting for it. Each second is a second less of this precious life that it cherishes. Until that moment, it had no idea it was condemned to this fate. It thought it would live forever. When we see an animal like this, it really looks as if it knows what is going to happen; it looks terrified. The closer to the butcher it gets, the more its terror increases. Finally, it is there, and the assistant holds it while the butcher raises his cleaver and cuts into the goat's neck. Perhaps it takes a few blows to sever the head, and the goat screams with pain throughout.

We are that goat, being pulled down the road to the butcher. Trapped in a false illusion of permanence, we had no idea this would happen. Now we are bound by the rope of karma, and there is no escaping unless we can cut that rope and be free from karma and delusions. This is possible. But only if we become aware at this very moment of how dangerous our situation is.

Every Step Is a Step Closer to the Grave

Like an arrow shot from a bow, from the moment we are shot from our mother's womb—from the moment of our conception in fact—we are constantly flying toward our target, death. This is not some hypothetical piece of psychology or some religious trip designed to scare us into being good. It is simply a fact—one of the few undeniable facts of life. We can't escape it. We have put ourselves into this situation and there is no way we can change it now that we are experiencing this result. If we see that no lasting happiness can come while we are caught in this kind of existence, then we should be smart and do something to prevent being caught in this situation again before it's too late. So, although we may not currently be experiencing extreme suffering, like so many other sentient beings, we shouldn't think that we are immune from it. As far as impermanence goes, all samsaric beings are the same, whether they are at the top of samsara, like the highest gods experiencing the most incredible pleasure, or in the lowest hell. In his text *Instruction That Is Good in the Beginning, Middle, and End*, Patrul Rinpoché says,

> What can you say about years, months, or days?
> Look how things change every moment, right now!
> Each moment that passes brings you closer to death;
> now, this very moment, recite the six-syllable mantra.
>
> As your life runs out like a setting sun sinking away,
> death closes in like the lengthening shadows of evening;
> now what's left of your life will vanish as fast as the last fading shadows;
> There's no time to waste—recite the six-syllable mantra.[83]

The six-syllable mantra here, of course, refers to Chenrezig's mantra OM MANI PADME HUM, which Patrul Rinpoche says to recite as a way of exhorting us to practice the Dharma.

We see our life as lasting many years and we celebrate our birthday each year as some kind of prize, a special mark to say we made it this far. While we are happy to have lived for so many years, we rarely think that each year lived means one less year that we have left. Many of us think of our age in years, each birthday making us one year older—and we are that old—and no older—until the next birthday comes. We don't realize we are aging second by second.

I really recommend that you think like this all the time. When you walk, you should meditate on impermanence and death as you walk. Think that every step you take is a step closer to the grave, that for each step you take away from your room, that much of your life is gone. With the first step, that much of your life is gone; with the second step, that much more of your life is gone, and the same with the third step, the fourth step, and so on. When you go shopping, think that every step closer to the shops is a step closer to the grave.

When you return home, think the same thing: that much of your life is finished.

You can do this with any and all of your activities. When you write a letter, think in the same way. As you write "Dear," think that is one less "dear" you will ever write; you are that much closer to death. For every word you write, think that much of your life is gone. When you reach the end and you write your name, think that you have come that much closer to death. It is the same when you are gossiping. With each word you say, see it as that much of your life has gone. With every breath that you spend engaging in idle speech instead of in activities that are helpful for you and others, that much of your life has been wasted. When you read a book, every word you read brings you one word closer to death; every page brings you one page closer to death. When you finish that book, it is one less book you will read in this life. When you eat a plate of food, each time the spoon goes to the mouth, think of it as a spoonful of life that has finished. For every mantra and every mala of mantras that you recite, think that your life has become that much shorter, that you are that much closer to death. You can also do this when you are driving, seeing your life racing past with each passing mile. This can be a particularly effective version of this meditation because you can feel the speed and so can really feel how you are racing to death. The faster you drive, the quicker you reach the hells. You might be driving to work or to a restaurant, but you are really driving to your place of execution.

By practicing like this, something as simple as a walk can be a profound Dharma practice.

The nature of impermanence is that we are all dying every moment. In the hospital, there are people who are terminally ill who are said to be "dying." That is definite. They might have only a few days or a few hours left; they just don't know. But, in truth, it is the same for us. We think that *we* are living and *they* are dying, but we are all in the process of dying. Some of us have only a few hours left, some a few days, some a few years. No matter what age we are, there are many examples of people who have died when they were the same age or younger. Life is full of danger, and death can happen at any time.

When we look truthfully at our life, it's kind of frightening. We seem so strong and solid, but we are actually so fragile. This body is like a machine that can break down at any moment. We rely on the air going in and out of our lungs to keep us alive, and that breathing can finish at any time.

There will be nothing we can do when death comes. There will be no way to fix it then. If we are writing a letter and we make a mistake, we can correct the mistake or even start over. If we fail an examination at school, we can retake it. If our car breaks down, a mechanic can fix it. But when we see we have wasted our life, we cannot fix it as easily as that. When the time comes for our mind, the guest, to leave the guesthouse of the body, as Thokmé Sangpo says, we must do that. There is no way to change the past. We can change the present and the future—we have that freedom—but we cannot change the past that we have already wasted.

We Must Practice Dharma

The conclusion of the first root truth is that we must practice the Dharma. If we fail to remember death, we die without having practiced Dharma during our life. Perhaps we feel that there is plenty of time left for us to practice Dharma in the future. But as we have seen, that is not the way it is at all, and if we hold to this mistaken belief, we will waste the years that we do have left with mundane concerns. With so much time taken up in our worldly activities there is no time to practice Dharma. This is very nicely summed up in *The Descent into the Womb Sutra*:

> Half of the one-hundred-year life span is covered by sleep. Ten years are childhood. Twenty years are old age. Sorrow, lamentation, physical suffering, mental discomfort, and

> agitation take up time. Many hundreds of different physical illnesses also consume your time.[84]

Look at how much time we *don't* spend practicing Dharma now. Even if we live for a hundred years, half of each day is spent asleep, and because it is very difficult to create virtue while we are sleeping, we are effectively only talking about fifty years. We spend the first ten to fifteen years of our life as children, sleeping, shouting, playing, without the wisdom to make life meaningful at all. For the last fifteen to twenty years of life people often suffer from debilitating conditions that make it difficult to do the things that they want to do. We can see this with the old people we know, like our grandparents. Even if they wanted to do prostrations to gain merit and purify their obscurations, their body wouldn't let them. Or if they wanted to read a Dharma book, they may not be able to see the words or focus on their meaning. All this is to say that we should not wait until we are very old to start practicing Dharma, because by then it may be too difficult.

Of the fifty years of our waking life, that leaves twenty years where we have the opportunity to practice Dharma. Unfortunately, we usually spend most of each day engaged in mundane activities, and even if we have a set meditation practice—say an hour a day out of our twenty-four—we are often distracted and dull during that time, leaving us unable to concentrate and, thus, unable to practice purely. Geshé Kamapa describes this, saying,

> You say, "My contemplation is not working." But when did you contemplate? During the day you are completely distracted. During the night you are sleeping. So don't tell lies! This can happen to anybody. In the daytime you are busy with all sorts of things concerned with this life.[85]

When we do a positive action, it is usually clouded by some negativity, such as pride when we have been generous or anger that somebody hasn't thanked us enough for our help. We would be lucky if the time that we spend doing Dharma practice over the course of our life would add up a single year.

This is why meditation on impermanence is vital; it reminds us that we have no time to waste. Watching our breath, watching the second hand on our watch, we should always see these as signs that our perfect human rebirth is constantly running out. This will motivate us to stop wasting our life and to do only what is meaningful, what will assure us of at least another positive rebirth. Unless we develop this motivation, we won't make any preparations, and then life will be gone.

The Heart's Utmost Need

One of the most powerful teachings is *The Heart's Utmost Need* by Pabongka Dechen Nyingpo. In it, Pabongka Rinpoche says,

> I must keep this heart advice for myself—
> *The Heart's Utmost Need*—in the core of my heart.
> Don't be distracted! Don't be distracted!
> I'll reflect upon the state of my life from the depths of my heart.
>
> A fool who pretends to be capable, smart, and clever
> While clinging to the child's play of this life's appearances,
> Suddenly I'm overcome by the terrifying Lord of Death
> And, filled with despair, I'm unable to bear it.
> This is going to happen to me!
>
> Thinking, "I won't die, I won't die for quite some time,"
> While I'm distracted by the never-ending activities of this life,
> Suddenly the terrifying Lord of Death arrives
> And announces, "Now it's time for you to die."
> This is going to happen to me!
>
> Though I put effort into making arrangements saying "tomorrow" and "tomorrow,"

Now, suddenly, I have to go.
This is going to happen to me!

Without freedom, leaving behind in disarray
All my unfinished work, food, and drink, I have to depart.
This is going to happen to me![86]

We are so busy chasing the objects of our craving and desire that there is little time to practice Dharma. This is how we have cheated ourselves in this life. This is the essential advice of *The Heart's Utmost Need*: don't be distracted by what is meaningless. This is the heart advice of Pabongka Dechen Nyingpo.

We can compare our worldly activities to the play of a child whose only interest is to attain some fleeting happiness in a toy or a game. Clinging to this life is the "child's play" that robs us of true happiness and throws us into an unhappy rebirth after we die.

We might appear very intelligent and clever, having attained a high degree in university, and might be considered brilliant by others; we can be famous for having incredible ideas and for being hugely successful in business. But in reality we are still very foolish. All these impressive achievements are really nothing more than the play of a child because they are all solely about the appearances of this life. Just as child in the middle of a game does not consider others or worry about the future, a worldly person does nothing that benefits others at all or even benefits themselves beyond this life.

Then, while we are chasing the fleeting goals of this life, distracted by the activities of this life that never get finished, like a child at play, suddenly, unexpectedly, we are overwhelmed by the terrifying Lord of Death. This is going to happen to us.

A year comes and goes, and we think we are not going to die for a while. Then another year comes and goes, another birthday, and still we think we are not going to die for a while. And this goes on each year, each month, each day, while we live with the thought that we are not going to die for a while. Then, suddenly, while we are totally occupied with the meaningless works of this life, the Lord of Death is there and the time to die is now.

We haven't finished traveling, we haven't finished building our house, we haven't completed our degree, but the Lord of Death does not wait patiently until we have finished everything we want to finish. We cannot bargain; we cannot put off our death until this important work is done. There are no arrangements that can be made, no letters or phone calls we can make that will make him wait.

In the middle of writing a book, while having a meal or drinking with friends, before the television program finishes, without choice we must leave everything behind. I have even heard of somebody dying in a plane crash on the way to a meditation course.

Pabongka Rinpoche says that this will happen to us. One day, unexpectedly, shockingly, we will have to leave all we are doing behind.

The Heart's Utmost Need continues,

> I fall like an old tree trunk upon my last bed,
> Which I made and slept on just today.
> And, unable to turn over,
> I tug convulsively at my clothing and friends.
> This is going to happen to me!
>
> Though I'm completely wrapped in my last inner and outer clothes,
> I lack freedom to wear them other than just today.
> When I become as rigid as earth and stone,
> I see the beginning of my own corpse.
> This is going to happen to me![87]

This will happen, whether we want it to or not. At present, our living body sleeps in its bed, comfortable and warm, but there will come a time when, as Pabongka Rinpoche describes, our body will fall like a dead tree. That's how it will seem to others who find us there. Even though they tug and pull at the sheets and blankets, our corpse will not respond.

I have seen people who have died this way. As the elements are absorbed,[88] first the heat of the body leaves the head and goes to the heart, and then the heat from the feet travels to the heart. The person is no longer able to speak, and after a while the eyes roll up, showing the whites. Then the body becomes very cold and stiff. When somebody touches the head, it is like touching a log of solid wood in the bed rather than the person who was there before.

When the person was alive, they were the object of attachment for people, especially their partner. The body looked and felt so attractive, and people commented on its beauty. But when that same body becomes a corpse, people are immediately repulsed by it. They are too afraid to even touch it. From object of attachment to object of fear and aversion is a very small step.

The custom in India, and evidently in many other countries, is for the family and friends to sit around the body until it is time to be buried or cremated, weeping and crying. Making lots of loud cries seems a big part of the process, even if they don't feel particularly sad. In some countries, bereaved families even hire people to wail. I suspect people will think badly of somebody who is not sad enough, and so they act as if they are in agony.

In Italy there is a very strict Christian monastery where no outsider is allowed in and where the monks never go out. When somebody in the monastery dies, the monks have a huge party, with everybody enjoying themselves greatly. I think the meaning here is that because he has been guided by God, the person will have no trouble at all and will go straight to Heaven, and so this is a reason for celebration. The body then gets buried in a courtyard inside the monastery with a gravestone with the person's name on it. Then, every day, when the other monks pass the grave, they are reminded of impermanence and death. I think this is a very good practice.

Again, *The Heart's Utmost Need* says,

Though I struggle pitifully to say
My final words and last testament and to express my sorrow,
When, with my dry tongue, I can't make others understand,
I'm overwhelmed by intense despair.
This is going to happen to me!

Though others put my last food—holy substances and relics—
into my mouth with a trickle of water,
Since I'm unable to take even a single sip,
It remains in the mouth of my corpse.
This is going to happen to me!

Though encircled by loving and distressed relatives and friends—
Those close to my heart, heart friends, and those I keep in my heart—
Crying and clinging sadly to me at the ending of our being together,
Now I have to separate from them forever.
This is going to happen to me!

Though I'm tossed by waves of horrific hallucinations
And overwhelmed by excruciating, unbearable torment,
In this pitiful state where there's nothing I can do,
The appearances of this life disappear.
This is going to happen to me![89]

Some people plan to write a will but die before they do. They might try to convey their wishes as they die, but their mouth is so dry and their thoughts so muddled that they cannot say it clearly enough for others to understand. We struggle to say those last vital words to our loved ones, to ask forgiveness for our selfishness, but our tongue has dried up and no words come.

Overwhelmed by mundane concerns, we will be in no state to die in a positive way. This is why Pabongka Rinpoche exhorts us so forcefully.

It can be horrifying to realize that our body is breaking down, as Pabongka describes, and that death is happening, but it will be so much more horrifying if we are full of regret.

After describing the terrible death that awaits us, unless we transform our mind, Pabongka then describes the great suffering that will follow, in one of the three lower realms. He finishes each of the verses with the question "What to do?" because when we are in those states there is absolutely nothing we can do. After describing various sufferings of the hell realm, he says,

> When I fall into the miserable state of a hungry and thirsty preta,
> I have to remain there starving for many years—what to do?
>
> When I become a stupid, mute, unfortunate animal,
> I'm eaten alive or eat others alive—what to do?
>
> When the extremely unbearable sufferings of the lower realms
> Actually befall me—what to do?[90]

Finally, he says,

> I'll one-pointedly apply my three doors to practice to see who is faster:
> Me in my practice to reach the essence of my final goal—
> The works of self and others—as much as I can each day,
> Or Yama, the Lord of Death.[91]

The "essence of my final goal" is the mind of bodhichitta, that precious mind that thinks only of the welfare of all other sentient beings. Even if we are striving for it, still the selfish mind overwhelms us and we harm ourselves and others. Which will arrive first, the mind of great compassion and love, or our death? As Pabongka Dechen Nyingpo says, we must do as much as we can each day to ensure that the mind of compassion, love—and if we can, the mind of bodhichitta—will be the winner of this race.

This is the advice that Pabongka Rinpoche gives us in this text. Following only the thoughts of this life, we totally cheat ourselves our whole life, as if we are heartless—not heartless in not having a physical, beating heart but heartless in being without the mindfulness of what is important in this life, missing out on the heart of our life. This is why this text is called *The Heart's Utmost Need*; it is the heart advice of this great teacher. This is the advice we should take into our heart and keep there, constantly reminding us to never be distracted by the meaningless affairs of this life.

6. THE SECOND ROOT TRUTH: THE TIME OF DEATH IS UNCERTAIN

It is not sufficient just to recognize the fact that one day, in time, we will die. We could feel quite strongly that we will die, but that would still not be enough to motivate us to transform our mind. We need to further understand that not only will we definitely die, but the time of our death is uncertain. This most precious opportunity we now have in our hands—this perfect human rebirth with all its potential—could be snatched from us at any second, and so we really need to make the most of it at this very moment. We don't have a second to spare. The first meditation, that death is certain, gives us the energy to not waste our life but practice Dharma instead. This meditation, that the time of death is uncertain, gives that resolve the urgency it needs to really be effective.

Death can occur due to the end of our natural lifespan, which is indefinite; due to the factors that sustain life like food or heat being unavailable; or due to ignorance, such as with accidents or suicide. This loosely corresponds to the three sections of this part of the death meditation we are following:

- The lifespan of human beings in this world system is not fixed.
- More factors endanger life than support it.
- Our body is extremely fragile.

The Lifespan of Human Beings in this World System Is Not Fixed

There are other world systems where the lifespan is definite, where the beings in that world, because of karma, will live for a specific number of years. For instance, beings of the northern continent[92] have a fixed lifespan of a thousand years and those of the eastern continent live for two hundred and fifty years.

There is no fixed lifespan in our world system, the southern continent. Vasubandhu, in his *Treasury of Knowledge*, says,

> Here the lifespan is indefinite. At the end of the eon the lifespan declines to ten years. At the beginning it is measureless.[93]

Even within that lifespan, we have no way of knowing when we might die, even if we die naturally of old age. Karma from our previous lives determines how long the natural lifespan of this life will be. In these degenerate times, the duration of our life is even more indefinite as the factors that determine our death increase. Of course, we have no way of knowing this, and on top of that, karmic seeds are ripening all the time. Many of them will cause us suffering and some can bring an untimely death. There are many more factors that contribute to death than to life.

More Factors Endanger Life than Support It

As well as our natural lifespan, we can so easily have an unnatural death. Think of all the people who died on the planet today. How many of them died of old age? How many of them woke this morning with no expectation to die today? How many of them were prepared for death when it happened? How would we face death if it were suddenly, unexpectedly there before us? This is the purpose of this aspect of the nine-point death meditation, to prepare us for that time that can happen at any second, to prepare us to expect what for most people is totally unexpected.

In *Precious Garland*, Nagarjuna says,

> Hence while in good health create foundations of doctrine
> Immediately with all your wealth,
> For you are living amidst the causes of death
> Like a lamp standing in a breeze.[94]

Life is like a candle flame in the wind. Just as a flame can be easily extinguished by the wind, our human life can end for any reason. The flame and our life, filled with the conditions for death, are both unstable and fragile.

There are more factors that harm life than support it. There are many living beings and nonliving things that can harm us. We see this all around us. A son kills his father, a husband kills his wife, the vehicles we drive cause injury and death, the food we eat poisons us. Because the body's elements can so easily become imbalanced due to its fragility, it is easy to encounter suffering and death.

We can die at any time due to many conditions: in our mother's womb, as an infant or teenager, in adulthood, or in old age. We just don't know. We can die from any cause. There are so many potential causes everywhere we look: disease, accidents, murder, disasters.

So many people are dying at this moment. People who were perfectly healthy yesterday are dying today. They will die in car accidents or be killed by other people. We could simply feel thirsty but be dead before we reach for the glass of water.

Even the things we have in order to support our life can become the cause of our death. Our house can kill us by collapsing in an earthquake or burning down. There can be a gas leak that kills us. The more material possessions we have for our own enjoyment, the more chance that we'll be robbed and maybe killed for them. Many people in the US keep guns in the house as protection but are killed by those same guns.

Considering the risks we face every day, we should be thankful we have lived this long. In *A Guide to the Bodhisattva's Way of Life* Shantideva says,

> The untrustworthy lord of death
> waits not for things to be done or undone;
> whether I am sick or healthy.
> This fleeting lifespan is unstable.
>
> Leaving all I must depart alone.
> But through not having understood this
> I committed various kinds of evil
> for the sake of my friends and foes.
>
> My foes will become nothing.
> My friends will become nothing.
> I too will become nothing.
> Likewise all will become nothing.[95]

Some people never even have a chance to be born, dying in their mother's womb because of a miscarriage or an abortion. Babies die though the mother not being vigilant. Many sick people die on the way to hospital, without having the chance to reach a doctor. And many patients in the hospital die without having the time to go home. Even doctors working in hospitals, trying to cure people, can die before the patient does. This can happen to us.

Some people go on vacation and never return home. People go mountain climbing to get a reputation but the only way they get in the newspaper is in the obituary column. People work so hard at university, planning a big career that will bring them fame and wealth, but their life finishes before they graduate.

Many play football for relaxation, but when the game is over, they leave the field on a stretcher. Many people die before the big wedding they have planned for years. Even driving to the supermarket to get some food, to a cinema, to a party, many never make it there, dead in a car accident. This can happen to us.

The food bought from the supermarket, sitting on the kitchen table to be prepared for lunch, never gets eaten because the person has dropped dead. The many clothes people have bought—winter clothes, summer clothes, party clothes, work clothes—are never worn. People die eating a meal or drinking a cup of tea; they die halfway through a conversation or a business meeting. Office workers die before they have a chance to receive their salary. Shopkeepers can be shot dead by a thief. This can happen to us.

We might plan to attend a meditation course but never make it. This happened to a student called Teresa. After the California meditation course, where she drove us to the venue three or four times a day, she told me she was going to Nepal to do lots of retreats because her husband had left her. She planned to do the eighth Kopan meditation course, but she stopped in Thailand on the way. Somehow it was her karma that while there she was drugged and drowned in the sea.[96]

Another student, an Australian boy, returned to Australia after a course to finalize things there before becoming a monk. He even had a whole set of robes made, but he never had a chance to wear them; he didn't even reach Australia. Some hindrance occurred in his mind, and he threw himself from a high building and killed himself. Things like that happen.

Even in dangerous situations, such as a war, people never expect to die. Soldiers buy homes and plan holidays for when they return home as if they were completely sure that they could never be killed.

Billions of people are busy making plans that they have no certainty of seeing completed. For hundreds of thousands of people each day, this sense of permanence will cheat them, and they will never wake up again in this body. For them, this body they so cherish will be a corpse by tomorrow, something that the family needs to dispose of.

There are many people we can see in the morning that we cannot see in the afternoon. There are people going to work, people shopping, people watching television, people meditating, people sitting in restaurants, people harvesting crops—people we can communicate with today who won't exist tomorrow. Very few of them are expecting to die.

Reading the obituary column of a newspaper is a very good reminder. Perhaps they should rename it "All the people who didn't expect to die today but did," because that is the situation for most of the names we read. Reading a newspaper like this is a complete course in impermanence and death.

Stories of Plans Unfinished

There is the traditional story of a servant in Tibet who saved a little from his monthly wage for many years until he could buy a big sack of barley. He hung it from the ceiling of his room by a rope and happily contemplated all the things he could do now that he was rich. He thought he should get married and have a child, and he wondered what name to give that child. Just then the moon came out, and when he saw the moonlight in his room, he cried out he would call the child Famous Moon (Dawa Dragpa). He was so happy that he got up and started dancing around the room, swinging his walking stick around. The stick struck the bag of barley and it dropped down on his head, killing him instantly. All his great plans were for nothing.

We can start a court case but die before we win. This is what happened with Ang Nyima, a Sherpa businessman who was instrumental in starting the Kopan courses. He had been a monk with Tashi Lhunpo monastery before but had become a very successful businessman selling thangkas. He gave me a thought transformation text composed by Kachen Yeshe Gyaltsen,[97] which somehow gave me the inspiration to teach Westerners.

When I checked with Lama, he agreed I could try if I thought it would be beneficial, and so I gave the first course, just one or two pages from the text. And from there came the first month-long Kopan course and then all the others, and from them came all the FPMT centers around the world. Ang Nyima had been the spur for all this by giving me that text, although of course it was Lama's blessing that was the main cause.

Ang Nyima was imprisoned for stealing a sacred pot from Pharping, a very holy place of Vajrayogini not far from Kathmandu. He spent a year in prison awaiting trial, and while there he taught the prisoners how to carve tables and make thangkas. I think in many ways he was a very religious person. However, the day before his court case started, which he was confident he could win, he suddenly died.

There was a young Japanese man in Santa Cruz, California, who got cancer and within a short time was in hospital, dying. One of the nurses attending him told me that he became very bitter, thinking that with his whole life was in front of him, somehow the world had cheated him. He got angry and broke tables and other furniture and he shouted at the staff, overwhelmed by the thought that he was dying. Although he was very intelligent, he couldn't see how it was his mind that cheated him, not life. His world seemed permanent, and then it changed and that, to him, was not right. He could not accept that he simply got cancer and was going to die and that there was no external agent to blame for it.

This was how he related to the world and how we relate to the world. We live in a permanent world, with permanent houses and permanent people. Our friends appear permanent; our possessions appear permanent. We fail to see the impermanence of things and so, when they suddenly stop, we feel cheated, like that Japanese man.

Visiting a Cemetery

When I see a cemetery, it reminds me how impermanent life is. In India and Nepal death is very evident, with bodies being burned by the roadside and in the river. In Kathmandu by the Bagmati river there is a big Hindu temple, called Pashupatinath,[98] where bodies are always being burned. When I see a body getting prepared for the pyre, I think that that person probably went to bed the day before without any thoughts of death but with a head full of plans for today and his future. His family, who joked and chatted with him yesterday, now have no way to communicate with him. Something happened and now his consciousness is in the intermediate state and his body is a corpse waiting for the fire.

There was a cemetery quite near where Tushita Delhi[99] center used to be, which I sometimes visited. It was very interesting. A body would be brought in, washed beside the river, and prepared for the funeral pyre. Crowds of people, rich and poor, followed each body.

I could tell the social standing of the person who had died not just from the crowd around the corpse but from the quality of the wood for the funeral pyre. For a rich person the wood would be of very good quality, well cut and stacked so the body would burn easily. There would be a big and well-dressed crowd: family, relatives, friends, colleagues—sometimes hundreds of people, brought in cars and taxis and motorcycles. Some would take pictures like it was a holiday. Most waited until the body was burning well and then bowed, showed their respects, and left. They probably had many other activities to do. Many beat their chests and wailed. Many talked about the good qualities of the person who had died. When he was alive, they probably criticized him and fought with him all the time, but afterward they were sorry and upset. Some grabbed the body as if they would be pulled into the fire with it. There was much noise, but not one single benefit to either the people there or the dead person.

Once, a man, possibly the father of the dead person, saw me standing there and asked me if I was doing research. I thought that this would be the right time to discuss life, while he had the dead relative in front of him and the space to think of what was important in life. I wondered if he had any idea that this was what was going to happen to him some day. However, he, and most of the people I talked to, had no idea about what happened after death and were just sad and confused. There seemed no answers in their minds at all.

Standing there watching all the rich people at this funeral, I had the feeling that, although in a worldly way their lives were so busy and successful, they were totally empty. Nothing for them could become the cause for liberation or enlightenment. It saddened me how meaningless their lives seemed. They had no time to make a relationship with death, and therefore they gained nothing useful from seeing a dead person being cremated. In fact, it seemed like death was something to be hidden.

When a person lives like this, it is very difficult to generate a virtuous thought, such as compassion or loving-kindness. Of course, it depends on which sort of person is at the funeral. There are also some very generous and compassionate rich people in India, and I'm sure their funerals would be very different from the ones I witnessed.

A poor person's cremation was very different. The wood was of very poor quality, scraps of wood and twisted trunks that didn't burn well. With the poor person, there were only a few relatives to help the funeral arrangements, which were very simple and crude. The body was covered with a simple yellow cloth with some Hindu symbols on it.

Once, in England, I went to see one of the big cemeteries in Cumbria, near the Manjushri Institute.[100] There was an open gravesite waiting for the funeral, with a label there, reserving it for somebody. I thought that was very interesting. It was the exact opposite of the Kadampa training called *the ten innermost jewels*,[101] where the meditator trains to be unheedful of what happens to the body after death. Here, this person was very mindful, finding just the right spot under some lovely trees, spaced well away from other graves. Just like some people take trouble choosing their retirement home, this person wanted just the right place to be buried.

Some of the inscriptions on the gravestones where amazing: "laid to rest," "gone to sleep," or "gone away from us." People are scared of even saying the word "death" and so they resort to these euphemisms. All these people in the cemetery, tucked up in bed, sleeping for so many years!

In the West, cemeteries are like beautiful parks, places where you go to have a picnic. In many other countries a cemetery is a very fearful place, especially in places in Tibet where they perform the "sky burial," cutting the body up and feeding it to the vultures. It is a wonderful place to practice the chöd practice but fearful for a normal person.

Our Body Is Extremely Fragile

Previously we looked at the external factors that can kill us. Another aspect of the uncertainty of the time of death is that our body itself is so fragile that it can be damaged and destroyed easily. Our body is like a water bubble riding on a stream, so fragile that the least breeze will pop it. A tiny hair touching it can cause it to pop.

There are countless conditions that cause death, not just a few. There are so many diseases that we can die from. There are various viruses and flus; there are stomach diseases and diseases of the blood; there are skin diseases and diseases of every sort of organ. Besides the old diseases like cholera, leprosy, and TB, every year scientists are discovering new diseases we can catch like SARS, Ebola, and COVID-19.

Tibetan medicine recognizes 424 diseases, which all result from the four elements within our body, earth, water, fire, and air,[102] becoming imbalanced. There are said to be 360 types of spirits, called *dön* in Tibetan, that can cause us harm and even kill us. These are the malevolent beings that can take possession of us if we are vulnerable, causing pain, mental anguish, even madness. Our mind becomes foggy and deranged, and we lose the ability to think for ourselves. There is also another type of spirit called an *interferer*, or *gek* in Tibetan. There are 80,000 kinds of this *gek* spirit. These are also malevolent and will try to harm us even if we try to please them.

Since we are generally more aware during the day, we can usually see when harm is coming. If somebody comes into our house with a weapon, we probably know whether we can protect ourselves. It is not so easy to be aware at night, when we are sleepy or asleep, and so when we are unconscious and the gross senses are absorbed, these spirits can harm us much more easily. That is why sicknesses often start at night; it can be a sign that we have spirit harm.

If the body were a machine, it could be fixed; when broken, we could make it function again. But once the breath has stopped, we can do nothing. One time there will definitely be an out-breath without an in-breath. Seeing how the breath can be stopped at any time for countless reasons, we see how our life is very fragile. Anything can affect this delicate machine.

There are many ways that food can kill us. Lack of food is a huge problem with literally billions of people on this planet, and conversely we can die from overeating. An unhealthy diet can lead to illness and death. We can choke to death with a glass of water, and of course alcohol causes so many deaths each year. If we don't walk properly, we can twist our ankle and fall over, and that fall can kill us. A thorn can get into our foot and become infected. Even a bee sting can be fatal. That's how fragile our body us.

The climate can kill us. Not just climate change, but even when the weather changes from hot to cold and back again, we can easily get a fever, and if our body is weak that can lead to our death. Many people in both the poor and rich countries freeze to death every year.

Cancer or a heart attack are not the only things that can shorten our life. Even without these very serious diseases, there are so many other conditions that bring death. With the heart pumping and the breath going in and out constantly, we feel we are alive, like a very solid, concrete thing, something that is very permanent. But our life is totally dependent on that breath, on the air continuing to go in and out, allowing this machine of our body to function. That is what we call "life," the inhalations and exhalations of the breath. How long this continues is not our choice. If it were in our hands, we could keep the breath going in and out forever. But it is not under our control; the breath can be stopped at any time. Seeing our life as a candle flame in the wind is a much more realistic way of thinking than the solid, permanent way of viewing it that we now have.

One Day It Will Be Us

Our friends seem so permanent. We see them every day, we talk to them on the phone every day, and then one day we will receive a phone call—but it won't be *from* our best friend but *about* our best friend; it will be somebody else telling us they are dead. Then, all that connects us to them is a gravestone with their name and the date of their death on it. We can no longer communicate with them. The only way we can keep their memory alive is to take flowers to their grave, stay silent for a few minutes, and leave. And slowly our memory of them will get vaguer and vaguer and they become just one more grave in a cemetery, next to all the other graves.

For me and for many students of the FPMT the greatest lesson on impermanence and death was the death of Lama Yeshe. It seemed to us, with our thick skulls, that he would always be there for us as our inspiration, as our father, as everything that was special, but then one day he wasn't there anymore. He looked so permanent and truly existing, even though he repeatedly told us he wasn't, and then he proved it to us, giving us the best possible example. Besides a few relics that were left after he was cremated, there is nothing more of Lama's holy body. To think of Lama passing away should alone be enough to remind us that we ourselves are also going to die, sooner or later. At any time, at any hour on any day, we will be forced by some circumstance to leave this body. It all depends on karma.

Just as one day we will get a telephone call telling us that our dear friend is dead, so one day all our friends will get the same sort of phone call, but the name that is spoken will be our own. One day we will be doing some activity, drinking a coffee, playing a record, reading a book, doing the gardening, and the water bubble that is our present life will pop and that activity will never be finished. If it's me, people will turn to each other and say, "Have you heard, that crazy monk, Zopa, the Mickey Mouse lama, is dead." Pop! Like a water bubble. Who can say who will be first to pop, you, me, our friends? Nobody knows.[103]

There are various things we can do to help the dead person, such as ask lamas to pray or do practices ourselves, but there is nothing that will get that person back. And similarly, no matter how much people might love us, there is no way they can bring us back. After that final breath we have only one destination, and that is our next life, wherever that is.

The body is taken to the cemetery and the funeral held. Then our friends and family will leave with tears falling, but our consciousness will already be in the intermediate state, probably on the way to the lower realms.

There will be nothing left of this life's existence but our name, recorded in a register somewhere and used by our friends when they remember us. After some time, those people too will die and so even the name will become nonexistent. Then, one day even the book where our name is written will cease to exist. Many people born on the same day as us are already in another life. When will it be our turn? Maybe tomorrow, maybe later. Many among our gurus and family already have new bodies. We will experience the same impermanence.

If that had already happened to us by now, where would we be in the six realms? We could be a frog, a lizard, a fish destined for the hook of a fisherman. We could be a hungry ghost or a hell being. Our stupidity could have secured us a rebirth as a dumb animal; our anger could have bought us a snake's body and have us slithering along the road, looking for frogs to kill. We could be a mosquito desperate for blood. Or an octopus or jellyfish. We just don't know. We can't swear with complete certainty that we will awake tomorrow morning in this body. We can't put our signature on an iron-clad guarantee.

Thinking of how many times in this life we have been nonvirtuous and how many times we have been compassionate, examining our mind like that—isn't it crazy to even contemplate getting angry or becoming attached to somebody or something?

We should not feel that death only happens if we contract some terminal disease. Because we are currently free from cancer we will live for a long time—this is deluded thinking. Many people who are completely healthy will die today. I don't know the statistics, but I suspect that more healthy people die each day than sick ones. Death can happen in so many different ways.

We Must Practice Dharma Now

Unless we are aware of our own impermanence, it will be very difficult to practice Dharma, and if we are not aware that we could die at any moment, then there won't be the urgency to practice Dharma *now*, which is the conclusion of this second root of the meditation on death.

Accepting we can die at any moment, healthy or not, immediately brings peace. Freeing ourselves from the concept of our own permanence allows us to relax. Because of our attachment to this life, we have many expectations about gaining happiness, wealth, power, and fame, and when these expectations are not fulfilled, we experience worry and fear. Remembering that we could die today, we see that none of these things has any meaning. We therefore eliminate all the expectations that only bring us problems and immediately find peace, happiness, and satisfaction.

Unaware of the fragility of this life, we find it so hard to think beyond the mundane existence we are trapped in, making it difficult to effectively practice Dharma. As Shantideva says,

> "Death shall not come today"—
> I have no reason for feeling so smug.
> The time when I will cease to be
> most surely will come.
>
> Who will give me shelter?
> How will I escape?
> Surely I will cease to be.
> How can my mind be at ease?[104]

The Kadampa geshés firmly held the attitude that they would die, thinking, "I will die this year, I will die this month, I will even die today." They lived their lives with this fundamental attitude, bringing them great happiness. If we live with the thought that we are going to die today, so much fear is cut off. Lama Tsongkhapa explained that living with this attitude is the best thing because then we can prepare well for our future lives and we don't die having led a meaningless life. We practice Dharma strongly. Then, if we do die today, having this attitude is of course the best, but if we don't die today, this is still the best attitude because it stops all distractions to our Dharma practice and makes our life so worthwhile.

7. THE THIRD ROOT TRUTH: NOTHING CAN HELP AT THE TIME OF DEATH EXCEPT DHARMA PRACTICE

As we have seen, the traditional way of meditating on death is the nine-point death meditation, divided into three sections or root truths. We have covered the first two, that death is certain and that the time of death is uncertain. Now, fully understanding that we will die and that we might die at any moment, we need to address the most important question: what will help us at death? The three points raised in this section are that, when we die, our possessions cannot help us, our friends cannot help us, and even our body cannot help us. At death, all these things cease to exist for us. The conclusion, then, is that only the Dharma can help.

When we die, we leave all material things behind and move into another life with only the positive and negative imprints left on our mindstream. The negative imprints lead us to a suffering rebirth, whereas the positive imprints lead us to a fortunate one. Which one will ripen at death depends on our state of mind. Just as Dharma is the only thing that can help us if we want to be happy in this life, it is also vital if we want to be happy at death and in the next life.

Wealth and Possessions Cannot Help

We horde our possessions and are so attached to them, and yet we can't take them with us when we die. We can't take even one strand of hair or one grain of rice into the next life. The poorest beggar and the richest king are exactly equal in what they can physically take to the next life—nothing.

The king who lives in a vast palace and sleeps on a golden bed will die on that golden bed. He has a great treasury of jewels, mountains of material possessions such as the most expensive silk clothes, and enough food to last a hundred or even two hundred years. Living in such luxury, when he dies, he takes none of that with him. Without choice his bare consciousness slips from his body like a hair pulled from butter without leaving a mark.

When a beggar dies on the street, they only have their stick and begging bowl, and yet there is no difference between them and the king; both leave everything behind, taking not even an atom into their next life. At death, the king's body becomes a corpse, just like the beggar's. If the beggar has created more merit, although they are materially poor, they are really the rich one. From the Dharma point of view, the one who is prepared for the journey into the next life has the real riches.

Even if we have food stored that would last a hundred years, not one crumb would help us at death. Even if we have a million wardrobes full of the most expensive clothes, we leave this life without any of the clothes we have bought. Even if we own three galaxies full of possessions, not a single atom can accompany us into the next life.

We have no choice but to leave everything behind. What we possessed will now belong to others. They might say, "Oh, this thing belonged to..." and they will say our name. That is what we have been reduced to, a name. The house we lived in will have a very empty feeling, without us or our possessions, all the things we worked hard all our life to acquire.

How much work has been involved in obtaining those possessions? All the years studying and working, earning more and more money to buy more and more things. Think of what negative actions have gone into acquiring all those things: all the energy, the anger, the desire, the jealousy, and so forth. And yet, when we die, all the things we have acquired over our lifetime will be left behind.

Not only do our possessions not benefit us at the time of death, but our attachment to them also disturbs us greatly. Sensing we are separating from all these things we have loved, we become terrified, causing us to be born in the lower realms. This is the great danger at death. Attachment—to our possessions, to our friends, and especially our body—has the power to disturb our mind terribly at death and can mean that we die with a strongly negative mind, ensuring misery at death and a suffering rebirth after death. The things we loved in this lifetime become enemies at death. They are not enemies from their side; it's our attachment to them and the fear of separation that causes such strong fear and anger.

Like in a dream where we have a billion dollars only to find we have nothing when we awake, at death, no matter what material possessions we acquired in life, we go to the next life with nothing.

These possessions are meaningless in this life, and our attachment to them is profoundly dangerous when we die. Not one can be taken with us, not even a single hair. Therefore, why should we take so much time and effort into acquiring them when we will only lose them in a short time, when we die?

Friends and Relatives Cannot Help

Not only are our possessions unable to help at our death, but neither are the people around us: our loved ones, our relatives, our friends, and so forth. All our lives we have lived with and relied on other people to give us a sense of happiness, but rather than helping us be happy as we die, people can actually hinder our death. Even if we are surrounded by hundreds of people at our deathbed, not one can help us, not one can make our transition to the next life less lonely. We can't take even one with us as a companion.

A king might have thousands of servants and advisors, bodyguards, and soldiers, but not one of them can be of help as he dies. No servant can make death more comfortable, no advisor can explain death away, no bodyguard can fight off the Lord of Death. The most skilled doctor is useless at prescribing medicine to eliminate death. The king is utterly alone as he faces death. Even his family around him at his bedside can only make his death more painful.

We might not have the servants and bodyguards a king has, but in this aspect we are the same as a king. Unless they are very skilled at Dharma, the people around us as we die can be a great hindrance to our death. Our partner and children we love and who love us dearly are helpless in the face of our death. Unable to let us go, they wail and scream and beg us not to die, but it has no effect. Their attachment to us and our attachment to them just make it more difficult for us to die peacefully. We see the faces of our loved ones, and knowing we will never see them again, tears pour down our face and we howl in misery. Just as we are unable let go of our life, we are unable let go of the attachment to the people of our life, and that hold makes death incredibly difficult.

As we are dying, it's much better to not have such people around. If there are Dharma friends or lamas who know how to help at the time of death, that is something else. They know what to do to help us transform our mind, to not allow attachment or anger to arise. But otherwise, because it is so important to have a quiet mind as we die, it is better to not be surrounded by people or possessions. Then, if we want to remember some meditation practice, it's easy because there is not much distraction from outside.

Our Body Cannot Help

This body that we feed and take so much care of is supposed to be a constant source of pleasure for us, never causing any suffering at all, but of course this is completely untrue in life, and when we separate from our body at death it causes us great fear and suffering. Our greatest possession, our greatest friend, becomes our greatest enemy at death.

If we found out that a sweet-talking friend who was acting so friendly to us really planned to kill us, our attachment to them would disappear immediately! Perhaps we must remain in contact with them, but we would be incredibly careful around them and skeptical of what they tell us. Our body is that sweet-talking friend and we need to see how all the trouble we lavish on the body, the ties we have to it, can hinder our death terribly.

In some ways our greatest possession is our body. This is the thing that we cherish the most in this life. We go to school and then to university, getting the best degree possible to ensure we can take lavish care of the body, feeding it, clothing it, giving it a house to shelter from the weather, giving it medicine when it is sick. We go to work, spending so many hours each week just to earn money for what it wants. After we are paid, we need to shop for the food, taking it home and preparing it before we can feed it to the body. And then we need to clean up afterward.

Think of how much time, energy, and money has gone into protecting the body and making it look beautiful. We buy it the best possible house and the most expensive clothes. We spend so much on getting our hair to look just right, first this color and then that, first this style and then that. We have shoes for every occasion—indoor shoes, outdoor shoes, shoes for parties, shoes for dancing—so many shoes! With so many clothes and shoes we might even have to buy a bigger house to fit them all in! There is nothing we would not do for our master, the body. It is our greatest possession, but we are its slave.

We get married in order to be happy, but so many marriages are besieged with problems and confusion. Feeling our partner is lacking in some way, we quarrel and cause each other pain, and we come to feel trapped in the relationship. When we investigate, we can see that so many people get married because of attachment to the body; it is the needs of the body that enslave us, not the marriage.

Without the body there would be no need for marriage at all and no need for homes, careers, and all the things that surround a relationship. Think of what life would be like if we didn't have this body. There would be no sicknesses related to it; there would be no need to work; we would never get tired or have to shop for food or make kaka and pipi. And there would be much less trouble with other beings.

All these problems that arise from attachment to the body seem a bit strange when any day now that body will just be a corpse. In life, we took such care of it, buying it the best clothes and feeding it the best food, but soon that body will be laid out on a bed and covered in a shroud, looking very fearful to others, even if it was attractive in life.

Borrowed from our parents, destined to become a corpse very soon—why should we place so much importance on this body? As we have seen, Thokmé Sangpo compares the body to a guesthouse that the temporary guest, the mind, will leave soon enough, to take residence in another temporary "guesthouse" and then another and another, continuously until we break the cycle. At present, we have no choice but to take a new body and we have no choice what kind of body we take and in what realm we are reborn. It all depends on karma.

Meditating on Attachment to Possessions, Friends, and the Body

It is good to frequently do an analytical meditation on your attachment to your possessions, friends, and body where you imagine you are actually dying.

At this time, imagining the time of your death, consider how you would feel about your possessions. Consider the things you now possess that will soon no longer exist for you. Do you have strong feelings for them? Check your mind truthfully, whether you care or not, whether you have attachment for them and you are afraid to lose them.

When you have a strong sense of what it would feel like to be dying and leaving all your possessions, maybe when you're feeling some of that fear, then think of the shortcomings of holding on to your attachment to your possessions. Not only are the possessions not the cause of happiness now, but they are the cause of being continuously reborn in samsara, and most probably in the lower realms. Try to see how this is true and then think that therefore you should not be attached to possessions at all.

Now, think of your relationship with your loved ones, with your family and friends, and again imagine that you are just about to die. Soon, you will be separating forever from your partner and children, from your relatives, from the friends you love. You have no choice. How do you feel? Will your attachment to them bring you great distress as you are dying?

As with your possessions, check how this attachment causes suffering now and will cause great suffering at the time of death, tying you to samsara even more, causing you to be continuously reborn in the lower realms. If that is so, why should you be attached to those you love? Loving them is wonderful, but there is no reason to be attached. After pinpointing the problems this attachment brings, determine not to be attached.

Finally, carry out the same analysis with your body. Feel that you are about to die, that death is actually happening. How do you feel about leaving your body? If there is fear of leaving the body due to attachment to it, think in the same way about the shortcomings of being attached to the body, how it doesn't bring the happiness you think, how attachment to it only causes suffering now and will cause great suffering at the time of death. You have no choice but to leave the body when you die. When you have pinpointed this problem, think that because attachment to this body only brings unhappiness and suffering without any benefits at all, there is no reason to remain attached to it.

When you use this technique of strongly visualizing that death is really happening and identifying how attachment brings such suffering, you see there is no reason to be attached. Each time you do, there is a sense of relaxation, like when you have eaten too much and your belt is digging into your stomach, and then you let it out, causing you to sigh with relief. Even just strongly imagining you are about to die like this, your mind becomes more peaceful when you imagine letting go of your attachment.

Losing your attachment for these things—your possessions, friends, and body—brings a real peace, but for that peace to be lasting, it has to be established; it cannot happen all of a sudden. Remembering death like this frequently in this sort of analytical meditation is extremely helpful in overcoming problems.

We Must Practice Dharma Purely

Of the three outlines of the death meditation, after seeing how death is definite and its time is indefinite, and after seeing that our possessions, friends, and body cannot help at the time of death, we can be left feeling that nothing can help us to have a happy death. Is there any method?

There is one. The Dharma is the only method that can definitely benefit at death, that can stop the worries and suffering of death. Since death is definite and we don't know when it will happen, and since the Dharma is the only thing that can help us at the time of death, we must practice the Dharma and practice it purely.

Perhaps we might know this logically, but another part of our mind tells us it doesn't really matter, how death is far in the future and something will happen that will let us be happy. Like the arrogance of the king who thinks he is immune to suffering, this mind is controlled by the king-like sense of "I" that sees itself as the controller and the other negative minds such as attachment, pride, and jealousy, as its servants. This ignorant, lazy mind can see the worth of the Dharma but still think it is not that necessary.

There is no other question we need to ask ourselves other than "Do I want to have a happy or a miserable death?" Death has to happen; that is easy to accept. But none of us wants a miserable death. If we knew for sure that after death there is just blankness, just dark nothingness, like an infinitely moonless night, there would be nothing we could do and we could relax and maybe have a happy death, but nobody can be sure of that.

If we try to really get a sense that we are about to die, how do we feel? If we have any sense of fear, that shows we are not fully confident we will have a happy death. We must prepare for death. Understanding that, life becomes very simple. Every choice we face from now on is a choice between a happy death and a miserable one.

When we examine it, it is very, very clear that the only way to have a happy death is to have a completely virtuous mind, which will come by only ever acting virtuously, and that is what "practicing Dharma" means. We must practice Dharma purely and abandon any actions tainted with the eight worldly dharmas.

That doesn't mean that we should never make plans, but we need to ensure that whatever plans we make are positive plans, ones inspired by a Dharma motivation rather than selfish ones ruled by the wish for temporal comforts. Our temporal plans should be stopped right now, and our Dharma plans, plans for a happy death, should begin right now. At least we should try to make any plans we have as positive are possible. Just as it is pointless renovating a building that is about to be demolished, we should not waste our time on the comforts of a life that will surely end soon.

To start to practice Dharma as we are about to die is too late. I met many old, retired people in New York who had obviously led very active lives, keeping their bodies fit and their minds alert. They had a lot of energy for life and were very intelligent. Many had had great success in life. The one thing most of them had in common, though, was how unhappy they were. The problem was not having worked hard all their life, the problem was doing it in a way that was not meaningful, and so as they became old, they could see very clearly just how they had wasted their time. They saw a whole life of incredible effort and what people would call great success and they knew, when it was too late, that all this meant nothing.

If they had understood, they would have seen how retirement is a wonderful opportunity to put time and energy into Dharma practice, but they had not met the teachings and understood karma. Many would go to the park and stare at the young people passing by, still actively leading their lives, while they themselves were just waiting to die. Sometimes they would go window shopping and then go home and stare out the window are the passing cars or sit out the front watching the sun set, waiting to die.

I met an old lady in Australia whose routine was to come down from her room, have breakfast, and then push her chair to the window and stare out at the street for the rest of the day. Really, she was very comfortable; she had good food to eat every day, but her life was so empty. This perfect human rebirth she had received this once was being completely wasted. When I saw her, I thought of the poor Tibetans who were beggars in India, wearing rags and often starving. How much richer they were than this old lady, because they had the Dharma all around them and they were always saying mantras. They had refuge in their hearts and complete trust that they would have a better future rebirth. Even without the intelligence and the success of the New Yorkers or the comfort of the Australian, they had great richness because they had the Dharma.

When we have the Dharma, we might look externally like everybody else, but the quality of our mind is different. Our way of thinking is completely the opposite to those without the Dharma.

Advice for My Mother

There's a cave in Lawudo, the place where I was born, where people said my previous reincarnation practiced Dharma. I'm not so sure. I suspect I might have been a mouse stealing the Lawudo Lama's food. Anyway, because of my connection with the place, I helped establish a school and a retreat center in Lawudo, and my mother and sister both worked there, cooking and looking after the place.

Many years before my mother died, I gave her some advice. I had gone back to the Lawudo Retreat Centre to attend the annual *nyungné*, the Chenrezig fasting retreat, where there is intensive practice for two days, involving total fasting—not even drinking—on the second day. While I was there my mother came to see me. I joked with her and teased her but didn't have time to have any serious discussions with her.

Just before I was leaving, between the fire puja that finished the retreat and having to rush to the plane, while we were having breakfast, seeing how old she was and how she could die soon, I decided I would like to tell her something that would really benefit her in case she died that year. She had always been so incredibly kind to me, and I couldn't think of anything else to do to repay that kindness. (I needed a translator! My Sherpa is very rusty and my mother often had trouble understanding me, so my uncle came to translate. I have many uncles, but this is the young one who always works at Lawudo and he understands me better.)

What I told her was this. There are three things that she should remember every day:

- Today I am definitely going to die.
- Therefore there is no reason to be attached to possessions and people.
- The only thing that can benefit me at death is Dharma.

I asked her to think about this every morning when she got up and again after she had lunch and then again in the evening. When my uncle had translated, she said she would do that. I wrote these three things down on some paper and gave them to my uncle so he could remind her. When I went back there later, I asked if she had continued to think on these three things, but I don't remember what she said.

I really wanted to help my mother and this advice was the only thing I could think of that would really benefit her. To be able to have a happy, unattached mind at the time of death is the most important thing, and if I could help my mother have this in some way, that is better than giving her lots of money or warm clothes. No matter how comfortable I made her, if she died with clinging and attachment to her possessions and the people around her, it would be so difficult not to be reborn in the lower realms. Giving her that advice meant that she would be fine, whether I was there with her or somewhere else in the world when she died.

By training the mind like this, she had the ability to stop anger and attachment arising at death and to take a fortunate rebirth. As I mentioned, she spent some time in a pure land before being reborn as a human back near Lawudo. This was through her devotion to Chenrezig and the millions of mantras she recited in her life.

To think not only that we are going to die but that we are definitely going to die that very day is so beneficial. If we can have that conviction, then automatically everything we do that day will be preparation for our future life. Holding that thought, everything we do becomes Dharma, and we get so much done in one day. And if we don't happen to die on that day, then that is excellent, because we then have another day to fill with Dharma practice.

We Need to Practice Dharma Now, Before It's Too Late

The Buddha advised us that the Dharma is nothing more than not harming others, helping others, and thoroughly subduing our mind. The unsubdued mind is a very rough mind, like a bush full of thorns, one you cannot touch without tearing your hand. This cruel, painful, unsubdued mind causes us to suffer, to be unhappy. This is what we need to pacify, to purify. We cannot attain enlightenment with an unsubdued mind; we cannot even attain the mundane happiness of this life.

To meditate on impermanence and death frequently is the best way to remind ourselves of the importance of practicing the Dharma. Because there is nothing that can benefit us at the time of death except the Dharma, and because death can occur at any time, we must not only practice the Dharma, but we must do it now without delay, and we must do it purely.

Practicing Dharma is not about buying an expensive mala or shaving our head, or about wearing robes or sitting in a damp cave for years. It is solely about transforming our mind from nonvirtue to virtue. We need to know exactly what virtuous actions are and always do them and conversely know exactly what nonvirtuous actions are and always avoid them. That's the best preparation for death.

The Dharma we learn must be in the heart. If we intellectually know the Dharma well but have not integrated it, it is very difficult to make is useful when we die. Practicing the Dharma, rather than just understanding it, is vital. Only we can look after ourselves at death.

Pabongka Dechen Nyingpo told the monks he taught that there was no need to give up the various activities they did in the monastery and go to a cave to practice Dharma; instead, they should ensure that whatever they did was Dharma, whether it was studying, praying, debating, or whatever. For instance, he advised them that after having recited the refuge prayer a thousand times, they should check to see whether they had reflected well on the meaning even once while reciting it. A Dharma activity is determined by the motivation, not the outward form.

Considering our life is full of thousands of life-threatening hindrances and how easy it is for death to happen, it's incredible that when we go to sleep we wake up the next morning. Having this perfect human rebirth, every second is more precious than the whole sky filled with wish-fulfilling jewels. We are so unbelievably fortunate; it's like a miracle.

This is why it is so important to develop the firm conviction that we could very easily die at any moment, that we might go to sleep tonight and not wake up tomorrow. We must reflect again and again on this nine-point death meditation with the three main points: death is definite, the time of death is indefinite, and the only thing that can help at death is the Dharma.

8. DEATH AND REBIRTH

REINCARNATION

It is important to define what death is. When we are unsure of that, we will also be unsure about reincarnation. In the West, death is when the heart stops beating, but according to Buddhism it comes later than that. Death happens when the mind disconnects from the nonfunctioning body and enters the intermediate state, the bardo.

If we didn't have a mind that was distinct from the body, that would be the end of us, but the mind is not the body. If the mind were to stop with the physical body, like a flame being extinguished when the candle is spent, there would be no argument, but it is not like that. The mind is nonmaterial energy whereas the body is matter, and although the mind connects with a body for a certain period of time, when we die, when the physical body ceases to function, the mind continues and takes another body. This is what is called *reincarnation*.[105]

What kind of body we take in our next life depends entirely on karma. There are only two ways to go: to be reborn in one of the three fortunate realms, as a human, a god, or a demigod, or in one of the three suffering realms, as an animal, a hungry ghost, or a hell being.

Is there reincarnation? Does the consciousness cease the moment the body dies? For many of us, there is no clear answer to this. If you sincerely look at the question and answer, "I don't know," that is a very honest answer. Or perhaps you feel that there is no reincarnation, no karma, that everything finishes at death. Or perhaps you intellectually believe that, but the heart doesn't feel it. You could harbor a deep dread of what happens when you die. Or you might feel, whether you are religious or not, that something good will happen after death. It is very important to think about this and to discuss it with others.

I have often led students in a meditation on the continuity of the consciousness. In this meditation, we see that this moment of consciousness must be the result of the previous moment of consciousness. And that moment of consciousness is the result of the moment before that. In that way, we can trace the moments of cause and effect all the way back to the first moment of this life, and further, to the consciousness in the womb and the first moment at the time of conception. But even that first moment of mind of this life must have had a cause, and that cause must have been a previous moment of mind, the mind of the last moment of our previous life.

Many people have done this meditation and really been able to make that link with their previous lives. I remember once a Western student with very stable concentration was able to remember right back to his mother's womb and then went even further to his previous life in Tibet. He had a very strong image of the room of his previous life's family, the blocks of tea and the churn that churned the butter. If we can't remember our previous life, it is because our mind is too clouded, not because there was no previous life.

Reincarnation Cannot Be Disproved

It is illogical to claim there is no such thing as past and future lives simply because we have no personal experience of being reborn. By that reasoning we can "prove" we have never been in our mother's womb. Empirical reasoning simply cannot cover this subject. Scientists can explain birth on a physical level, they can measure the growth of the fetus and show how it is nourished, but that is only one small part of the story.

While it can be scientifically shown that we were once in a womb, what caused us to enter our mother's womb? This can be explained on a physical level, but there is no scientific explanation of the mental experience. If we can't fully explain the evolution of mind in this life, how can we explain past and future lives? Based on the reasoning that the only things that exist are what we can see, we should say that there was no mind in the womb and there is none at death, because there is no experience of it. If we have to be skeptical of past and future lives, we have to be skeptical about mind too, because we are unable to accept what mind is.

The fact is we suffer because we have created the causes to suffer, and the imprints of our past nonvirtuous actions ripen in our mindstream when the conditions come together for them to ripen. This would be impossible if there were no mind. And if we had no mind, we would have no past or future lives.

We are skeptical where we shouldn't be and not skeptical where we should. What we need to do is escape from ignorance in order to be free from suffering, and skepticism of past and future lives does nothing to help us do this. We have no logical proof we will exist tomorrow—our mind does not have the power to see tomorrow—but then why aren't we as skeptical about tomorrow as we are about future lives?

Our physical and mental constituents are not one, but they are very closely related. Not addressing this is the reason the science books are incomplete. Science states that life started in the ocean, that the beings we are now emerged from early life forms that came from the ocean, but that is an explanation of the physical evolution of living beings on this planet; it has no ability to explain the beginnings of the evolution of the mind, and therefore it is limited.

How can we believe in the other realms, especially the hell realm, when we cannot see them? We need to rely on the explanations of the enlightened beings, and we need to investigate to see whether the Buddha is indeed a reliable source. This is not something we should take lightly, because the more convinced we are in the words of the Buddha, the more faith we will have in all his teachings and the more we will be able to transform our mind.

When we investigate, either through our own analysis of his teachings or the fact that countless practitioners have been led from suffering to full enlightenment using his guidance, we will see that the Buddha is the perfect guide. Just look at the high lamas such as His Holiness the Dalai Lama. What they know is faultless and totally based on the wisdom of the Buddha. On the other hand, because they only ever work with empirical knowledge, even the top scientists are limited.

As the great yogis of the past progressed along the path, their understanding of reality improved and they saw things that we can't even imagine. This was all the product of the mind, not of machines. The great Indian yogis such as Milarepa had minds so powerful that they could influence their bodies, being able to fly and take many forms and so forth. They could clearly see not only past and future lives but also the different realms, just as we can see the table in front of us. These were not logical possibilities to them but actual objects of knowledge, things that they experienced as very real. In Tibet, the great bodhisattva yogis had control over where they reincarnated and so could choose their future rebirth to be of most benefit to others. Everything they experienced confirmed the truth of the Dharma that the Buddha taught.

Because reincarnation is not an accepted part of Western culture, many people think it can't be real. But now people in the West are hearing about reincarnation more and starting to accept it. If there is a person who doesn't suffer from goiter in a country where almost everybody else has it, they are considered strange. Our beliefs are shaped by what kind of culture we encounter as we grow up. Because something is accepted by society doesn't necessarily mean it is correct. We need to analyze what we have learned and decide whether it accords with reality and then accept or reject it, whether or not society tells us we should believe in it.

Many of us have feelings at birth that come from the previous life, but as we grow we quickly cease to remember them. There are plenty of accounts of people who have actually remembered past lives. I have been given the title "Rinpoche," which in our tradition means a reincarnated lama, but I have no recollection of anything before my childhood. When His Holiness the Dalai Lama was a child, on the other hand, he could recognize his past servants and his past religious items. There are countless stories of lamas who have remembered previous lives, and additionally, there are many very ordinary people who, because of some karma ripening, have been able to remember the house they lived in or their family from a previous life. Many of these cases have been verified. There are many examples of Tibetans, Indians, and Westerners who have remembered past lives.[106]

Whereas reincarnation is not that accepted yet in Western culture as it is in Asia, my feeling is that, in their hearts, many Westerners are questioning this assumption of only having one life. They are not sure.

The Body Does Not Reincarnate

Some people, on seeing a body cremated or buried, argue that it is impossible to reincarnate because there is no more body. That is because they don't differentiate the mind from the body. The body has color, shape, and form; it is substantial, whereas the mind is colorless, shapeless, and formless. It is a phenomenon without form, whose nature is clear and knowing, in that it can know an object. So, these two are completely different; one is substantial and the other is insubstantial.

The body does not reincarnate. The body disintegrates completely after death, rotting in the earth or becoming ashes. This doesn't happen to the mind. Even if the entire world were to be destroyed, leaving only space, with not an atom left, the mind would continue. When we talk about "transmigratory beings," it is the mind, the consciousness, that leaves the dead body and transmigrates, to take another life, either in the suffering lower realms or the upper realms. The consciousness does not stop but continues.

We naturally associate the mind with the brain, but while there is an incredibly close interrelationship, the brain is not the mind; the two are still separate entities. There have even been instances where people have been able to live without a head and presumably without a brain. When Kyabjé Zong Rinpoché[107] (the previous one) once visited Pagri in Nepal, he saw a person with no head, just a hole in the neck where his family fed him and kept him alive. He was evidently able to make some rudimentary communication with his hand, rubbing his stomach for hunger and shaking for feeling cold and so forth. It might seem nobody can live without a head, but this is what Rinpoché saw. If we have the karma to die from a simple cut finger, we will; if we have the karma to survive without a head, we will.

The Death Process

What happens when we die? Due to craving and grasping, the mind leaves the dying body and jumps into its next existence, but before that there is a whole process that happens, as the body dies and the mind is absorbed, becoming more and more subtle. This process is important to understand.

Craving and Grasping Cause the Next Body

As we have seen, the whole of samsara operates through the mechanism we call the twelve links of dependent origination. The two links that particularly relate to reincarnation are *craving* and *grasping*. Whereas they are certainly operating in our daily life, in the context of the twelve links, craving and grasping have more to do with the connection of one life to the next.

When we understand that we are being separated from this body in death, strong fear at the separation arises. The thought of leaving this body is terrifying, no matter how much suffering the body has caused us in our life. This attachment to our body is craving.

Grasping is another form of attachment. Along with the strong craving not to be separated from the current body, the dying person can feel incredibly cold and grasp at heat, destining themselves to be reborn in the hot hells. We see this with some people who are dying. No matter how many blankets we give them or how high the heating is turned up, they still feel unbearably cold. This can be due to the heat element being absorbed during the death process, but this need for heat can be the condition to be reborn, right after death, in the hot hells. Similarly, some people feel incredibly hot, which is the condition for rebirth in the cold hells.

To receive a human body, the craving is the same—not wanting to be separated from the current body—as is the grasping onto the next body, but the close condition is the strong wish to have another human body. We also need perfect morality and great generosity.

Due to the basic ignorance, craving and grasping arise, which leads to *becoming*, the next link of the twelve links, where the consciousness or mind actually joins with the egg and sperm and becomes a fetus. After that there is only *birth* and *aging and death*.

If we were free from the unsubdued mind and karma, there would be no way we could take a samsaric body. There would be no reason at all to do so. Then, we would never have to experience the suffering of rebirth, the suffering of aging, the suffering of death, and all the other sufferings that make up this samsaric life. However, we are bound by karma and delusions. This is the fundamental suffering of samsara. It is like the foundation of the house, like the ground.

Because of karma and delusions, the consciousness joins with the sperm and egg and a new life is formed. Wherever the consciousness goes, the self goes. The consciousness is the base for the self. The body exists for some time and then dies, but the consciousness continues, tied in bondage to karma and delusions.

The Absorptions of the Elements

Until the consciousness separates from the body, the brain might no longer function and the heart might have stopped beating, but the person is not yet dead. A highly realized being can stay in meditation for days, even weeks, before the consciousness leaves, but even for ordinary people there is a gap between the last breath and the departure of the consciousness, which can be anywhere between a few seconds and a few days. A good indication of death is when heat has left the heart area.

During the death process, the elements that make up our physical body are "absorbed" into each other.[108] One by one, the four fundamental elements of form—earth, water, fire, and air, representing the corporality, liquidity, heat, and wind energies that constitute our body—lose their ability to function. The element does not actually dissolve but the psychic wind that is the basis for the mind to connect with that element ceases to function due to the deterioration of that element, and then the more subtle elements become more manifest. And so, for instance, as the earth element weakens, the mind can no longer associate with it, and the water element, the fluid factors of the body, becomes more manifest.

The mind withdraws and becomes more subtle as the gross minds dissolve, giving way to more and more subtle minds, and finally to the extremely subtle mind, which is what leaves the body for the next life. Great meditators are able to remain aware of the whole process of death; we quickly lose the ability to control it.

The extremely subtle mind possesses our buddha nature, free from all gross and subtle delusions. This is what we are trying for when we meditate and work toward enlightenment and this is what naturally occurs at death. Unfortunately, death does not mean all our delusions evaporate and we are enlightened; all the manifest gross and subtle minds dissolve, but the karmic imprints of everything we have ever done remain on the extremely subtle mind. They go with us to the next life and, as we have seen, they determine what that next life will be.

The wind energies[109] are more subtle than the air that we breathe; they represent the various energies that run through our body in psychic channels, channels that resemble our physical nervous system. The mind rides on these wind energies like a rider rides a horse, and at death the mind is absorbed, moving with the ever-more-subtle winds, until it is absorbed into the center of the central channel, where the extremely subtle mind resides.

The absorptions are also related to the five aggregates (*skanda*). They are form (the body) and the four mental aggregates of feeling, discrimination, consciousness, and compositional factors or compounded phenomena. The minds of *compositional factors* include all the deluded and virtuous minds we have in our normal life such as greed, shyness, caution, ignorance, jealousy, and pride, as well as patience, love, and wisdom. There are traditionally fifty-one mental factors, both positive and negative, and those minds that are not feelings and cognition are considered to be part of the category of compositional factors.

The first aggregate to be absorbed in the death process is the *aggre-*

gate of form. At the same time, the mirror-like wisdom—the ability to see many objects simultaneously, as a mirror reflects many objects together—is also absorbed. The earth element is absorbed, and the dying person feels as if their body is heavy and sinking into the ground. The physical body becomes very thin and the hands and limbs become loose and unmanageable. The inner sign—the vision that is experienced by the dying person—is like a mirage, like water shimmering in the heat.

Next, the *aggregate of feeling* is absorbed. The dying person can no longer experience physical feelings, whether pleasure, pain, or indifference. At the same time, the wisdom of equality, which sees all feelings of happiness, suffering, and indifference as having the same nature, is absorbed. The water element is absorbed and all the liquids of the body—urine, blood, and so forth—dry up. The inner sign is that they experience a vision of smoke, like a room filled with incense.

Next, the *aggregate of discrimination* is absorbed. The dying person no longer recognizes their relatives and friends or knows their names. The wisdom of discriminating awareness is absorbed, and the fire element is absorbed. The heat of the physical body disappears. The inner sign is that they experience a vision of sparks, trembling like starlight, or a sky filled with fireflies.

Then, the *aggregate of compounded phenomena* is absorbed. Their body can no longer move. At the same time, the all-accomplishing wisdom is absorbed. This is the wisdom of attainment that is mindful of external, worldly activities and worldly success and their need. The dying person loses the idea of the need and purpose of external activities. The air element is absorbed. This is the moment the breathing ceases; Western doctors would consider this the moment of death. The inner sign is that the dying person experiences the vision of a flickering dim red-blue light, like the last spluttering of a candle.

Finally, the *aggregate of consciousness* is absorbed. This consists of the eighty gross superstitions and the winds that act as their mounts. "Superstitions" means the gross illusive minds, the dualistic wrong conceptions. At this point, they have the following visions. First, they see the *white vision*, which is like a very clear sky, like that in autumn, full of the brightness of the moon. Then they experience the *red vision*, which is like a copper-red reflection in the sky. Then they experience the *black vision*, which is a vision of empty darkness, like a dark and empty sky. Lastly, they experience the *clear light vision*. This is a vision of complete emptiness, very clear, like the sky of an autumn dawn. This is the vision of final death.

These inner visions of death are experienced by animals as well as by humans. What we are discussing here is the process of a "natural" death, which means a death not brought about by sudden, traumatic conditions, such as a car crash, where there is no time for the sequence of the various visions, and the mind goes straight to the intermediate state.

As for the moment of death, rather than occurring when the breathing stops, it actually is when the very subtle consciousness finally leaves the body, usually shown externally, by a trickle of blood or white fluid from the nose or the sex organ.[110]

The Great Yogis Choose Their Rebirth

At the point in the death process where the clear light is experienced, yogis who have spent their lifetimes in meditation use the methods they have been practicing all their lives to remain in meditation in the clear light for many days or even weeks. The duration varies depending on the meditator. During that time, far from being a smell of decay in the room, there is a fantastic, sweet smell due to the power of their realizations. Also, they look magnificent, totally different from an ordinary person dying.

Many Tibetan lamas have passed away in meditation since coming to India. Ordinary Indian people never believed that such a thing as passing away while in meditation was possible because they never saw it happen. In their way of thinking, the moment a person died the body should be taken out and burned before it began to smell. Because many Tibetan monks living in India ended their lives in Indian hospitals, it was difficult to receive permission to leave the body alone for a while because the doctors would never listen.

The death process meditation is an important aspect of a highest yoga tantra deity practice, where the meditator visualizes going through the death process, going through the intermediate state, and then being reborn as the deity. This is called *taking death, intermediate state, and rebirth into the path as the three bodies (or kayas) of the buddha.*

Our mind is full of distractions. To try to stay on an object in meditation in ideal circumstances for even a few minutes is extremely difficult, and while we are going through the trauma of dying, it is even more so. Being able to use tantric methods at these times depends on possessing great control and having done much purification. This is why it is so important to train as well and as often as possible, using the tantric sadhanas, purification practices, and, most of all, destroying the self-cherishing and developing bodhichitta.

The most important part of the meditation is the visualization of the clear light of death, which is conjoined with the understanding of emptiness. The vision of clear light occurs to all of us on many ordinary occasions, such as when we yawn, sneeze, have an orgasm, or pass into sleep, but the time is too short and we miss it. On the other hand, the great yogis, at the end of the completion-stage practice of highest yoga tantra, are able to stay aware as the vision happens. By concentrating on this mind without distraction, it is possible to reach enlightenment either at this time or during the intermediate state.

For such a practitioner, this union of clear light and illusory body is the moment when ordinary death is completely purified, as is ordinary intermediate state and ordinary rebirth. This is when the practitioner actually realizes the three bodies of a buddha. The ordinary death is transformed into the dharmakaya (wisdom body), the ordinary intermediate state is transformed into the *sambhogakaya* (enjoyment body), and the ordinary rebirth is transformed into the *nirmanakaya* (emanation body).

This is where Vajrayana practice is essential. In the highest yoga tantra practices with this kind of meditation, the visualization of the clear light is called *the son*. If we are able to combine this tantric meditation with the actual death process when we are dying, then this is called *mixing the mother and son*. It requires a very advanced meditation practice to be able to hold the tantric practice right through the death process. For a meditator who can do this, based on a realization of emptiness, the mixing of the mother and the son means that the practitioner becomes enlightened in that lifetime—without waiting for the intermediate state, as Lama Tsongkhapa did, or the next life, or going to a pure land where they can become enlightened.

Many great practitioners have become enlightened in the intermediate state or have gone to a pure realm. Many others have reincarnated in human form again in order to help all sentient beings, as Lama Yeshe did. Lama was able to experience these visions during meditation and did not have to wait until death. In his daily tantric practice, he was able to open the chakras[111] and allow the winds to flow in. For great practitioners such as Lama, reincarnation in a womb is completely different from normal people. They can choose the reincarnation, choose the parents, and choose the environment they will be reborn into, in order to be of most benefit to others.

The Intermediate State and Rebirth

As we have seen, craving for a physical form determines that we will take another body in samsara when we die, but before that, when the mind leaves the now-dead body, it enters the intermediate state, the bardo.

In the same way that the last stages of death were the dissolution of the aggregates with the three visions (white, red, and black), when the intermediate state commences, the visions reoccur in reverse order: the clear light, the black near-attainment, the red increase, and white appearance, with the eighty superstitions arising during these three visions, and then the other visions up to the mirage.

The evolution from death into the intermediate state is like passing from sleep into a dream. The intermediate-state body is formed by previous karma and delusions. The principal cause of the intermediate-state *mind* is the subtle mind, and its cooperative cause is the wind energy that accompanies the subtle mind. Similarly, the principal cause of the intermediate-state *body* is the wind energy, and its cooperative cause is the subtle mind.

Generally, an intermediate-state being can see the world, the relatives, and the past dead body, but karmically does not recognize any of this, so there is no desire to get back into it. The form of the intermediate-state body is that of the next rebirth. The being has many psychic powers, such as the ability to fly or do anything else it thinks of. Without a gross body like we have, it has no resistance to matter, and as soon as the being thinks of a place, no matter how far away it is, the body is there.

The longest length of existence in the intermediate-state body is seven days, although the being can take rebirth in a physical body at any time before that. After seven days, the intermediate being dies—this is called a *small death*—and takes rebirth in the same form for a further seven days until another small death occurs or a physical body is found. The longest intermediate-state existence is forty-nine days. Therefore, for that length of time after somebody has died, Tibetans do a puja every seven days for seven weeks, coinciding with the longest time that person would have to undergo existence in the intermediate state. There is usually a big puja on the forty-ninth day.

It is said a being destined to be reborn in the god realm has a vision as an intermediate-state being of going up a steep road; for a being destined for the human realm, the vision is going along straight; and for one destined to be reborn in the lower realms, they have the vision of being upside down, like the yoga pose where you raise your legs high above your head.

For a mind clouded with nonvirtue, the intermediate state is a terrible place. Already in the form of the next life, if it is going to be in the lower realms, the being must face many of the tortures of the lower realms, such as being crushed by huge mountains. The being has visions but doesn't realize that these are projections of its own mind, so it experiences great fear. It feels as if it is being blown about from place to place by a strong red wind or a fierce storm, or caught in a noisy fire, with the air filled with a terrible deafening sound like burning wood crackling. Or it may be tossed on huge waves, smashed into the water again and again and lifted up again and again. It may be tormented by karmic guardians, *yamas*, monsters with terrible bodies and fearful animal heads, such as lions, sheep, and scorpions, all of them chasing the intermediate-state being, screaming at it and beating it. The being has no respite from this at all.

Even if the person has created much negative karma and is destined for the lower realms, due to the power of the Three Rare Sublime Ones—the Buddha, Dharma, and Sangha—and due to the power of the truth of karma, if we strongly and purely do pujas or prayers for the dead person, we can definitely affect the intermediate-state being, helping lighten their suffering a little or even helping them pass from that state into an upper rebirth. There are also many special tantric and sutra methods to lessen the suffering or cause a rebirth in the upper realms more quickly for those dead. Generally, however, they have no choice where they are reborn; that is according to their karma.

Just as death is like falling asleep and the intermediate state is like dreaming, when we are born it is like waking up. If we are reborn in the hell realm, then the awakening is a terrible one.

For the intermediate-state being to take rebirth as a human, there must be three favorable conditions that exist and three faults that are absent:

- The mother must be healthy, free from any of the six diseases, such as having things wrong with the blood, and must not be having a monthly period.
- The intermediate-state being must wish to enter the sperm and egg in the mother's womb.
- The male and female must be engaged in the sexual act.
- The mother's womb must not be misshapen or obstructed by bile or the like.
- The sperm and the egg must not be diseased.
- The intermediate-state being, the male, and the female must all

be free from the fault of not having the karma to become child and parents.

Unless these six conditions are there, the being cannot begin its next life. If the male and female do not have the karma to become that being's parents and the being does not have the karma to become their child, it will not happen. I see so many couples unsuccessfully try for many years to have a child, checking with doctors, taking tests, unable to explain what is wrong. Generally, besides the other five conditions, it is because there is no karma for it to happen.

The cause of rebirth is seeing the future parents in sexual union and having attraction toward one of them. If somebody is going to be reborn as a female human being then the intermediate-state being develops strong attachment for the father and aversion for the mother; to be reborn as a male it is the opposite. This attachment is enough for the being to leave the intermediate state and take rebirth. The being wants to have sex with the one it is attracted to, but when it starts to embrace them, it doesn't see any part of the person except the sex organ, which causes frustration and anger to arise. So, first attachment and then anger become the conditions for the death of the intermediate-state being and the rebirth as a human being. It's easy, therefore, to see how ordinary birth is caused by karma and delusions.

As I mentioned, we have many different winds within us that cause the mind to travel through the body. When the male and female are engaged in sexual intercourse, the downward-voiding wind moves upward, generating heat, causing the white and red drops to melt. There is a release, which the couple take as pleasure, and the sperm and egg come together. The mind of the dying intermediate-state being enters this, like cream coming on top of boiling milk. When this happens, the new life has begun.

When the mind of the intermediate-state being joins with the sperm and egg, it sometimes enters through the crown aperture of the man (a sensitive area by the crown chakra) and sometimes through the mouth.

Then it travels down through the penis into the mother's womb. It can also just enter the mother's womb directly.

Again, as with the start of the intermediate state, the visions appear in reverse order; first the clear light, then the black, red, and white visions, and then the eighty superstitions that were absorbed with death re-manifest. The wind that accompanied the mind of the intermediate-state being starts forming the psychic energy channels of the new body, starting with the central channel and then the right and left channels, then slowly the other 72,000 channels, and the fetus develops around these.

With the development of the body, and particularly of the sense organs, the consciousness starts to re-establish feelings of attachment and aversion. By the end of the gestation, the baby's senses have developed enough for the womb to seem cramped and uncomfortable, and for the baby to be disgusted with the smell and feel of the womb. A wind energy moves the fetus into a position ready for birth with the head toward the mouth of the womb. This wind strengthens, and the downward-voiding wind of the mother commences the job of pushing the child out of the womb. This is the actual birth.

From the moment of conception, the person is aging, but this is not generally recognized. A baby seems a perfectly new thing and it is not until middle age or later that we label a person as "aging" or "old."

9. PREPARING FOR DEATH

THERE ARE MANY METHODS in Buddhism that help us avoid a premature death, such as animal liberation and long-life pujas, and of course, if we have a life-threatening illness, it is better to try to save our life than to simply accept the fact and wait to die.

Animal liberation is a wonderful practice.[112] As well as saving the lives of many kind mother sentient beings, it is a very practical and effective way to prolong a life threatened by premature death. It's also very easy. The essence of the practice is to take a number of animals that are going to be killed—usually small ones like fish or worms—and release them in an area where they will be safe. In Asia, people liberate tens of thousands of animals. How many you release and how big they are depend on how much you can afford to spend. It is such a wonderful thing to do.

People usually combine releasing the animals with a practice where they recite prayers and mantras to them and walk them around holy objects such as texts and stupas, thus giving them incredible imprints and helping them to have not only a better life but also and more importantly a better rebirth where they will meet the Dharma.

Saving animals as part of the FPMT's practice started many years ago in Kathmandu when we bought some calves and chickens that were going to be killed and took them to Kopan, and it sort of grew from there. There is now a separate area called the Animal Liberation Sanctuary, under the direct care of FPMT's Enlightenment for Animals project, that is home to dozens of cows, sheep, and goats. The organization has done many large animal liberation practices for the long life of His Holiness the Dalai Lama. There are many centers within the FPMT that regularly liberate animals and there are even a couple of projects to save animals and help them have a good life. The idea is to keep them in a nice environment where there are many holy objects and where mantras are played to them, thus planting the seeds of enlightenment in their minds. They become very fortunate animals. It is wonderful how we are able to benefit not just people but also those suffering, pitiful animal sentient beings.

Besides animal liberation, there are many ways of eliminating obstacles to life and thus prolonging it. In some ways, explaining the Dharma is the best way. If somebody is going to commit suicide or has a destructive lifestyle, taking drugs and so forth, hearing about the Dharma can transform their lives—that is definitely saving a life.

Within Tibetan Buddhism there are specific practices for prolonging life, such as White Tara or White Heruka. People often make *tsatsas*[113] as a method of eliminating obstacles to life. Eliminating obstacles to a long life is not preparing for death, however, which is something we should be doing every day.

The Need for Purification

To have a happy life and a happy death, it is vital to do the practice of purification.

If our mind is clouded with negativity, we will be terrified at death, whereas if we manage to purify it during our lifetime, our death will be tranquil and happy. This is totally logical. The essential technique is letting go of attachment, which means stopping viewing "my" and "mine" as important and seeing the happiness of others as more important than our own. This is the vital role purification plays in our life.

There are many methods for purifying the mind, including making offerings to the sangha and holy objects, making stupas and statues, doing prostrations—especially to the Thirty-Five Confession Buddhas and the Medicine Buddhas—doing intensive practices like the two-day nyungné retreat, and major retreats like the three-month Vajrasattva retreat.

No purification technique can be perfect without the four opponent powers:[114]

- the power of the object
- the power of regret
- the power of resolve
- the power of remedy

When we do a particular purification practice, we often reverse the last two powers, doing the visualization of the purification deity such as Vajrasattva and reciting the mantras—the *remedy*—and then, before the deity dissolves into us, we make the *resolve* never to do the action again. With these four powers we can purify even the karma that would otherwise definitely result in experience of the heaviest suffering of the hell realm. Pabongka Dechen Nyingpo said that whether this is going to happen to us depends on whether we have faith in karma.

Based on strong refuge in the Buddha, Dharma, and Sangha, the *power of the object*, we look at the negativities we have committed, reflecting on the shortcomings of creating negative karma. We think about a specific negative action we have done, or our negativities in general, and seeing how this causes so much suffering to ourselves and others and how it interferes with our achievement of realizations of the path to enlightenment, we feel great regret, the *power of regret*. The more regret we are able to feel, the more powerful our purification becomes and the more we purify our negative karma and obscurations.

This naturally leads us to determine to not do such actions again—the third power, the *power of resolve*. Based on this we do a purification practice such as reciting Vajrasattva mantras or prostrations. This is the *power of remedy*. Any virtuous practice that we do is a remedy to our negative karma, and so this fourth power can be reading a text that explains emptiness, meditating on bodhichitta, or any virtuous action of body, speech, or mind. It doesn't have to be a specific practice, as long as we combine it with strong regret and resolve not to do the negative action again. While any Dharma action purifies our negativities, incorporating it into the practice of the four opponent powers makes it incredibly powerful.

This is very good to do three times in the morning, then three times later in the day, perhaps after lunch, and then again at night before falling asleep. Alternatively, we can do the practice three times in the evening. Powerfully and continually purifying helps stop whatever negative karma we have committed from manifesting in suffering. Even if the negative karma we created that day is not completely purified by that one purification, it will certainly be lessened, and so it is incredibly worthwhile to make purifying with the four opponent powers a regular part of our Dharma practice. Purification is like a fire and negativities are the grain burned in that fire.

The Real Solution Is a Good Heart

Besides purification practices, the other method to stop the fear of death is to stop creating the cause of that fear, which comes down to one thing: developing a good heart. No matter how many problems there are in our life, the solution is the good heart, the altruistic attitude that cherishes other sentient beings. If we really love ourselves, we should love other sentient beings. The best way to cherish ourselves, to take care of ourselves, is to cherish other living beings. Instead of renouncing others, who are the source of all our past, present, and future happiness, we renounce the I, which is the source of all problems.

It is very good to practice the awareness that all others are the source of all our happiness. We should always practice this mindfulness, at home, in the office, in the street, wherever we are. And that leads us to understand that we are here to bring others happiness. With our family, we see we are here to cause them happiness; with friends, we are here to cause them happiness, and the same with our colleagues, with strangers on the street, and with the animals we see. We live with the thought that we are here to bring happiness to these cats, these dogs, these fish, these insects. That is our job.

Whoever we meet, we should think our job is to bring that person happiness. From the moment we wake up to the moment we go to sleep, everything we do should be done with this attitude, unstained by self-cherishing. In that way, every daily activity becomes a service for other sentient beings. Even eating food or taking medicine is for the happiness of others—we are doing it not for our comfort but in order to have a long and healthy life so we can be of benefit. We make money in order to have the resources to benefit others.

Then, as a byproduct, without expectation or desire for it, we effortlessly achieve whatever we need: comfort, health, leisure, protection, financial security—what normal people fight for all their lives—but we get these things not for ourselves but so our life is best suited to serving others. Everything comes from having a good heart. With a good heart everything is Dharma.

There are different levels of how we can be useful to others, how we can ensure their happiness. We can try to bring them a little mundane happiness, helping them get what they need in this life. For those with no understanding of the Dharma, this is excellent. They will respond to our good heart and start to see the worth of having a good heart. However, to really be happy, they will need to understand the Dharma; therefore, helping them learn the Dharma is very important. In that way, we can lead them to the happiness of future lives, to the renunciation of samsara and liberation, and to full enlightenment.

In doing this, our own mind naturally becomes more subdued, more patient, softer. We develop more tolerance and compassion for others. We become kinder. These very basic qualities give value to our human life, making this body highly meaningful.

The good heart is the wish not to harm others but instead to help them. Within that lies the whole of the Dharma. Within that, there are all the beneficial minds that we need to cultivate: equanimity, generosity, patience, loving-kindness, compassion, and especially bodhichitta, the mind that wishes to attain enlightenment in order to benefit each and every sentient being. If we can aspire to this mind, then we are living our life in the best possible way, and we can be confident of dying with a happy, peaceful mind and having a good rebirth.

One of the best ways of protecting ourselves from harmful minds is by taking the various levels of vows that we can take as a Buddhist. Living in the vows does not mean that everybody has to become a monk or a nun. As a layperson, we can live purely and morally. There are lay vows we can take for life that are a wonderful protection, such as the five lay vows of not killing, stealing, lying, committing sexual misconduct, or taking intoxicants. Even if we can only take one or two of these, based on refuge in the Buddha, Dharma, and Sangha, we will cease so much harm to others. There are also the one-day vows of the eight Mahayana precepts,[115] which are very powerful, creating limitless skies of merit. To live purely, mindfully for twenty-four hours can profoundly transform our mind.

For instance, refraining from sexual misconduct not only brings happiness to ourselves and others in this life, by making our relationships more harmonious and protecting us from cancer and other dangerous diseases, but it also means that, because karma is definite, we will definitely have harmonious relationships in our future lives and so be more able to practice Dharma.

We generally take vows in front of our guru. This makes it very powerful, far more powerful than just deciding that it would be a good thing not to commit these nonvirtuous actions. This is because of the very powerful relationship we have with the guru. Once we've made a sacred vow in front of the most important person in our life, breaking it would not only hurt the sentient being involved but also hurt the relationship with our guru.

If we fail to protect our mind and continue creating more negative karma, the purification practices we need to do will be endless. We might do practices such as Vajrasattva or prostrations to the Thirty-Five Medicine Buddhas, but by always creating more negativity we will always have to face the consequences of those actions. There will be no end to getting sick, to going to hospital, to having operations, and to all the medical expenses and psychiatrist's bills.

This is why purification alone is not enough. We need to purify the imprints of negative actions already on our mindstream, but we also have to stop from creating any further negative actions.

Among all these practices, awareness of impermanence and death is paramount. Then, with a good heart, whenever somebody criticizes us or angrily provokes us, we can respond with a calmer, more compassionate mind. Even doing this just once protects us from creating the negative karma of anger, which contributes to a happy life and a happy death. The more we can turn from self-cherishing to cherishing others, the happier and lighter our life and death will be.

The great lama Chöden Rinpoché once explained that people's natures can easily change as death approaches; habitually angry people can become very kind hearted, and conversely normally kind-hearted people can become very resentful and angry, even violent, if they feel that their death is somehow unfair. He explained the importance not only of taking the vows we can take as a Buddhist, but of renewing those vows, such as when we retake the bodhisattva and tantric vows in a self-initiation[116] of a highest yoga tantra deity. If we can do that, there is no chance we can ever go to the lower realms and we can be assured that when death comes, we will be able to face it with a happy mind.

The Transference of Consciousness

Rebirth in a pure land is possible through a practice called *powa*, the practice of the transference of consciousness at the time of death. Although powa can be done by a lama on another person, it is mainly used by very advanced practitioners when they see that they are dying and that they won't become enlightened in this lifetime, and so they forcefully push their consciousness from their body just before death and send it to a pure land. This is one of the six yogas of Naropa.

Some Westerners think that powa is a simple technique that anybody can do at any time. They think that if somebody is fed up with a relationship or cannot find a job, they can decide to head for a pure land, just by visualizing a seed at the navel and shooting it out the top of the head. It's not at all like that.

If the practitioner has had definite signs of death and has failed to eliminate the life obstacles through the usual means to prolong life—mandala offerings, purification practices, and so forth—and if it is clear that there will be heavy pain and mental suffering that could obstruct a good death, then the practitioner can choose powa rather than wait for that to happen. It is often suggested to practice powa when the signs show that death is about six months away. If a person does powa at the inappropriate time—either earlier than necessary or too late—it is compared in the texts to killing the deity, so timing is crucial.

Having decided to practice powa, the person trains with a guru. It needs to be done in conjunction with the five powers that we will look at below, especially the power of the white seed; they must attain complete nonattachment from everything around, including friends, loved ones, possessions, and even the body, and then make extensive charity to other sentient beings and the Buddha, Dharma, and Sangha.

If a dear friend is dying, you can request a lama to do powa for them. It is said that if you do, you should never touch the body until the powa has been completed, and that the powa can only be done after the breathing has stopped but before the heat has left the heart, which means while the consciousness is still in the body. Before that, there is the risk of taking a life. This is different to somebody who does powa on themselves, where it is recommended to do it six months before death. If the lama is practicing powa for that person from a distance, you should also tell them exactly which direction the head is facing and the exact time of death. It is also recommended that you do an astrological reading for the dead person.

Although generally this practice should never be done until the person has stopped breathing, I heard that once in Tibet, when a lama heard a group of Tibetans was going to be executed by the Chinese, he asked the soldiers to wait and then sat down and did powa for them. (Whether he was one of the people to be shot I don't know.) Anyway, he sat in meditation and did powa and the people waiting for the execution simply collapsed in a heap, their consciousnesses having left their bodies, presumably for a pure land. They had no need of the bullets of the Chinese soldiers! The lama not only saved the people from whatever rebirth was awaiting them, he saved the soldiers from the negative karma of killing.

If we have received teachings from a guru during our lifetime and if we feel strong devotion for the guru, then our guru can remind us of the core practices as we are dying—of bodhichitta and letting go of attachment—and reconnect us with our particular deity. If we can meditate on the deity we have practiced during our life, such as Chenrezig or Tara, and strongly wish to be reborn into their pure land, then we have a good chance of attaining that wish.

Similarly, for a dying friend, we can recite the prayers and mantras of the deity that they practiced in life. Helping them hold on to the connection as long as possible is the best gift we can give them.

Even without a strong practice, their guru can assist them in attaining a pure land. It is also said in the teachings that being able to remember the guru is the best method of transforming the consciousness and that they will receive enlightenment very quickly. This is incredibly powerful.

Even if they have created one of the five immediate negativities,[117] because of their devotion for the guru, or somebody shouting the name of the guru into their ear, their consciousness can be transferred to a positive rebirth. If they do not have a strong devotion, then that person can shout at them to remember the Three Rare Sublime Ones.

When they have a very strong connection, in some circumstances it is possible for the guru to move their consciousness away from nonvirtue and toward virtue, even in the intermediate state, toward a better rebirth and even toward a pure land. When a high lama transfers somebody's consciousness to a pure realm, many special signs happen, such as rainbows or white light emitting from the body.

The Five Powers

The five powers are five ways we develop our life and prepare ourselves for death. The mind-training texts describe two different orders to the five powers, one to do in life and one to do at the time of death.[118]

The order in life is the power of intention, habituation, the white seed, destruction (blaming the self-cherishing), and prayer. The order at death is different:

1. the power of the white seed
2. the power of intention
3. the power of blaming the self-cherishing thought
4. the power of prayer
5. the power of habituation

Practicing the five powers at death is the fundamental practice; it is the real powa, making our death meaningful and beneficial for all sentient beings. Underlying all the other practices we can do during our life—sadhanas, mantras, prostrations, and so forth—this is the foundation; this is what destroys our self-cherishing and stabilizes our guru devotion. And so, it buoys us during our life and prepares us for death.

The Power of the White Seed

The first power is the *power of the white seed*, which, in our lifetime practice as well as the practice at the time of death, means accumulating the white seeds of positive karma. Accumulating merit during life means creating positive karma and purifying negative karma, but at death it is too late for that, so accumulating merit at the time of death mainly involves cutting the attachment we have to things.

There are various signs of death that come: outer, inner, and secret signs. If we recognize them, such as the signs of death that come in dreams, and realize we are soon going to die, with the power of the white seed, we determine to stop clinging to our possessions and loved ones, and above all, to our body. Knowing the suffering that clinging to them will bring us as we die and afterward, we renounce them and give them away, either mentally or actually. By applying the meditation of renunciation, we are able to cut the grasping mind and free ourselves from the bondage of attachment. With that freedom, there is nothing that makes it difficult to experience death.

Whether we physically get rid of our possessions or not, we must mentally free ourselves from them. We can systematically give away everything, we can write a will leaving them to others and so know they are no longer ours, or we can mentally separate from them in some way. We can dedicate everything we have to all the holy objects in the world, such as Dharma center and teachers, or to all the living beings, healthy and sick, rich and poor. Dedicating our possessions to help all other beings helps to free us from clinging, which is a great release for our mind.

Dedicating our possessions is not to make monks or nuns rich; it is to create the maximum amount of merit as we die. The more powerful the object of our charity, the greater the merit we accumulate, and the happier the mind will be at death. While making gifts to other sentient beings makes us happy and peaceful, when we offer our possessions to the Three Rare Sublime Ones, we accumulate so much merit.

There are so many stories of miserly people who have died clinging to their possessions and have subsequently become spirits, or even dogs, stuck to the property or possessions that they were attached to, causing so much harm to the beings living there.

Clinging to the things of this life is very foolish. Doing so is compared to a child playing in the sand, creating houses and cars, thinking they are "mine," and never thinking beyond that. Then, when they are destroyed, such as when another child kicks them over, they are devastated. We are childish when we cling to the appearances of this life, to comfort, praise, reputation, material possessions, and so forth. Of losing the objects of our eight worldly concerns, Shantideva says,

> Like a child crying in pain
> when his sandcastle is destroyed,
> my mind weeps
> when it has lost praise and glory.[119]

The childish ones cling hard to what they see as theirs and suffer miserably, whereas the wise ones see clinging as suffering and renounce it, knowing that their life, their body and all their possessions will soon be no more.

The Power of Intention

The next power, the *power of intention*, can also be called the *power of motivation* or the *power of the attitude*. It is the same practice at death as in our lifetime, although the texts list it in a different order. During our lifetime we constantly check our motivation to ensure it is as vast and positive as possible. Every morning we think, "The purpose of my life is to free all sentient beings from all suffering and its causes and bring them every happiness. Today, that is my job, and I will do nothing else but that." As we die, that intention becomes more specific. We tell ourselves that we will certainly maintain our good heart even in the intermediate state and the next rebirth. Thus, the power of intention as we are dying is to think,

> From now until I achieve enlightenment, especially up to the point of my death, while I am dying, in the intermediate state, and in all my future lives, I will never allow myself to come under the control of self-cherishing and I will never allow myself to be parted from bodhichitta.

If we have this intention and are able to remember this altruism all the time, there is no suffering, even as we die. Our life, which has been a very pleasant journey, becomes very beneficial for other sentient beings as we die. We are then able to have a meaningful rebirth and further develop our mind in order to benefit so many sentient beings.

Unless we can keep a pure, altruistic motivation, we can slip back into self-cherishing, which means we will be unable to achieve the three great meanings: the happiness of future lives, liberation, and enlightenment. Furthermore, it means we will be unable to help all other sentient beings attain those great meanings. We will be unable to help those numberless beings suffering terribly in the hell realm in any way—even one of them—and the same with the hungry ghosts, animals, humans, and gods. Think of a fish in the water, moving toward a worm with a hook stuck through its body. Because of our selfish attitude, we will be unable to help the terrible suffering of both the fish and the worm, let alone cause them to attain the three great meanings. Our job is to free all sentient beings and we must hold that thought all day every day; otherwise it is so harmful.

With the power of the bodhichitta motivation, we can do anything. Not only will we achieve the three great meanings, but we will be able to cause all other sentient beings to achieve them as well. This attitude, which is so important in our daily life, is crucial as we face death.

The Power of Blaming the Self-Cherishing

The next power is called the *power of blaming the self-cherishing* or the *power of destruction.* What we blame is self-cherishing; what we destroy is the ego. When we examine the source of all the problems in this life and of all the problems we will face during death and in our next life, we see that they all originate from the self-cherishing attitude.[120] We will see that every undesirable thing comes from this self-cherishing attitude: the failures of this life, the problems in our Dharma practice, and all the diseases and unwanted situations. Although they might have external conditions, they all stem from self-cherishing.

On the basis of self-cherishing, desire arises, anger arises, jealousy arises, ill will arises, all the dissatisfied minds arise. These minds cause us to harm others, who then naturally retaliate. We have given them the target of our self-cherishing, and so it is natural we will receive the arrows of their harm. But the real source of that harm is our own self-cherishing.

We need to see this clearly. Whenever somebody harms us, we need to see that we are experiencing that harm because sometime in the past we have given that harm in that same way. In *A Guide to the Bodhisattva's Way of Life* Shantideva says,

> I myself during my past lives brought
> similar torments upon other beings.
> Therefore it is only fitting that this same tribulation should fall
> upon me,
> who is the cause of injury to other living beings.[121]

This is the opposite of how we feel at present. We feel we are blameless and the rest of the world is causing us unwarranted suffering. By seeing the real cause of all our suffering, our self-cherishing, we can target the real culprit and destroy it completely without harming others or ourselves.

When people don't love us, when obstacles occur, when we encounter problems at work, we need to remind ourselves that whatever problems happen in life, we are experiencing the results of karma we have created in the past. If we had not created the karma to be harmed by others, it could not possibly happen. We cannot blame others. There is no reason to get upset, no reason to be angry with them. The karma that caused us to harm them in the past is being returned to us, causing us harm now.

This power of destruction that places the blame on our self-cherishing is very liberating. Instead of blaming others or blaming ourselves, we place the blame firmly on our self-cherishing. Instead of taking the problem on ourselves, we give it back to the self-cherishing. As soon as we do that, there are big differences in our life. Perceiving the real enemy, our own selfishness, we see it has robbed us of every happiness over our countless lives. Not only must we blame it for all suffering, we also must also do everything we can to destroy it.

If we understand how karma works, we can then see how all our negative actions are the cause of all the suffering we now experience and will experience. The *ripening result* of karma means that because of our nonvirtuous actions we will be reborn in a lower realm, whereas the *possessed result* means that, even if we are reborn as a human, the environment we are reborn into will be hostile and unsupportive. Because of the karmic aspect called *experiencing the result similar to the cause*, whatever negative action we have done that has harmed others will ripen in the same way at some stage in the future, and so if we have stolen, for instance, we will be the victim of theft. And with *creating the cause similar to the result*, we are habituating ourselves to repeating those nonvirtuous actions again and again, strengthening and perpetuating our suffering.

Putting the blame on the real enemy is a fundamental thought transformation practice. We shift our focus completely around from the supposed harmer to the real harmer, and we determine to destroy the real enemy. With the self-cherishing mind there can only be dissatisfaction; with the mind cherishing others, immediately there is satisfaction.

Free from the self-cherishing mind, we can take on the suffering of all other sentient beings, and so our death can be truly meaningful. We have the power to transform our death into a joyful and rich experience.

The Power of Prayer

In context of the five powers in life, the next one, the *power of the prayer*, comes last because this is how we set up our day. At the time of death, however, the power of prayer is listed as the fourth power. This means praying to never be separated from bodhichitta, the supreme altruistic mind.

We pray something like this:

> In all circumstances—happy or suffering, good or bad—and at all times—at death, in the intermediate state, and in all future rebirths—I will never allow myself to fall under the control of self-cherishing. Not even for a second will I ever lose this precious mind of bodhichitta. Not even for a second will I stop cherishing others and working only for their benefit.

We pray that we will be able to remember bodhichitta at the time of death, in the intermediate state, and in all future lives, and that we will be able to practice in order to again meet the guru who reveals the teachings on thought transformation and bodhichitta. Having such a strong prayer in our heart sets up the motivation for everything we do. This is the attitude in our normal life we should start and finish each day with and the attitude we should have at death.

The Power of Habituation

The last power is the *power of habituation* or the *power of acquaintance.* In life, this means mainly training in bodhichitta but at the time of death it refers to the way we die.

When we know we are about to die, we should lie in the lion's posture, the posture the Buddha assumed when he showed the aspect of passing into parinirvana at Kushinagar. For that, we lie down on our right side, with our right hand under our head and our ring finger pressing the right nostril closed, which reduces attachment, the main cause of a miserable death. Then we lay our left arm along the top of the body and stretch our legs out straight with our feet together. If we are too weak to assume this posture as we die, we can ask others to help us get into it. It is also mentioned that keeping a lamrim text by the pillow at the time of death helps us to remember the teachings and so avoid the lower realms.

This special posture is itself a protection; it helps us die with a positive, happy mind, not with anger, attachment, jealousy, or any of the other disturbing thoughts. In that way, our experience of death becomes a path to enlightenment.

While in that position, if we can, we should meditate on the suffering of others and generate compassion, taking on their sufferings and giving them all our happiness in a *tonglen*, or taking and giving, practice.[122] Even if we are unable to meditate on emptiness or do a highest yoga tantra practice as we die, to be able to experience our death on behalf of the numberless other sentient beings is so beneficial. Taking refuge in bodhichitta is the greatest benefit when we are living a normal life, whether we have problems or not, whether we are healthy or ill, and likewise it is the greatest benefit as we die.

We can also meditate on the emptiness of the I that is dying, which can be something like "My body is not the I; my mind is not the I; the collection of body and mind is not the I. The I does not exist anywhere on this collection, but that does not mean that the I does not exist at all. How does the I exist? The I that experiences death is nothing except what is merely labeled by the mind, dependent on this association of the body and mind. If it is analyzed, that is all the I is. Therefore, the I is empty of existing from its own side."

Another similar and quick method of meditating on the emptiness of the I that is dying is to think, "I am dying" and analyze what it is that is dying. We will see that if there were no mind labeling this I that is dying there would be no I, therefore the I is merely labeled based on the aggregates of body and mind, constantly changing, and death is one of those changes. The I does not ultimately exist anywhere; such an I is a total hallucination. It is completely empty. That emptiness is the ultimate nature of the I. If we could die with this thought, it would be a very powerful and positive mind.

Of course, bodhichitta and emptiness are minds we should be developing every day, but they are particularly vital at the time of death. The power of acquaintance in life is to develop these minds, and the power of acquaintance at death is to hold these minds.

To practice these five powers at the time of death is better than powa. Powa can help us attain a pure land, but to do all the practices involved in powa with the purity and intensity needed for success is very difficult. Using the five powers during the life and the five powers at death, on the other hand, will definitely ensure a better future rebirth. It helps us prepare for our own death and it helps us help other people to die well.

Helping People with Terminal Illnesses

Every day in the world tens of thousands of healthy people die. Many die from car accidents or from other causes; there are dangers from fire, water, earth, wind, and so forth. If we are trying to help somebody with a terminal illness like cancer, we need to help them see this. (I will use cancer here as an example, but this can refer to any terminal illness.) Somebody overcome by such a disease will commonly feel that they are the only person in the world suffering in that way, and that the rest of the world is healthy and free from all problems.

The basic psychology for helping a cancer sufferer is the same as meditating on impermanence and death. As we have seen, normally in our life, and especially when we are overwhelmed by confusion, worry, and fear, remembering that death may happen at any time can be of great benefit. This is no different with the cancer sufferer. That is not to say meditating on impermanence and death will cure the cancer, but it will cure the suffering mind that brings so much misery. It even means that their life can be enriched by the disease, forcing them to look at reality in a way they never have before.

There are three points we should make in order to help somebody overcome the despair of having an incurable disease:

- It is a misconception that their disease means imminent death whereas everybody else has a long and healthy life.
- Having a long and healthy life is not the main purpose of life.
- Everything comes from the mind, including the disease itself and the suffering that the disease brings.

Many people with cancer live for many years and have very worthwhile, productive lives while alive. Conversely, many people not suffering from a specific illness die for a million different reasons every day. Just because we are healthy and fit does not mean we will definitely have a long life. As we have seen, there are far more causes for death than for life, and any of us can die from any of those causes at any moment. For somebody with a disease like cancer, it's too easy to have the fixed idea that they alone will die very soon, while all others are healthy and will living long while. It's simply not like that.

Destroying this misconception can greatly help. From there, we can show the ill person that death itself is not the problem, but rather it's the *concept* of death that is the problem. There is no real frightening death that exists from its own side; what frightens us and makes it so hard to deal with is our own concept of what death is. Our misunderstanding, our attachment and clinging to the appearances of this life, blocks us from letting go of our body, our sense of I, and our very life. This is like being attached to things that appear in our dreams, such as if we dream we have the body of a god or the wealth of a billionaire. We cling to these dream objects on the basis of the hallucinated concept that they are real, and we create attachment and hatred based on that hallucination. Just as in a dream, in life we hallucinate and create negative emotions based on a sense of a concrete reality, a reality that is not there.

According to Buddhism, because we have had numberless lives, each of us has gone through every experience numberless times. Death, like everything else, is completely natural, like birth or a sprout coming from a seed. What creates the fear is not the cancer or even death itself, but something else.

There are many people with diseases like cancer who are very content and happy. They can even use the disease to enrich their lives and benefit others greatly. Many of my gurus died of cancer, but contracting cancer wasn't a cause of fear for them. They had no fear or worry because, understanding the nature of reality, they could see how death is just a transition from this state to another state. They could even use the experience of the disease to develop their minds further on the path, leading them yet closer to peerless happiness and full enlightenment.

I have met many people in the West, too, who have faced a terminal illness like cancer without fear or worry, and who have in fact been very happy. This shows that the disease is not intrinsically frightening; it's how the mind reacts to it that makes it frightening. Clinging to false concepts of a permanent healthy body and a life that will never end, we cannot accept when that concept is shattered. We need to give up our clinging. With a contented mind we are happy, whether we live for another hundred years or just a few minutes more. There is no clinging to permanence and so no suffering when impermanence becomes manifest in this way.

The second point to explain is that being healthy and having a long life is not the main purpose in life. The main purpose in life is to benefit others. This is what makes life meaningful and this is what brings us true happiness. This has nothing to do with how well we are or how long we are destined to live. To live one day with the mind cherishing others is to have a full life; somebody with cancer might indeed die in a short time, but if they spend their time benefiting others, then they are fulfilling the true purpose of life and have had a full and good life.

With this attitude in their everyday life, real happiness comes. They have great strength in their heart, so it doesn't matter what happens to them. This attitude immediately cuts off so many problems, which have come from deluded concepts.

First, it is important for them to be aware that without feeling compassion for others, no matter how much wealth they have, there is no real happiness in life; they can never be satisfied. After making a million dollars, the millionaire wants two million. And after making two million, they want ten million. And it goes on and on like this until the time of death. Without compassion, being wealthy has no meaning. On the other hand, with compassion, the sick person ceases giving harm and only ever benefits others; as a consequence, they experience real peace and happiness. In that way, compassion is the source of all worldly *and* ultimate peace and happiness.

We are one, others are infinite, so if we, this one person, achieve liberation, it's not much to be excited about, or if we are reborn as a hell being, it's not much to be depressed about. Whatever we do, we should do it for others. We can help the cancer sufferer see how experiencing their illness or death on behalf of others is the bodhichitta attitude, the one that makes their experience beneficial for all sentient beings.

When we take on the suffering of others in a practice like tonglen, we can use our own illness to develop compassion for others. When it is done very well, it can even relieve their physical suffering, but the important thing is that our tonglen practice purifies the imprints that are on our mental continuum. We are purifying our mind and destroying the cause of suffering, leading to the cessation of all problems—even that of death and rebirth. And ultimately it leads us to enlightenment. This is far more important than trying to ensure a long life.

Somebody with cancer, like all of us, must understand that everything comes from the mind. The disease comes from the mind; the suffering caused by the disease comes from the mind.

To the cancer sufferer, the disease itself seems to be the main cause of why they are suffering, but the disease is caused by an imbalance in the four elements of the body: earth, water, fire, and air (the solid and liquid constituents of our body, the heat that keeps us alive, the wind energy, and the air that we breathe). When the mind is not disturbed by delusions, the wind, the vehicle of the mind, is not disturbed, so the elements stay in balance. Delusions, however, disturb the wind, and when the elements fall out of balance, illness results.

The cancer is not the problem; even death is not the problem. The mind clouded with ignorance and delusion is the problem, and this is what needs to be addressed. This is exactly the same with a healthy person as with a sick person. We are all sick with the disease of the deluded mind. Being ignorant of the ultimate nature of the I, we all create negative actions that cause suffering to ourselves and others, which can manifest as illness and ultimately death. If we were free from delusions, we would be free from death itself.

When the consciousness leaves the body, the mind makes up the label "death." That's all it is. There is no death coming from outside, existing from its own side, something real and frightening. There is just the death created or labeled by the mind.

This is the same when any unwanted thing happens. When there is a change that our self-cherishing does not expect or want, we label it as a problem. Having labeled it that, it appears to us as a problem. And we believe it! We believe there is a real problem in our life. In fact, this "real problem" is just a creation of our own mind. If we had not labeled this situation a "problem" and believed that label, there would have been no problem at all. So, whether we have a problem in our life depends on whether it is labeled as such. If we were able to label the same situation as "good," we would see it as good. We can change the way we see things.

Although labeling something as "bad" is the creation of our mind, it is not the creation of our entire mind, just of self-cherishing and attachment. Our patient mind does not see a person as bad; it can even understand how somebody who harms us is a kind friend, allowing us to diminish our self-cherishing. The healthy mind of loving-kindness wants only happiness for that person.

"Cancer" too is a label. It is a concept. Even what is called "cancer" comes from the mind. But whereas there is no such thing as cancer existing from its own side, there is a merely labeled cancer, and somebody suffering from cancer does not necessarily have to give it a label to feel the pain.

The ultimate goal of life is to free all beings from all suffering and cause them every happiness. The purpose of our life is not just to be healthy or have a long life, but to be beneficial to others. When we know that, whether we are healthy or not, whether we are dying of not, nothing else matters.

FPMT Hospices

Another very practical way of helping people with terminal illnesses is the hospice movement. In the FPMT there are many students who are interested in this, and I feel this is extremely important to do. The first FPMT hospices started in Australia, with people like Venerable Pende Hawter doing incredible service creating the organizations that grew into full hospices.

This is not only a great service for those people who are terminally ill but is also a wonderful education for the people who work for the hospice. By guiding others faced with death, they are learning about death wisely and they will be able to guide themselves when their time comes.

The Root Institute's Shakyamuni Buddha Community Health Care Centre in Bodhgaya, India, grew out of seeing a sick old man on the road to Rajgir north of Bodhgaya, the place where the Buddha gave the great teachings on emptiness called *The Heart Sutra*. Kirti Tsenshab Rinpoché was traveling there to give teachings on emptiness. We were having lunch at a restaurant when Rinpoché saw an old, sick man outside, naked and crawling with flies. Rinpoché asked if there was some way we could get the man to a hospital, but one of the students, an American doctor, explained that, because he was so poor, there was no way he could get adequate treatment in an Indian hospital. After discussing it, I managed to persuade the Root Institute to take him in and care for him. While doctors cared for him, he improved, but in the summer most people left, and he got sick again and then died.

After that, I saw an old man who shook so badly he couldn't even walk with his two sticks. When I saw him, he had fallen onto a pile of firewood, and I thought that even if he wanted a drink of water, he was too weak to walk to where the water was. Remembering that other old man, the thought came to me that we should start a home for destitute people. The idea was that it would be for everybody, but we would tell them plainly that it was a Buddhist organization, that the place wasn't just to look after the body but to take care of the mind as well. And especially when they were going to die, to help them die with a positive attitude, full of loving-kindness and compassion.

That was how the destitute home and the community care project started in 1991, and it has done such a good job helping the poor and ill people of Bihar, the poorest state of India. For the people who work there, serving the poor people there becomes a great teaching and an expression of bodhichitta, putting bodhichitta into practice, and in that way, it becomes a great purification and accumulates extensive merit.

Helping Others Die Well

Because we have delusions, we have death and rebirth. Because we have delusions, we have suffering. Our body is built to experience pain. When we pinch our flesh, it hurts. If our body did not have this nature, there would be no way we would feel any pain. We are very vulnerable; even drinking a glass of water can cause us to choke and have sudden pain unless we are careful. Because this collection of body and mind comes from impure causes, from karma and delusions, we must experience suffering.[123]

Knowing this is vital if we want to understand how to overcome our own suffering and how to help others, especially when they are dying. They need an education on death: on what death is, on how to deal with death, and on how to have a happy death. Depending on the dying person's mental capacity, background, religion, and situation, if we can skillfully introduce them to this and help them develop their compassion and devotion to their religion, and if we are able to help them generate a positive mind and die well, we can be of incredible help to them. It is much more important than giving a home to a homeless person, giving food to a starving person, or giving medicine to a sick person. We are giving that person a rebirth as either a human being or a god. That is our gift to the dying person, the most precious gift possible.

We need to know not just the ways of helping them be physically comfortable, but also psychologically, how they can generate a positive mind despite their situation. Even if they call themselves a Buddhist, that does not mean that they practice purely all the time. As we have seen, as long as the attachment to the eight worldly dharmas is there, any action, including a so-called Dharma action, is just nonvirtue and the cause of the lower realms. If they were to die and be reborn as an animal or worse, there is nothing we could then do to help. As Shantideva says in his *Guide to the Bodhisattva's Way of Life*,

> By conduct such as mine I will not reach again the human condition.
> If I do not attain again human birth,
> I shall only meet sin,
> whence would arise then what is meritorious?[124]

Therefore, if we are able to help somebody to die with a positive attitude, we are saving them from eons in the lower realms.

Developing a positive attitude is something that can help anybody: Buddhist, Christian, Hindu, Muslim, Jewish, or somebody with no beliefs at all. Even for somebody who believes that there is only one life and that they will soon cease to exist entirely, breaking their attachment to the body and this life is an important step in dying in a peaceful and happy way. Somebody suffering great pain can still die peacefully.

Death is a crucial time. The person who is dying needs so much help. Understanding the nature of the mind, simple meditation techniques, common sense advice, hospices—there are many tools to help those who are dying, but they all lead to the person being able to let go of the clinging to this body and this life.

There are two aspects to helping a dying person: helping them to understand what death is and how to deal with it, and the practices and things we and they can do to help make their transition to the next life a smooth one.

While making a dying person physically comfortable by giving them the proper medicine or making their room beautiful is very good, if the person has faith in the Buddha, Dharma, and Sangha, we have many opportunities to help them, by reminding them of their practice. However, even if they do not have faith in the Three Rare Sublime Ones, we can explain to them that they are not the only dying person in the country or in the world, that so many others are dying on that same day, and everybody has to go through this experience. In that way, we try to help the dying person generate compassion for others, thinking in a broad way, instead of only themselves.

If the dying person could remember bodhichitta as they die, beyond any doubt they would be saved from the lower realms. But even a strong degree of compassion is such a positive mind to have. It is our responsibility, if we are that person's loved one or friend, to help them in this. To be thinking of the happiness of others as they die, rather than their own terrible circumstances, is an amazing thing to do, and it will ensure a positive rebirth. We can encourage them to feel compassion and loving-kindness even as they are dying.

Whether the dying person has faith or not, the best way is to help them transform their mind into compassion and loving-kindness is by generating a mind of tonglen, a mind that willingly experiences the suffering of all other dying people. Help the person to think, "I'm going to dedicate my experience of death to all sentient beings. To allow them to be free from the fear and suffering of death, I will experience all their problems by myself." They take upon themselves the suffering of death of all other beings and experience their deaths for them. "How wonderful it would be if I could experience this for other sentient beings, so that they could be free from these sufferings."

If somebody is not Buddhist, it would be unskillful to try to explain Buddhism to them when they have held a different belief all their life, but if we know what kind of mind they need to have at death, it is relatively easy to use their own belief system to stimulate a positive mind. We can help the dying person generate devotion to whatever belief system they hold by talking about and bringing out the positive qualities of that religion.

For example, if the person is a Christian, it is easy to help them generate faith in Jesus by describing his great qualities: his infinite compassion, his fully knowing mind, and his perfect power to guide. By reminding the dying person of this, they can feel that Jesus with all his great qualities is there in their heart. We can help them see that the nature of their mind is pure, so that they don't have to feel guilt. We can show how their mind is oneness with God, and that the nature of their mind is pure, like God. In that way we are leading them to a sense of the clear-light mind but using different images and different terminology. This way we are skillfully using the faith in their heart to bring forth compassion and happiness and to help them let go of their attachment and aversion, protecting their mind and making death easier.

It is important that the dying person is as peaceful as possible, so we need to make sure that we don't inadvertently spark attachment, anger, or any type of distraction. We can show the disadvantages of desire and hatred and how attachment to their possessions will not help them keep them one minute longer. We can help them accept the situation they are in and to learn from it, even though these are the very last moments of their life. Whatever advice we give needs to fit the level of the mind of the dying person and be suitable for them to hear.

The family around the dying person needs to maintain harmony and to not display strong emotions that could upset them. To wail and scream and plead for them not to die will not keep them alive and will only agitate them and make their death more difficult. I cannot emphasize enough the importance of a tranquil and supportive environment for a dying person.

Whether the dying person can comprehend we are there or not, it is very beneficial to sit quietly with them holding a strong bodhichitta motivation in our hearts. We can recite mantras, either aloud so they can hear if that is appropriate or silently if it is not, for instances if they are not Buddhist and might be perplexed or upset hearing these strange sounds. Whether or not they have any idea of Buddhism, the power of the mantra can definitely be of huge help as they are dying. The Medicine Buddha mantra, the Chenrezig mantra, or Shakyamuni Buddha mantra are very powerful, but also whatever you (or they) have a strong connection with. If they have slipped into unconsciousness, it is good to recite the mantras in their ear, blowing in it as well, as you recite. This has definite power to help. There are also the ten great mantras to be said at the time of death.[125]

It is very good to have pictures of the buddhas and many holy objects around the room of a dying person (or images from the person's particular religion) and to burn incense and make the environment as calming and positive as possible.

If you have any relics of the Buddha, bringing them to the side of the dying person ensures they will not have a lower rebirth, as does putting special blessed pills on their crown. Having a prayer wheel near the dying person is another very powerful way of ensuring a good death and a better rebirth. In fact, if there is a prayer wheel in the room, we don't need to do powa, as the prayer wheel itself becomes a form of powa. Simply thinking of a prayer wheel helps the dying person shoot the consciousness through the central channel and out of the crown to reincarnate in the pure land of Amitabha or Chenrezig. Simply touching a prayer wheel brings great purification. If a prayer wheel contains a hundred million OM MANI PADME HUM mantras, turning it once accumulates the same merit as having recited OM MANI PADME HUM a hundred million times, so turning it just once is the same as having done many years of retreat. Therefore, it is very good to encourage a dying person to have a prayer wheel and to turn it as much as possible.

When a Person Has Died

It's good to chant whatever mantra we know or have a special connection to, or a mantra the dying or dead person had a special connection to. If, for instance, they were devoted to Tara then that would naturally be the mantra to chant. Shakyamuni Buddha's holy name mantra and of course the Medicine Buddha mantra and the Chenrezig mantra are very powerful at these times. The ten great mantras I have already mentioned are particularly powerful when we are with a dead person. We can place a sheet of paper with the ten great mantras written on it on the dead body. With a motivation of bodhichitta we can recite the mantra, silently or loudly depending on the circumstances, and blow on the person's body, which has the power to purify and benefit the person. This of course applies to dead animals as well as humans, but I am focusing on dying and dead people here.

Reciting prayers and mantras and doing pujas for people who have died is very important. Even if the person is not a Buddhist, or if they have not been virtuous and so are likely to be reborn in the lower realms, reciting prayers, mantras, and so forth can definitely help in some way. In general, it is all up to karma. No matter how much compassion the enlightened beings have, they are unable to alter the karma of a sentient being who has created the causes to be reborn in the lower realms.

But having said that, due to the power of the Buddha, Dharma, and Sangha, if we have a strong connection with the dead person and if we do the practices strongly and purely, because that person now is an intermediate-state being—which is a very subtle state—it is possible to influence the rebirth in some way; the terrible suffering can somehow become a little bit less. It is even possible that we can influence the intermediate-state being to be reborn in the upper realms instead. There are many stories showing that this has happened in previous times. Whether we are able to influence the rebirth or not depends on many factors—above all, on the strength of the karma for the lower realms. We can't change that person's karma, but we can influence which karma ripens, and if the karma to be reborn as a human ripens, then that person has the opportunity to purify the negative karma in that lifetime.

Where a person reincarnates is indicated by where the consciousness leaves the body, and we can influence that in some cases. It is very good, immediately after the breathing has stopped, to place a stupa or special powa pills on the dead person's crown to help the consciousness leave through the crown, which will ensure a better rebirth. If we have any holy relics of the Buddha, they are incredibly powerful to use in this way. It is very important when somebody is dying to not touch any part of the body other than the crown in case it influences the consciousness to leave by that part.

The best thing is to leave the body undisturbed for as long as possible, but if the body has to be disturbed, such as when it is in a hospital ward, it is good to place a hand on the crown with the hope that the consciousness will be attracted there and so depart from there and ensure a rebirth in a pure land or the formless realm. Giving a strand of hair on the crown a short, sharp tug will help. If a family member or a lama has the skill to perform powa for the dead person, then this is the time to do it.

There is a tantric practice called *jangwa* that is a very powerful method to purify the karma of a sentient being who has died. There are a few different ways of doing this, and it can be done with different deities, such as Medicine Buddha or Vajrayogini. The main idea is that we recite powerful mantras to bless mustard seeds, and then, while meditating on emptiness, we visualize hooking their consciousness back, while throwing the seeds on the deceased, or on a photograph of them, or even on the name written on paper. This can help the consciousness change direction and receive a human body instead of a lower rebirth, or even go to the pure lands.

A jangwa practice associated with Medicine Buddha is one that even we ordinary people can perform, without risking the possibility of creating further interferences for ourselves or for the deceased. Other jangwa practices associated with other specific deities require a high level of skill on the part of those doing the practice—skill in visualization, in self-generation, in ritual accuracy. If it is done by a meditator with very good concentration, it can influence that rebirth, allowing the being to attain a higher rebirth or even a pure land. Even if they have already been reborn in the lower realms, they can be freed from there.

The intermediate-state being has small deaths every seven days for a maximum of forty-nine days, and it has to be reborn within that period, so family must help that intermediate-state being as much as possible during that time. That is why the custom in Asia is to do pujas, or have them done by the sangha, every seven days for seven weeks after the death of the person. During that period, we can make extensive light offerings, do intensive practices, make Buddha statues, tsatsas, or thangkas. Practicing like that, with dedication, we can influence that rebirth.

When Lama Pasang died at Kopan Monastery, Lama Lhundrup, the abbot, and three or four monks recited the extensive Medicine Buddha puja every day for the forty-nine days. Something like that is an incredible thing to do. There is also a middle-length version of the puja available in English and other languages, and if the family members and loved ones can do that, if not every day, at least every week for the seven weeks, that is excellent.

We All Need an Education about Death

We all need an education about death. Learning how to die doesn't mean learning how to commit suicide. (I've heard there is actually a book written by a university lecturer on this subject!) The kind of education we all need is how to die well, how to have control over our death. If we ourselves can learn how to die well, that is the most important education we can gain in this life, and if we can help others die well, that is the most important service we can offer in this life.

To show somebody how to face death without fear and to control the mind is to do much more than close the door on the lower realms; it allows them to have a happy death and a better rebirth, where they can fully develop on the path. Irrespective of religious beliefs, the real key to a good death is to die with a mind freed from delusions, one full of compassion. If we can help somebody reach that level of mind, we have performed a very great service.

There are many examples of people who were not great meditators but who have died well. I remember an old monk living below the Everest center in Solu Khumbu who had been told by his abbot to continue his retreat on Chenrezig indefinitely. I think he was quite a fortunate person. After becoming sick, just before he died, he recovered a little. Not wanting to die in his room, he asked somebody to help him outside and to read the *Bardo Thodröl* (*Tibetan Book of the Dead*) to him.[126] He understood that as the death process starts it is extremely difficult to recall all the things that are beneficial to remember, and that hearing the words of this book are a great guide to keeping a positive mind right through the death process. In that way, he was able to have an extremely peaceful and positive death.

At the same place there was a nun who had no problems at all at the time of death. She simply laid down in the lion's posture and attained liberation. She evidently meditated for a certain number of days during the death process. When I checked with the other nuns in the nunnery about her, they told me that, while she had only taken a few lamrim teachings, she had done so much purification and had kept all her vows purely. She seemed to have been a wonderful person who, despite not having a deep understanding of philosophy, had a very kind and pure heart.

Even recently there have been many people who have died well due to having a good heart. The head lama of this same monastery had renounced this life and was living in pure Dharma practice, looking very simple and unassuming, always wearing the plainest, poorest robes and eating the simplest food. The story was that he was very ill, vomiting pots of blood, but when he heard good news about the Dharma he got better for a while. The one time I saw him, he was so frail I thought he was a nun. He was very pleased to hear we were building the Mount

Everest center nearby, but he admonished me, telling me I was thinking too small. "You shouldn't have a little mind, building so small because you think you can't afford more," he said. "You should have a huge, strong mind, and this monastery should be built as large as possible, so it will be very beneficial for the teachings."

Evidently, he died very well, and the money for the pujas for his death was easily supplied by all the people he had helped. On the day he died, he talked all night with the monks and then toward dawn asked for some good tea. After his bowl had been filled, he sent them out and closed the door, dying in the meditation position at dawn. I think he sat in meditation for quite a long time, and now his reincarnation has been recognized by His Holiness the Dalai Lama and many other high lamas in that area.

All of these examples show how important it is to develop the mind before death and to be able to die with a positive mind. Then, when death comes, we will be able to control our mind and have a good death, just like these monks and nuns. We must make our mind ready now, not leaving it until it is too late. We need to train our mind like we train our body. We would train if we planned to trek in the Himalayas, knowing we would be carrying a heavy pack for long distances each day (unless of course we cheat and have Sherpas carry it for us). When we die, we won't have any Sherpas to guide our mind and carry the weight of its karma. We need to make sure that our mind is perfectly fit for the journey ourselves. If our body is weak, we cannot trek; if our mind is drowning in self-cherishing, we can't prepare for a good death. Nothing can help. There is nowhere we can go where we can escape a miserable death. We can hide on the moon or under the ocean, but we will still have to face death with great fear.

If something suddenly happened like an earthquake or something else that brought us danger, would we be able to handle it? Would we be able to keep our mind virtuous, or would our self-cherishing rise up like a great mountain? To maintain a virtuous mind no matter what happens, we must train it in virtue, starting now.

We should at least always remember the name of Shakyamuni Buddha and say his mantra. If our last thought can be of the Buddha, we are assured of a positive rebirth. We will never be reborn in the lower realms as long as we remember the Buddha, or Chenrezig or Tara or whatever buddha we feel close to. If we make a habit of reciting the mantras now, we are more likely to be able to continue to recite the mantras when we are about to die—this helps so much. They have the power to save us from the lower realms. If even somebody else blowing on our dead body and reciting mantras can do this, then of course saying the mantras ourselves has that power.

Just as our life should be dedicated to others, so should our death. When death comes, we should resolve that we are experiencing the suffering of death on behalf of all other sentient beings and as much as possible try to stay in that state of awareness as the mind goes through the absorptions. As I have said, this is not something we can spontaneously do at that time; it is something we need to train in from now on. Then, when the day comes that we know we are going to die, we will be able to practice sincerely, from the heart. We will be able to die bravely and happily when we have sincerely trained in compassion and bodhichitta, feeling we are experiencing the suffering of death on behalf of others—the others who are countless whereas we are only one. No matter how much we might be suffering, it is lost in comparison to the suffering of others.

Every positive thing—every happiness, every enjoyment, every success, every goodness, including any realization on the path to full enlightenment—has been received only by depending on the kindness of all sentient beings. Therefore, each and every one of them is so precious, more precious than skies filled with diamonds. We owe every happiness to others, and so by experiencing the suffering of death for them we are repaying their great kindness.

If we can die with such a mind, our death will be like drinking nectar; it will be the most blissful thing. Just as anything other than serving others in life is meaningless, so dying without such an attitude is meaningless. And so the best preparation for death, the best protection, is to develop loving-kindness and compassion and, if we can, the precious mind of bodhichitta.

With such a mind, death will not be a big deal, because for us it will simply mean a change of body. Reincarnating will be like changing our clothes. Just as we leave our old, dirty clothes behind and put on a fresh, clean set, we will simply leave our present body, which has exhausted its potential, and take a new, young body in a family and place where we have every opportunity to develop our mind and generate the realizations of the path to enlightenment.

10. IMPERMANENCE

Gross and Subtle Impermanence

Death is a major transition from one state to another, from the body of this life to the body of the next life, but every causative phenomenon—everything that is the result of causes and conditions—is in transition all the time. This is impermanence, and one of the fundamental tenets of Buddhism is that that all causative phenomena are impermanent.[127] There is not a single thing created by causes and conditions that has even the slightest degree of permanence. Seeing things as permanent is a major source of our suffering; seeing our life as permanent is probably the greatest mistake we make in life.

In contrast, the meditator who has a deep understanding of impermanence and death will never be shocked by change; they know that life is change and so whatever happens is understandable and acceptable. Although understanding impermanence is not that difficult, realizing it is. Realizing impermanence brings great benefits; this is a jewel that makes our life so happy and easy.

Just as ordinary people regard money as the most important thing in life, the great meditators regard meditating on impermanence as the supreme richness. As we have seen, in *The Great Nirvana Sutra*, the Buddha says that among all the ideas, the idea of impermanence and death is supreme. Having achieved the realization of impermanence, great meditators' lives become meaningful and pure because their minds are protected from distraction. For us, even if we wanted to meditate for five minutes, so many other things would arise—the mind goes all around the world, remembering all kinds of objects we feel either attachment or aversion for.

There are two levels of impermanence taught in the texts:

- gross impermanence
- subtle impermanence

Gross impermanence is the change that is noticeable and happens over an extended period of time, whereas subtle impermanence is too subtle to discern—these changes take place within every microsecond. Nothing remains the same for even that brief amount of time. The change is too small and too brief for our mind to comprehend, and so we think that there is a degree of permanence that there is not. The great meditator Gampopa[128] says,

> This vessel-like world that existed at an earlier moment does not do so at a later moment. That it seems to continue in the same way is because something else similar arises, like the stream of a waterfall.[129]

We can see gross impermanence. We can see buildings crumble and people getting older, plants blooming and then dying, years passing. Nature, the seasons, and everything around us shows us this gross impermanence if we just care to pay attention.

We can see we are changing and getting older, and logically we know that in a hundred years we will no longer be here. In the same way we can see that in a million years the cities and even mountains will be nonexistent. Just because we fail to live our life with these ideas does not mean we cannot logically see them.

Even though we understand things are impermanent, the latent belief we hold and believe in is that they are permanent. Our logical understanding and our way of living are in opposition. Even though a river is constantly changing, with never the same water there for one moment as it flows past, we see it as one thing. Although it is forever coming and going, we see it as permanent. We see ourselves and others as we see the river, as separate permanent entities.

Because this subtle impermanence is not apparent, things appear as permanent. Our body is permanent, this beautiful flower is permanent. This is how it appears to us and this is what we believe.

Our Sense of Permanence Cheats Us

The basis of all our problems in life is very strange; it is something that does not exist at all. We create a fantasy, something that is the opposite of the reality, and we believe in it. From this, all wrong conceptions and discriminating thoughts such as anger and attachment arise. With these wrong conceptions, these wrong thoughts, we create so many problems in our life, problems for ourselves and for other beings.

We see an object and believe it to be permanent, but then it disappoints us by being just the opposite and so we blame it for making us suffer. There is no reason to create problems; there is no reason to make up this wrong conception of permanence, to look at impermanent phenomena as permanent. There is no benefit to us and no benefit to other sentient beings. We build up this concept of permanence and we follow it, becoming the causes of our unhealthy mind and unhealthy body.

It is like that Japanese man we looked at earlier who felt so cheated when he found out he had cancer. He truly believed that he was healthy and deserved a long life and somehow the world has deceived him.

The nature of causative phenomena—form, sound, smell, taste, tangible object—is impermanence. Not only do they change over a long period, such as flowers wilting, fruit becoming rotten, and so forth, they are changing, decaying, moment by moment.

What exists in this moment does not exist in the next moment. This beautiful body or this beautiful flower that exists this moment no longer exists in the following moment. Everything is continually changing, but there is a continuum where something similar arises, like water in a waterfall, never the same water but seeming the same.

However, because we don't expect things to change, we are shocked when they do. Say, we meet somebody for the first time and think they are attractive; attachment develops for them. But over a long time, the nice shape changes, the wrinkles come, the hair goes gray, and so forth. We don't notice how they are constantly changing. If we don't see that person for many years, when we see how they have aged and are no longer attractive, we feel quite cheated.

Similarly, the other deluded minds like anger, pride, and jealousy arise based on the hallucination of permanence. If we could perceive all phenomena as transitory, we wouldn't be deceived when they revealed their transitory nature to us.

See Conditioned Things Like a Flash of Lightning

In *The Vajra Cutter Sutra*, there is the famous verse:

> A star, a defective view, the butter lamp flame,
> An illusion, a dew drop, a water bubble,
> A dream, lightning, a cloud:
> See all causative phenomena like this.[130]

Each of these similes is a pointed reminder that we cannot trust the appearance of things. It is worth looking at each in turn.

Like a star at dawn, all causative phenomena, including this life we cherish, are there one minute and gone the next. Like a candle flame, flickering in a strong wind, it can be extinguished at any moment, and like an illusion, it gives us the sensation of solidity where it is not. Each simile points to the same truth in a slightly different way.

Like a Star

The first simile in the verse is a star. Some commenters have taken this as a star at dawn, others as a shooting star, but the lesson is the same. It is something that is there in front of us and yet before we know it, it's gone. This is our life. This is everything that we have in our life: our possessions, our reputation, our loved ones, even our enemies and problems. At this moment, because we cling to the notion of permanence, it looks like these things will go on and on, but they are a brief flash in the night as a shooting star streaks across the sky. They appear so real and solid, and huge, and yet they are like the morning star on the horizon, a tiny prick of dim light, soon to be extinguished by the light of the sun.

Like a Defective View

Our view of reality is distorted. This is the second simile used, the defective view. When we have some kind of eye condition like a cataract, we can see things such as fine hairs in front of our eyes that in fact do not exist; if we have jaundice, everything can seem yellow, when in fact it is not. The object of our sight exists but we mistake how it exists because of the disease.

Commentators also use the analogy of a mirage for this. In the desert, we see water which, because of our great thirst, seems so attractive, but it turns out to be a mirage. This is how appearances trick us. We are fooled by the appearance and dismayed when it lets us down.

Things that appear to the uncritical consciousness as real start to seem less so when we analyze them. Nagarjuna said that the mirage appears as water to the direct perception from a distance, but if it really were water, the closer we got to it, the more it would appear as water. In fact, the opposite happens; the closer we get, the more we can see it is an illusion. The independent, permanent nature of things is the same. Unexamined, things naturally seem to exist this way, but when we explore whether this is so or not, we slowly start to see that the way we have been viewing things is in complete contradiction to how they actually exist.

The masters compare the mind to a mirror: it has the potential to reflect back reality, but it is covered in the dirt of our delusions and so incapable of reflecting that reality accurately. Everything we experience is distorted by our misconceptions.

The route to the direct realization of the absolute nature of phenomena is through what is called *valid inference*. We cannot see the reality at this stage, but we can use our logic to understand that phenomena must exist like that. There are said to be three levels of objects: obvious, hidden, and very hidden objects. Obvious objects are things that we see with our direct perception that are unmistaken, such as when we see smoke, we know it to be smoke. The second level, hidden objects, are not objects of our direct perception, but we can ascertain them through logic. If that smoke is coming from the chimney of a house, we can deduce that there is a fire in the house, and so from smoke we can use a valid inference to show that there is fire. This is a vital technique used in Buddhism to analyze the nature of things and see the reality below the false surface of what we perceive.

Very hidden objects, such as the most subtle aspects of karma, are beyond even the logical understanding of normal people. For instance, we cannot use valid inference to deduce the age of the person living in the house with the fire. It is said that only buddhas can understand this, and we must rely on valid sources, namely the scriptures, for an understanding of these very hidden objects.

Valid inference will take us a long way, though. Using our logic, we can see that things and events have not the slightest permanent nature. When we explore this, we will see this clearly and no amount of argument to the contrary will change that understanding because it is the truth. In the same way, through logic we can see that nothing at all can have any degree of independence. From there, it is a small step to understand that all our suffering stems from failing to live our life within these truths. The logical understanding of these vital truths might be easy enough, but to *realize* them—to integrate them into our lives at a depth where they influence everything we do—is far from easy and requires years and years of deep meditation.

The most subtle understanding we can have is of the lack of inherent existence of things and events, and in particular our own sense of self. Buddhism talks about the emptiness of self and the emptiness of phenomena. Until we have reached a very advanced level, whatever appears to us will appear as a real, concrete, inherently existing thing, something that exists from its own side without causes and conditions, without parts, something that is permanent and separate from our own perception of it and from all other things. Whether we logically know this to be false or not, we will still perceive it as such, and our habituation will almost certainly make us act toward the object as such.

Here is the beauty of this instruction from the masters to see the world as like a mirage: Even at our stage of development, when we are very far from realizing emptiness directly, we can still stop becoming involved in the false appearances of things and events and stop making mistakes based on that involvement. In short, although we still see things and events as truly existent from their own side, we are no longer fooled. We see the mirage, but we don't run to it.

Like a Butter Lamp Flame

Causative phenomena are also compared to a flickering flame of a butter lamp. Although the flame might seem bright and strong, it is so unstable that the merest breeze can extinguish it. This is how our life cheats us. We feel we will live forever, that nothing can stop this life of ours, and yet there are so many causes for death and so few for life. Our life, our possessions, our friends, and family are all like a candle flame in a strong wind, likely to cease to exist for us at any moment. And similarly, like a candle flame, they are changing with every moment.

If everything were permanent and hence unchanging, how could we ever progress? Overcoming negative emotions would be impossible; liberation and enlightenment would be impossible. We would be like an armless person trying to climb an ice mountain, constantly slipping back. And not only could we never reach the top of the mountain, but we could also never help any others climb that mountain. Therefore, this is a very important point to meditate on.

Unless we train our mind to let go of solid appearances while we are alive, how can we even expect to be able to let go when we are dying? At that time, when there is incredible fear and sadness because we feel we are losing everything, it will be so much more difficult.

Like an Illusion

The next simile is an illusion. Here we need to be careful. The Prasangika philosophers[131] tell us that life is illusion-*like*, not that life *is* an illusion. All of the similes used in *The Vajra Cutter Sutra* point to ways we can view our life, but they do not tell us that there is no reality to life, that it is a total fantasy.

If we look at the moon and squint our eyes, we can see two moons. Are there really two moons in the sky? Of course not; this is an aberration of our sight caused by squinting. When we see two moons when we squint, we are not fooled into thinking there are two moons, but unfortunately in our normal life we are too easily fooled into thinking that nonexistent things, such as permanent phenomena, actually exist. Permanent things do not exist any more than hairs in our eyes or yellow mountains or two moons, but we are fooled by our own ignorance into believing that things have a permanence.

We are not asserting that things do not exist, but that they do not exist in the way that our deluded mind perceives them. This is a huge difference. The object is there, but it is dependent on causes and conditions, and it is impermanent in nature. What we see, what we are cheated into seeing, however, is an object that is independent and permanent, an object that does not exist at all. All our other mistakes grow from this, causing us the incredible suffering that we must face in this realm and in all the other realms we have lived in and will live in.

That concrete quality of objects is the great deceiver. It is the magician that tricks us into believing in what isn't there. In fact, another favorite simile the great teachers use is the magician.

A skilled magician will take a rope or a stick and say a mantra, and his audience will see a horse or an elephant. He could even make a whole city or a beautiful man or woman appear, and the audience will totally believe in the illusion. He has "illusioned" these objects based on an existing base, but the thing that the audience sees is a total illusion.

It is important to see this hallucination we pull over the top of the objects of our world, like a carpet over bare floorboards or a tablecloth over a table. Reality is like a beautiful painting we have left for too long, and now it is covered in dirt and the colors are faded and shapes indistinct.

The way an object exists in reality and the way it appears to exist to our deluded mind are complete opposites. The way it exists is dependent on causes and conditions, on parts and whole, on label and base, as well as being impermanent in nature; the way it appears is a single entity, independent of anything else, existing out there without any dependence on the mind, and it is completely permanent.

This nonexistent object—this independent, permanent thing—that we believe in is what we have to understand. It is what is called *the object of refutation*. We must see it very clearly and see that it doesn't exist in the slightest.

By believing the false view of the object to be reality, we exaggerate its qualities, seeing one object as "good" or "beautiful" and another as "bad" or "ugly." Society tells us having big muscles and a well-toned body is beautiful, so we see a person with those qualities as intrinsically beautiful. If fat is beautiful in our society, that is how we see it; if thin is beautiful, that is how we see it. From that, we develop attachment to that false view of the "beautiful" object or aversion for the "ugly" object. In reality there is no such inherent, permanent, truly beautiful or truly ugly object, but on the basis of our belief in it, all these negative emotions arise and with them come all the harm we experience.

That is not to say that because objects do not exist the way we perceive them, that they have no existence at all. Conventionally, they exist. There is ultimate truth—how objects exist by being merely labeled on the valid base—and conventional truth—how they appear to a deceptive mind that sees them as inherently existent—and on that conventional level they function and bring pleasure and pain to us.

If you know *The Heart Sutra* you will know that after the crucial verse that says that "form is empty, emptiness is form; form is not other than emptiness and emptiness is not other than form," the sutra goes on to list all phenomena in the same way, stating that there is no feeling, discrimination, compositional factors, and consciousness—the other four aggregates that make up what we are—and then listing no eye, no ear, no tongue, and so forth. The bodhisattva Chenrezig, the person explaining this in the sutra, is not saying we have no eyes or ears, but that we have no eyes that are not empty of inherent existence. Negating objects in this way gets to the core of the ultimate level of reality.

We can do that wherever we are. When we are in a supermarket, we can add a "no" to whatever we pick up—there is no butter, no milk, no washing powder, and so forth—and by doing so remind ourselves that there is no permanent, independent butter or milk that exists from its own side. When we see our desirable friend, we can add a "no." They are no friend, meaning they are not a friend who exists from their own side; the self-existing, permanent desirable friend is a complete hallucination, a dream that our delusions have created.

By putting a "no" over the hallucination, we are using a simple, two-letter word like an atomic bomb to utterly destroy the wrong conception of a self-existing permanent thing. And by doing so we destroy the real enemy, ignorance.

Like a Dew Drop

We should see life as being like a dew drop sitting on a flower in the early morning. Either the weight of the drop will cause it to fall from the flower, or the sun will warm the air and it will evaporate—but whatever the cause, that lovely dew drop that we admire at dawn will not exist as soon as the sun rises. Like this, all causative phenomena, and especially our own life, are transitory.

If we look at the friendships we have had in our life, we will probably see that some have lasted but most have come and gone, like that dew drop. But even the lasting ones will disappear at some stage. That is the nature of things.

Even very solid seeming things will at some time in the future be no more. The great cities of the world seem like they have always been there and will always be there but that is not so. Look at how New Orleans was devastated by Hurricane Katrina. This big, solid, permanent thing—something nobody thought could ever change in any way—was suddenly destroyed in a day.

Nobody could have dreamed that the World Trade Center in New York would ever not be there, not in thousands of years, let alone be so nonexistent in such a short space of time. It was a huge shock to millions of people when those two planes flew into the twin towers and completely destroyed them. The poor people working inside never thought as they went to work that morning that they would have to jump from the top story windows, falling like little dolls to their deaths. This is a very cruel example of impermanence and the fact that we can die at any moment. We start a journey with no thought that we might not finish it. Everybody does, including all the hundreds of people that die every day in traffic accidents. All the people in the emergency wards of every hospital in the world have the same story. They had no idea it could happen to them.

Like a Water Bubble

Similarly, we should see life as being like a water bubble, so fragile, so easily destroyed. As Lama Tsongkhapa says in *The Foundation of All Good Qualities*,

> This body and life are changing, like a water bubble;
> Remember how quickly they perish and death comes.
> After death, just like a shadow follows the body,
> The results of black and white karma follow.[132]

Lama Tsongkhapa is exhorting us to not waste a second of this perfect human rebirth, because it can be finished at any moment and then we must experience whatever karma ripens at that moment, positive or negative. Life seems so firm, solid, stable, and the things of this life seem so important, but it is all like a water bubble, so perishable and unstable, so insubstantial.

Just as our shadow follows us in this life, when we die our karma follows us in the next, to determine whether we are happy or miserable. None of us wishes even the slightest suffering, and yet we act as if our actions have no consequences at all and we will live a thousand years. How far from the truth this is. This verse from Lama Tsongkhapa is so important because it reminds us of what is important in life, creating only virtue and preparing for a death that might happen at any moment.

Like a Dream

Padmasambhava says,

> The appearances of this life are like last night's dream.
> The meaningless works of this life are like ripples on water.[133]

We are plagued by the eight worldly dharmas, drugged by attachment to the pleasures of this life such as comfort, possessions, reputation, and so forth, and made miserable by the undesirable situations we must experience such as poverty, discomfort, criticism, and so forth. Seeing our life as like a dream can really help to break the desperation that we often feel. Perhaps everything *seems* so important, so huge and concrete, but all this is like last night's dream.

When we wake up from a dream in which we won a million dollars, we recognize that the million dollars was a fantasy, and that all the pain and hard work we experienced to get it in our dream were for nothing. In the same way, we need to recognize the fantasy of the permanent "I" that we believe to be completely real from its own side.

When the time comes for us to face death, we will see how life is very similar to last night's dream. All the energy we put into the affairs of this world and all the emotions that we felt—the suffering, the craving, the excitement, and so forth—at the end of our life are revealed as the empty, trivial things they are. We see so clearly that we have wasted our life in pursuit of the meaningless and that all we have to show for it is a great mountain of negative karma on our mindstream, waiting to ripen into unbearable suffering in a rebirth in the lower realms.

When we think that death is very near, there is no point in being concerned with what will soon be gone. Illness, bad reputation, lack of money or possessions, and so forth—these disagreeable things will cease to be in a very short while, so what's the use of clinging to appearances? This is a very simple and powerful method to stop delusions from arising whenever there is a problem. Similarly, when we meet the four desirable objects—pleasure, possessions, praise, and a good reputation—we can use this method to control the mind.

Padmasambhava adds that we should see the meaningless affairs of this life like ripples on water. If we watch ripples on a lake or river, they come continuously to the shore and stop, always followed by more and more and more. As they hit the shore, they ripple back but nothing will stop them. In the distance they fade, but there are always more. This is a beautiful image of the affairs of this life. The work of samsara is endless because it never brings any satisfaction. We start a project and work hard at it and at some time we finish it, but even before we have finished, we are starting yet another project, thinking that this is the one that will make us happy.

Like Lightning

In the sutra called *The Play in Full*, the Buddha says,

> The three worlds are impermanent like an autumn cloud.
> Look at the dance of the sentient beings, with birth and then death.
> How a sentient being's life is here this moment and then gone the next
> is the same as a flash of lightning in the sky.

All causative phenomena are like a flash of lightning. This has great meaning. On a dark night we try to get home but because of the darkness we are unable to see anything at all. Then suddenly there is a flash of lightning and the path, the fields, and the trees are vividly illuminated, but only for a split second. It appeared and it is gone. That is just like the appearance of this life. All our possessions and property, all our wealth, our many friends and family members, our own human body, all these are like the appearance lit by a flash of lightning. They have appeared and then they are gone. The day death comes it will seem exactly like that; all these things we are experiencing now will be gone, just a memory.

This example shows us the very nature of impermanence, but it is also very useful for looking at emptiness in a very simple way. Imagine that flash of lightning in the night as we are walking home. From absolute blackness we suddenly see so many images vividly, just for the briefest second and then all is blackness again. When it is completely dark, we don't label things because we fail to see the base. But when suddenly there is lightning, we see them and think, "There is a tree and there is a person." Our mind labels each of these bases. With the sudden appearance of a base comes the further labels: good and bad, beautiful and ugly, this and that. Even during this short time, anger or attachment comes. As soon as the appearance of the base comes, we label it. From birth until death, everything is like this. Friend, enemy, or stranger, the whole thing, including ourselves, is like this.

This appearance is very brief. What is appearing to us now can cease tonight, tomorrow, at any moment. All these things are just appearances, just labels placed on bases—some called "enemy," some called "friend"—that will vanish very soon, so there is absolutely no sense in becoming attached to them or angry at them. Seeing the appearance as not only labeled but as so brief—seeing the brevity of this perfect human rebirth—we understand that these disturbing emotions are completely childish.

Lama Tsongkhapa's advice is to take the essence day and night. Having an awareness of impermanence and death becomes the fundamental practice. It is simple, easy to understand, and easy to feel, but it is still a very powerful way to counter uncontrollable desire, the attachment that brings constant problems in life and creates harm to ourselves and others.

The Dharma is vast and there are countless techniques for developing the mind within the Dharma, but which is most suitable for us, considering how little time we have? We are advised to lead our life just as a swan takes milk from water; we need to extract what we need for enlightenment and nothing else. This example might not be apparent at first, but it is a good one. I remember thinking about it while I was living in Buxa Duar, the prison where the Tibetan refugees were housed when we first fled Tibet after the Chinese invasion. I didn't have a swan, but there were two turtles in the camp. I found a big drum that was used to churn butter and filled it up with water and then poured a little milk into it. It didn't really mix with the water that well. Then I put the two turtles into the drum and watched. In a very short time the milk was gone, drunk by the turtles, but they hadn't drunk the water at all. This is the point of thc example. There is so much we can do with this life, but it's vital we take the essence and use that to develop as quickly as we can.

Like a Cloud

Returning to *The Play in Full* sutra, the Buddha compared the three worlds, or three realms, to an autumn cloud. Autumn clouds roll across the sky constantly changing with the wind, reforming and disappearing. This is our life, never remaining the same for one moment. The three realms—the desire, form, and formless realms—are the same. There is nothing constant, nothing permanent in any of the three realms.

In many countries autumn is a changeable season and the clouds that float across the sky are forever changing. They look huge and majestic but they are so insubstantial, just water vapor. For a short moment, we are here with a human body, having some kind of life, doing something, but this lasts for a very short time, though from our side it might seem long.

Perhaps one day we hear that a friend we'd just been shopping with has died. What a shock! We feel this can't be right; we were talking with that person a few hours ago in the supermarket, so how can they possibly not exist now? In the same way, we will have our time on this planet in this form and then be no more.

At the moment we are here, with this body. But soon, after death, we will be in a different place with a different body, having a different life. We will be in the hell realm, the hungry ghost realm, the animal realm, or the god realm, or maybe even as another human being. We will do that for some time, and then again after death we will take another body in a different place. Life never lasts; it is indefinite. We can never have full confidence in it. We are like an actor on stage taking many roles. As soon as one role is finished, we must change our costume and wear the new one for a for a few minutes, until that scene is over, and then we must put on another costume, and then another. Like an actor constantly changing costumes, we must constantly change bodies.

Samsaric work is never finished. Without practicing Dharma, we will never be free from having to struggle to have any happiness at all, and then, even though we never really succeeded, death will cut all that short. Then we find ourselves in a future life, in another body, and samsaric work continues, another cloud in another shape. When we watch the world, we can see that it's like that all the time.

The higher will become lower. That is the nature of samsara. People climb higher to become a president of the United States, only to end up lower; kings are deposed. Mao Zedong started out with such a good reputation and now he is vilified in China for the damage he did.

In the same way, relationships go from high to low. A couple seem so happy at the beginning, but in the end there is separation. Even a very harmonious couple who get along very well, rarely fighting, will definitely have to separate at the end of life. As the Buddha says,

> The end of all that has been hoarded up is to be spent;
> the end of what has been lifted up is to be cast down;
> the end of meeting is separation;
> the end of life is death.[134]

Every meeting ends in separation; there is no choice. That is nature. People start a relationship, trusting in its permanence, but in a number of years, or even less, the relationship breaks up. A man falls in love with somebody he thinks is the most beautiful woman in the world, buying her lots of expensive presents and taking her on wonderful holidays. They decide they cannot live without each other any longer and so they get married. Then she gets pregnant and even before the child is born their relationship is changing. She sees more and more mistakes in his personality, and even though she doesn't express her discontent, it collects there in her mind. If she is candid, she might say it out loud and then there are arguments. She accuses him of selfishness, of spending all his money on himself. After the first child there are more children and her life gets harder and more miserable, with her husband spending more and more time away from home. Finally, they split up. Something that seemed so permanent at the beginning did not last very long at all.

Unless we remember impermanence, there is no protection; the dissatisfied minds of attachment, ignorance, and anger can so easily take over, invading our mind, like the way the Communist Chinese army invaded Tibet. We become a slave to the delusions. Then, with no peace in our heart, even if the three principal aspects of the path—renunciation, bodhichitta, and emptiness—might seem like a good idea, we are incapable of practicing them.

When we keep our mind in the awareness of how causative phenomena are changing all the time, decaying and dying due to causes and conditions, suddenly there is no place in our mind for confusion. It cuts off depression, which comes from our expectations not being met, and it cuts off a mountain of problems. When we see that the nature of this I—this body, this mind, our belongings, the friends, enemies, strangers, and so forth—is impermanence, we are immediately free from problems. From having a mountain of problems due to attachment and anger, we suddenly see there is no reason to create these problems, that our old attitude was nonsense.

Subtle Impermanence

What we have been mostly looking at is gross impermanence, the changes that are noticeable to us if we observe them. These gross changes, however, do not come from nowhere; they grow out of the constant changes that all compounded phenomena undergo at every moment. Gross impermanence arises from subtle impermanence.

When we see a flower, it might appear permanent to us: the leaves permanently green, the petals permanently red. But it is changing even as we look at it. Within each second, within each split-second, it is changing. We cannot see this subtle change at first. However, in a few days we can see that the leaves are becoming darker and the petals are withering, and we then think that it is dying, that it is not permanent after all.

It is not that the flower was permanently fresh and then it started to decay. That decay was happening from its very first moment. The causes that produced the flower are the same causes that bring about its momentary changes and that bring about its decay and its death. The changes do not happen from their own side. This present moment's flower is the result of the previous moment's flower, which was the result of the flower a moment before that. Similarly, this moment's flower is the cause of the next moment's flower, which will be the cause of the flower a moment after that. And so, there is a continuum of moments of the existence of that flower, from its first moment to when it is finally dead.

The flower we look at now depends on many causes and conditions: on the seed, on the person who planted it, on the soil, water, and sun that nurtured it, and so forth. In that way, this moment's flower is a dependent arising; it arises in dependence on all these causes and conditions. The water, the sunlight, and so forth are conditions that have brought this about, but the main cause of the flower is the seed. This moment's flower has changed subtly from the previous moment's flower, due to causes and conditions, but because it is in the same continuum of causes and effects, we see it as the same flower and permanent. Only when the changes are visible do we understand it is not permanent.

A real flower is a simple example because we notice its gross impermanence quite easily, but even a plastic flower is going through the same process.

Thus, gross impermanence is merely the aspect of subtle impermanence that becomes perceivable. We can see this in a relatively short-lived object like a leaf or a flower, but this is also happening to us and everything around us. Everything is changing, decaying, second by second.

Until some gross sign happens, we fail to notice how our body is changing all the time. We look in the mirror one morning and see the first gray hair, or we start to notice wrinkles around the eyes. Signs of old age come slowly; they do not happen in one day. Each time we look at our body it has become older, but we just do not recognize it. Only when the changes are pronounced do we see this change.

The earlier Buddhist philosophical schools, the Vaibhashika (Great Exposition) and Sautrantika (Sutra) schools, accepted gross impermanence—it is impossible to follow a Buddhist philosophy without it—but they still asserted that atoms had no constituent parts and the smallest moment of time could not be broken down further. The later schools refuted this, saying that *nothing* can be permanent. Even within the snap of the fingers, causative phenomena have changed. That which was here yesterday is not here today. That which was here a thousandth of a second ago is not here now. There may be the continuity of that thing, but the thing itself has changed.

The most subtle school of Buddhist philosophy, the Prasangika Madhyamaka school, asserts that this change takes place within the shortest time scale possible, a "shortest moment," of which there are sixty-five in the snap of a finger. I suppose this would be the equivalent of a nanosecond. Things not only do not last, but they are also decaying within every nanosecond, and the causes that brought them into existence are the same as the causes that are causing the decay and their eventual extinction.

What is "real" to us ordinary people is a world of objects that totally exist from their own side, totally independent, totally permanent. When we can see through this hallucination, we see that there is no other root from which the delusions can grow. When we understand how from this hallucination all our delusions arise, which then cause suffering, then we can see how we and all sentient beings suffer.

We Have No Choice but to Prepare for Death

Perhaps we wonder why we should be surprised that life changes. "That's natural. Let it happen!" To think getting older is natural but then to entirely disregard impermanence is very foolish. We should not be like those New Yorkers I mentioned, who deny the impermanent nature of their lives and try to disguise their appearance in the eyes of others who also play the same game. No effort can change eighty years into sixteen. They harbor a double delusion: first, that chemicals, makeup, and plastic surgery can keep them young forever, and second, that a permanent phenomenon, such as their I, can exist. The first delusion causes them to believe in cures that don't exist and the second causes them to be lazy and not seek the correct solution, the Dharma.

The moment we think about impermanence and death, desire stops, anger stops, all the other delusions stop. The normal world, ruled by desire, where everything appears permanent and independent, and where attachment and aversion arise at every situation, is left behind. Everything—family, friends, possessions, our own body—are with us for the briefest moment and so there is no reason to cling at all. The valid mind understanding this finds no basis to become attached or angry. There is immediate peace. We find deep satisfaction in our heart, free from the chronic diseases of the mind, the painful deluded negative emotions of desire, hatred, and so forth. And this is merely reflecting on impermanence and death, without even considering emptiness.

This perfect human rebirth, which is extremely difficult to find, offers the greatest opportunity. If we waste it, we will be forced to endure the lower realms for so long that it will seem like forever. It takes a lot of energy and determination to break away from the habitual laziness that seeks only the pleasure of this life and to start to move the mind toward what is really important. For that reason, combining the understanding of the preciousness of the perfect human rebirth we now enjoy with the understanding of how this precious life can finish at any moment is vital.

If we could be assured of living for a thousand years, perhaps there would not be this urgency to practice the Dharma. And perhaps if there was no such thing as reincarnation—we simply cease to exist when we die—then the Dharma would be an interesting idea but not something we would have to worry too much about. But, as we have seen, the mind is a continuity; it continues after death, which might be at any moment. Where it continues *to* is entirely dependent on our karma, on the positive and negative imprints we have placed on our mindstream during this life and countless previous lives from our virtuous and nonvirtuous actions.

Death is a dangerous time, and we need to do everything possible to prepare ourselves. So far, we have not done this. Only when we are certain that we are free from the possibility of a suffering rebirth can we relax, but we have no such certainty. If we look at whether we create more positive or more negative karma in one day, we will probably see we create far more negative karma. If we look back to last month, last year, or our entire lifetime, we will see so much nonvirtue created, meaning we are almost certainly facing a lower rebirth.

In order to stop all this, we have to make preparations in this life. This means we must purify the negative karma already accumulated, create positive karma, and also refrain from creating more negative karma. Everything we do should be in preparation for our death. It's like making a runway so a plane can take off. Without it, our plane can never fly. Studying Dharma but not integrating it into our life by reflecting on impermanence and death is like having the plane but never building the runway.

As we have seen, there is a world of difference between a normal person's fear of death, which is debilitating and useless, and a Dharma practitioner's fear of death, which acts as a wakeup call, showing us exactly what we need to do in this life to prepare for the next. For an ordinary person, it is the fear of loss; for a Dharma practitioner, it is the fear of dying with a negative mind and facing a terrible rebirth.

By remembering impermanence and death, the person on the path of the lower capable being escapes a lower rebirth, one on the path of the middle capable being escapes samsara. Our delusions from so many previous lives can be completely destroyed, and we can obtain infinite merit. If we can remember death strongly enough, our distractions cease. A higher meditator, one who has achieved high realizations and has good control of their mind, is quite happy at the time of death, whereas even an ordinary Dharma practitioner can die unafraid, having full confidence that they will not be born in the suffering realms.

Therefore, we should not shy away from studying death and meditating on the nine-point death meditation, the death process, and other meditations that bring home to us the urgency of our Dharma practice. Even if it is terrifying for us, we need the courage to face it, in the same way we need to face the pain of a surgeon's scalpel when we have a tumor that needs to be cut out. Perhaps we cannot be exactly like Milarepa, but we can move our priorities from chasing the eight worldly dharmas to ensuring a good death by purifying our mind and accumulating merit.

That means moving away from the self-cherishing attitude that sees "me" as the center of the universe and developing a mind that cherishes others and places their happiness before our own. This is the only way to real happiness, and this is the way to ensure a happy death and a fortunate rebirth. Free from this selfish mind, we have the space to cherish others, to develop our compassion until it becomes bodhichitta, the wonderful mind that strives for full enlightenment for the sake of all others sentient beings.

In our daily life we need to be aware of impermanence and death. Death is a natural phenomenon. After birth comes death, just as plants grow and then die. Ignoring impermanence and death—which is ignoring the reality of our life—results in so many negative emotions and problems. Being conscious of impermanence and death and understanding that death is something we all have to experience, we can practice Dharma fully and purely.

APPENDIX 1
THREE MEDITATIONS ON DEATH

1. The Nine-Point Death Awareness Meditation

Below are the points made in chapters 5 to 7 in the form of the traditional nine-point death meditation. Thoroughly familiarize yourself with the teachings on these points and then do this meditation, either meditating on all nine points together or taking one root per session or over several sessions, whichever way is best for you. The nine points are these:

First Root Truth: Death is certain.
- No being has ever escaped death.
- Our lifespan is constantly decreasing.
- There is very little time to practice Dharma.

Conclusion: We must practice Dharma.

Second Root Truth: The time of death is uncertain.
- The lifespan of human beings is not fixed.
- More factors endanger life than support it.
- Our body is extremely fragile.

Conclusion: We must practice Dharma *now*.

Third Root Truth: Nothing can help at the time of death except Dharma practice.
- Wealth and possessions cannot help.
- Friends and relatives cannot help.

- Our body cannot help.

Conclusion: We must practice Dharma *purely*.

Death Is Certain

The first three points show you clearly that death is certain.

No Being Has Ever Escaped Death

Contemplate how you are trapped in the cycle of death and rebirth by the twelve links of dependent origination: how because of ignorance, karmic actions are created that lead to craving and grasping that assure another samsaric existence after this one has ended.

Death is a dependent arising. The separation of the mind from the body under the control of karma and delusions is the definition of death. As long as the mind is joined with the form aggregate you are alive; as soon as the mind separates from the form aggregate there is no life; you are dead.

Death is certain. You will die, your loved ones will die, your enemies will die. Nobody escapes death. Every samsaric being still trapped in the circle of death and rebirth is forced to take uncontrolled rebirth after uncontrolled rebirth. Every being has to die, to be reborn, to spend a certain amount of time in that body, and then die again, only to be reborn again, regardless of the circumstances of that life. All things perish, so of course your body must also perish. Contemplate this.

Nobody escapes death. Think of all the famous people who have died, all the great teachers who have died. There is nobody alive today who was alive even 150 years ago, let alone since the beginning of this world system.

Think of the people you know who have died. Not just your friends but your relatives, your aunts and uncles, your grandparents and great grandparents. All of them are just names, just memories. And of the family that are still alive, you make assumptions that certain ones will die first and others later, but that is not at all helpful; you just don't know.

Many friends have already died. They seem so permanent and yet now they no longer exist. People you know, people you think are so permanent, people you see often, suddenly in the middle of their permanent life they die, popping like a water bubble. In the water you see many water bubbles on the surface. You have no way of knowing which bubble will burst first.

Our Lifespan Is Constantly Decreasing

Even though there are many factors that can shorten your life, nothing can add to it. You only have so many years in your body, and every second brings you closer and closer to death. As soon as you were conceived in the womb, that lifespan started running out, like sand in an hourglass. Maybe your lifespan is five years, maybe ten, maybe fifty, you just don't know.

With each tick of the clock you are moving away from birth and toward death. The second hand of a clock moves around very quickly, marking off one more minute gone from your life, and soon a whole morning is gone, never to be recovered—and then, a whole day.

Look at a watch or clock as the second hand goes around. Around and around it goes, each tick of the clock bringing you closer and closer to death; every in-breath closer and closer to death; every out-breath closer and closer to death. In that way ten, twenty, forty, sixty years are gone.

Like water flowing past in a river, like rocks falling down a mountain in an avalanche, nothing can stop you racing toward death.

It's natural to think "I am living" but in fact you are not living, you are dying. Year by year, day by day, signs of aging are increasing. Your body is aging, your breathing is weakening, your health is declining; you are slowly winding down like an old-fashioned wind-up watch.

Like a criminal led to execution, you are racing toward your place of death. When the time of your death arrives, what will your state of mind be? Will you still be wrapped up in the thought of the eight worldly dharmas, and so will have to face death with terror, or will you have renounced worldly concern and be able to face death with a clear, calm, happy mind? It's all up to you.

There Is Very Little Time to Practice Dharma

With so much time taken up in worldly activities, there is so little time to practice Dharma. Say you live for a hundred years. Half of each day is spent asleep, and since it is very difficult to create virtue while sleeping, that effectively becomes about fifty years. For the first fifteen years or so of your life you were a child, spending most of your time playing, without the wisdom to make life meaningful at all. And for the last years of your life, you will be too old to do anything but wait around to be fed and washed. The very old and infirm are incapable of practicing the Dharma.

Of the little time you have left, how much Dharma practice can you actually do? Think about it. Much of each day is spent in meaningless activities. Even if you have a set meditation practice, say an hour a day out of our twenty-four, during that time you are unable to concentrate and so don't practice purely.

The truth is that the time to practice Dharma is very short and death will be soon upon you, and you must be prepared for it by having transformed your mind through Dharma. Thinking like this, determine never to waste a second.

The Time of Death Is Uncertain

The second three points show that while death is certain, there is absolutely no certainty about the time of death.

The Lifespan of Human Beings Is Not Fixed

Unlike other world systems where the lifespan is fixed, ours is not, and so, even though you might be lucky and not die from unnatural causes, you still have no idea when you will die.

Although logically you might know you will die, you instinctively feel you won't, and this feeling stays with you right up until the time when you actually face death. This is the greatest hindrance to Dharma practice. You must investigate how we all have this instinctive feeling that we will live for a long time and that we definitely won't die today. Because of this false conception of permanence, because you trust it completely, your Dharma practice never gets done purely. Think about how dangerous this thought is.

When you go to bed, you might not consciously think that you will wake up the next morning, but you instinctively feel that way. Think about how this is a false assumption and one that ties you to the sense of permanence that creates so much nonvirtue, trapping you in the thought of the eight worldly dharmas.

This concept of permanence becomes the basis for laziness, causing you to delay your practice. You need to reverse that assurance—from an assurance that you won't die to an assurance that you will. Generate a feeling that there is no certainty at all that you will wake up tomorrow, that you have no idea how long you will live.

More Factors Endanger Life than Support It

Our natural lifespan is itself indefinite, but of course you can also so easily have a premature death. Think of all the people who died on the planet today. How many of them died of old age? How many of them woke this morning with no expectation to die today? How many of them were prepared for death when it happened?

There are many more conditions for death than for life. People can die at any time: in their mother's womb, as an infant or teenager, in adulthood or old age. Nobody knows when. Think of how many accidents people have in a normal life, any one of which could potentially be fatal. Think of all the everyday things that as a matter of course people treat with caution to avoid death.

Think of the things you own to support your life that could become the cause of your death—your house, your car, and so forth—and how whatever you do there is the chance of death.

Think of all the people who just yesterday were doing the same things that you do every day—commuting to work, going on holidays, playing sports, and so forth—and who, just like you, had that sense of permanence, but who are now no more.

Think of all the people who died between sunrise and this moment, just today. Some were very sick and so knew at some stage they would die, but probably the vast majority had no idea at all this was their time. This is happening in every country.

Think of all the plans and preparations that will never be finished because the people involved are now dead: the buildings never to be completed, the weddings never to be held, the exams never to be taken, the daily shopping never to be bought. Billions of people are busy making plans that they have no certainty of seeing completed. For hundreds of thousands of people each day, this sense of permanence will cheat them, and they will never wake up again in this body.

The sense of permanence gives you a feeling of security that is utterly false. Anybody can die at any moment, no matter how young or fit they are, no matter how safe their environment seems. Contemplate this.

Our Body Is Extremely Fragile

There are not just a few conditions that cause death; there are myriad. In addition to all the external factors that can cause death, there is the fragility of your own body. It is like a candle flame in a strong wind.

Think of the many diseases that you can die from. There are various viruses and flus; there are stomach diseases and diseases of the blood; there are skin diseases and diseases of every sort of organ. There are old diseases like cholera, leprosy, and TB, and every year scientists are discovering new diseases you can catch like SARS, COVID-19, and avian flu.

Your body is an amazing machine, but it's a fragile one and anything can affect it. There are many ways that food can kill you: an unhealthy diet, lack of food, even overeating. You can choke to death so easily. The climate can kill you, with storms, with heat or cold.

You can die simply taking a walk, infected by a thorn, or stung by a bee. See how in this way your life, like the candle flame in the wind, is something so impermanent and so easily extinguished.

When that happens, this permanent body will suddenly be no more, and you will soon be joined with another body. What kind of body will it be? A fish waiting for a fisherman's hook? A worm waiting for a bird's beak? Will it be a body of a suffering transmigratory being or a body of a fortunate transmigratory being? Consider your state of mind and whether you have more positive potential than negative imprints on your mind and how that is the sole consideration when you leave this life.

Whether you have a life-threatening illness or not, there are so many conditions that can shorten your life. Consider this and develop a strong sense of the uncertainty of the time of your death.

Seeing how fragile this life is, determine that you will not only practice Dharma, but you will practice it now. You won't delay at all because you never know when you might die.

Only the Dharma Can Help

Given that death is certain and its time is uncertain, the next three points ask that you consider what is important: your wealth and possessions, your friends and relatives, your body, or the Dharma wisdom you have acquired before you die.

Wealth and Possessions Cannot Help

Reflect on how when we die we take nothing with us at all, and how in this way the richest person and the poorest are exactly the same. If a billionaire dies with covetousness and greed, all the possessions in the world can't help him; how only his negative karma will determine what his next life will be. Think on this.

You are in exactly the same position as that billionaire. In that light, consider the relationship you have with your possessions. Think of the incredible effort you have put into acquiring them and how that effort has been never ending. Ask yourself whether they have brought you lasting satisfaction.

Now consider what harm a mind of attachment to them will cause at the moment of your death. You can't take any of them with you, not even a hair, but attachment to them can cause you to have a terrible death and a terrible rebirth.

Think of how all the things you own and all the projects and experiences you treasure are meaningless, like ripples on water, to use Padmasambhava's expression. If that is so, determine to change the relationship you have with your possessions, not necessarily getting rid of them but getting rid of your attachment to them.

Friends and Relatives Cannot Help

In the same way, attachment to your friends and loved ones can only assure you of a terrible death. At death you can't take a single companion with you, no matter how much you love that person. You have to go into the next life totally alone.

On the other hand, the attachment you feel for them and the attachment they feel for you can be a huge hindrance at death. It will only increase the confusion and agony you feel at death.

Determine now to alter your relationship with people—not killing the love you feel for them at all but getting rid of the attachment, so that when you die you can die without attachment but with love, the best way to die.

Our Body Cannot Help

This body that you feed and take so much care of is supposed to be a constant source of pleasure for you, never causing any suffering at all. This isn't just a complete myth in life; when you separate from your body at death it causes you great fear and suffering. Your greatest possession, your greatest friend, becomes your greatest enemy at death.

Consider how you have been a slave to your body all your life: feeding it, clothing it, giving it everything it wants. Think of how many hours a week you work solely for the comforts of your body. Think of how much time, effort, and money go into protecting it and pampering it. Think of the education you have worked so hard to acquire, all those years of studying, just to get money to give the body things.

Consider how odd this really is, when in a very short while this body will be a pile of ash or a rotting corpse. You are a very temporary tenant in the "guesthouse" of this body, and yet you lavish such care on it. That is very strange.

Think of the nonvirtuous actions you commit in order to give the body what it wants. You lie, steal, commit sexual misconduct—in fact, there is not one nonvirtuous action it won't demand that you do.

Your body is your most cherished possession and so attachment to it will cause you the most pain when you have to part from it at death. Imagine that you are dying at this very moment, and you will soon have to separate from your body.

Now, consider the two ways you can die. First, think of dying full of attachment to your possessions, the people in your life, and your body. Think of how miserable you will be and what pain it will cause. Think of the consequences.

Next consider the alternative, dying without attachment. Somehow, through diligently practicing Dharma, you have managed to break all the attachments that have ruled your life, and you are dying free from attachment. Think how that would feel. You are still dying. You will still very soon be separating from your possessions, your loved ones, and your body, but you have managed to lose your attachment to all these things. Even in death, even though you will never see any of these things again, still there will be perfect peace. Your mind will stay relaxed because you know that death is just a transition, and because you are going into the next rebirth unobscured by the three poisons, it will be even better than this rebirth.

Imagine what it would be like to approach death with this great sense of spaciousness and peace. Imagine what the great meditators feel: a happy transition, like going on a picnic. Loving the people around you without attachment, you leave them with the best possible gifts, your love and your good death, and you know they will be all right.

Ask yourself the question, "Do I want to have a happy or a miserable death?" When you can truthfully answer that question and see exactly that you need to have the former and avoid the latter, then you will see that the only thing to do is to practice Dharma purely, avoiding all nonvirtuous actions and only ever doing virtuous ones.

Having worked through these nine points, determine not only that you will practice Dharma and practice it now, but also that you will do everything you can to practice it purely.

2. The Death Process Meditation at Bedtime

Sleeping is something we all do a lot, and it tends to be either a neutral action or a nonvirtuous one. Most of the time we are attached to the temporal enjoyment of the comfort of our bed and to the rest we are looking forward to. While going to bed doesn't usually have any higher purpose than that, we can make it worthwhile. By slipping into sleep with a positive motivation, our entire sleep, no matter how many hours we sleep, can be made into a virtuous action.

While you are dreaming you rarely recognize the dream as a dream, but it is possible to train your mind. There are practices that you can do that will train you to stay aware during the different sleeping states, from waking to sleeping to dreaming and back again, the most famous one being part of the six yogas of Naropa. Whereas at present you react to what happens to you in dreams, developing attachment in some dreams and aversion in others, by seeing them as what they are with lucid dreaming, you stay detached from them and therefore do not create negative karma.

One excellent practice you can do as you go to sleep is to go through the death process. As you lie there, imagine the whole process, with the mirage-like vision, the smoke-like vision and so forth, each stage taking you into an increasingly subtle state. When you visualize the clear light, try to see it underpinned with the knowledge that it is completely without its own identity, that it is empty of any independent existence.

Emptiness is not nothingness; it is not empty space. This clear light lacks the inherent existence that you attribute to it. If you can get some feeling for this, then, when you move from the waking state to the sleeping state, your entire night will be profoundly transformed and your ability to remain lucid during your dreams will be greatly enhanced. This, in turn, will be enormously helpful at the time of death.

Even if just for a few seconds you can hold the feeling of the oneness of the clear light vision and the emptiness of the self, this is a profound mind and a wonderful one to fall asleep with.

It is very good to lie in the lion's posture when you are ready to sleep. Lie down on your right side, with your right hand under your head and your ring finger pressing your right nostril closed, reducing attachment. Lay your left arm along the top of your body and stretch your legs out straight with your feet together.

When we lie like this, there is less distraction and less chance of unpleasant dreams, and somehow, by remembering that this is the position that the Buddha used when he passed into parinirvana, the position itself becomes a very positive thing. Then, as you feel sleep coming on, think, "Just as the Buddha passed into nirvana in this position, may I too pass into nirvana, for the sake of all sentient beings. Just as the Buddha showed the example of impermanence in this way and was able to enlighten so many sentient beings, may I do likewise."

Sleeping in this position gives you a lighter sleep and so you are able to wake up when you need to. For instance, if you are in retreat and you need to wake early, then by thinking about the time you want to awake you will naturally do so. Many people lie on their backs or their stomachs when they sleep, and this makes it easy to have fearful dreams, besides causing them to snore loudly.

As you feel yourself moving toward sleep, generate strong compassion for all living beings and then, if you can, practice some tonglen, some taking and giving. Imagine all the other living beings and their suffering, and willingly take on all their suffering with the in-breath, and then give them all your happiness and positive qualities with the out-breath. Then imagine dying with compassion, by thinking how all living beings are suffering, and determine to free them from all the suffering by yourself. Falling asleep like this ensures a very positive sleep, free from bad dreams.

Another very beneficial thing you can do is to imagine the Buddha as your pillow, very bright and shining. Think that your head is resting in his lap. Feel you are taking refuge in the Buddha and visualize radiant white light coming from his body and pouring into you. All your negativities are purified and you become one with the Buddha's holy qualities. Then the Buddha dissolves into white light and that white light is absorbed into you. Feel that with this, because the Buddha is completely empty, your wrong concept of inherent existence dissolves and you see everything as completely empty. Then try to feel that this bright white light that you have become is the clear light of death, and that, because you have completely purified all negativities, you will now become a buddha.

3. A Meditation on the Experience of Dying

A profound meditation you can do is on the experience of dying; you imagine that you suddenly find yourself dying, that the mind is separating from the body like a hair pulled from the head. The purpose of this meditation is to guide your mind from negativity by showing you the importance of this moment and the danger of attachment to the trivial concerns of this life. You must understand that death is not an end; it is not like a butter lamp dying because the butter is exhausted. Therefore, this meditation is more useful than the most expensive medicine, because it allows you to prepare for the most important moment of your life.

At the time of death, because attachment can become incredibly strong and obscure your view of what is happening, it's vital to stay aware of the entire death process. In order to do this at the time, you need to practice now, rather than then, when so many things such as fearful visions and terror of the future will crowd your mind.

This is not a meditation that you can do once and think it's finished. Just as it takes time to flatten a rocky mountain, you have to work with the mind throughout your entire life. This is not working with words alone, but with the mind. The rational understanding of the profundity of this meditation can be finished if you work on it for many years, but the inner experience of the meditation can never be finished, not until enlightenment.

The main part of the meditation is to visualize that you are actually dying and to examine the impact that will have on your mind. This can be done on its own or in conjunction with other meditations in a retreat, such as meditations on the different realms. Think of how horrifying it is to see a corpse, and yet that is how your body will soon be.

Start the meditation by thinking how there are many more hindrances than supports to life and therefore you could die at any moment. Then think that because you have been habituated to negativity for so long, you will surely die with a negative mind and be thrown into the lower realms. Don't just say the words—really explore what this means and feel deeply that this is in fact your situation. Determine that by your continued, strong practice, when you do really die you will be able to face death with the certainty that you have a good heart, free from selfishness, and that death will hold no fears for you.

Imagine that death is happening now. Perhaps it was a car accident (and you can imagine the scene at the roadside: the ambulance, the stretcher, the race to hospital with the sirens blaring) or a sudden and terminal illness. Think that you are in hospital, in a bed with white sheets, in a room with machines and oxygen bottles.

The realization that you are about to die hits you and you see clearly that your life is over. There is nothing you can do and nobody who can help you. You can't phone the Lord of Death to postpone this. No matter how scared you are, there is nothing you can do.

Imagine that all your family, your friends, and relatives are there by your bedside, but already they are fading from your sight. There is nothing they can do, and they cry uncontrollably. Your mouth becomes dry; your tongue becomes short and blue; your hearing fades and your recognition of things breaks down.

You know that very soon your body will be placed in a box and carried out of your home and very soon it will be buried in a grave or cremated. Perhaps your family performs a ceremony. If you are Chinese, for instance, there might be a lot of loud music, and paper houses and paper money will be burned to send you on your way—but you won't be aware of this at all.

This will definitely happen to you. In one way or another you will have to go through the absorptions and leave your body, and there will be nothing you can do about it. Whatever you were working on, no matter how important it was, will never be finished now. Nothing can help now but your virtuous mind.

The death process is happening. You can feel it. Your breathing is getting irregular, with the in-breaths becoming shallower and shorter and the out-breaths longer. Your body's appearance is changing, becoming like a log of wood. Your sensations are leaving you. The doctors around you are shaking their heads and turning off machines. There is nothing more they can do. Suddenly you are no longer a person; you're almost a dead body lying there and people are afraid to touch you. Even your family is scared of you now. Your partner, who was so attracted by your body at one time, can't even look at it now.

That relationship you had with everybody and everything is now ended. All the experiences of this life are now no more than last night's dream;

they're that insubstantial and that unreal. The things that you enjoyed are lost to you; you can never enjoy them again.

Like waking from a dream to find all the things of the dream have never existed, you will soon find that all the things of your life no longer exist. Think of all the experience of your life—meeting friends, buying objects, going on holidays—all these will be no more very soon. Similarly, all the important projects that you have been working on will now never be finished. If you are building a house, it's ended by impermanence and death; if you are writing a book, it's ended by impermanence and death; if you are traveling, it's ended by impermanence and death. Whether or not you have finished your business, it's ended by impermanence and death; whether or not you have finished studying at college, it's ended by impermanence and death. Even eating dinner, watching a television program, writing a letter—all will go unfinished.

Just as it is pointless to be attached to dream possessions, so in this life it is pointless to be attached to anything, and now, at death, it is disastrous. Soon, this thing you called "your body" will be a corpse, carried to the cemetery on its last journey, and your family and friends will return to their homes and continue their lives without you. You will no longer see your home, your clothes, your possessions; they will be left for your relatives to divide up. Instead of the mountain of material possessions that weighed your life down, you will soon be on your way to the intermediate state with a mountain of negative karma.

This body that has served you all your life, running for you, walking for you, doing jobs for you—this body is no longer capable of movement; it is fast becoming a corpse. It has served you, but on the other hand you have been its slave, feeding it and clothing it and pampering to all its many needs, and now it is letting you down. The most important thing to you, this body, has deserted you. This body is made of a million parts, has tens of thousands of hairs over it, and you can't even take one tiny hair with you.

Think that now death is actually happening. Think, "Now I am dying. I who am called (and use your name) am dying. This 'I' that I have cherished all my life is ceasing to exist. Everything that this I has worked for all my life is now ceasing to exist and I can see that it has all been so meaningless." No matter how much regret you feel now, there is nothing that can be done. Your time is finished; there is no time to do anything. You have to separate from everything you have known.

Now the actual death process is happening. First your body feels heavy, and the earth element is absorbed. Feel your body sinking, like it is pushing down on the mattress. Your vision blurs and you have a *mirage-like vision*, where everything seems watery and wavy, like a scene you see in a far-off mirage.

Then you feel incredibly dry; your mouth, your saliva, everything dries up. Your hearing goes and you can no longer distinguish sounds. The water element is absorbed, and the mirage-like image is replaced by an *image of smoke*, like the room is filled with smoke from burning green wood, swirling everywhere.

Next, your ability to discriminate diminishes, and you can no longer distinguish shapes and people. Those around you become blurs, without names or discernible personalities. You can no longer smell things. The smoke-like image fades and is replaced by the *image of sparks*, like fireflies filling the sky, or the sparks from a fiercely burning fire.

When that weakens, as the fire element is absorbed into the air element, your tongue contracts and turns blue, and you no longer taste anything. You have a vision of *flickering light*, like the flame of a butter lamp about to go out.

Your breathing has stopped. Now, as the gross superstitions dissolve, the vision of flickering light becomes the first of the visions: the *white vision*. This is like a snow-covered landscape on a full-moon-lit night. This is caused by the white seed descending from the crown chakra down the central channel to the heart chakra.

Next is the *red vision*, caused by the red seed ascending up the central channel from the lower chakra to the heart chakra. This vision is like a clear sunrise just before the dawn breaks. Then, as the white and red seeds are absorbed into the heart chakra, there is the *dark vision*, a sense of swooning and becoming unconscious.

Suddenly, like the turning on of a light, the *clear light* vision appears, a white light that fills the senses. Try to picture it like clear autumn daylight. It's a bit like when you sleep in too late and wake to a completely dark room and then pull open the curtains, and blinding sunlight floods in. The darkness immediately gives way to a light that is bright and clear. This represents the most subtle mind, and this is the mind that moves from this life into the next.

Now your body is a corpse. Now you are no more than your name on a gravestone and a memory for some of your friends. Now is the time to take the corpse to the cemetery and to distribute the possessions of this person who had your name. Now is the time for your relatives to put a ring around a date on the calendar so they will remember to put some flowers on your grave once a year.

All the hundreds of shoes and all the clothes that you used to wear at different times in different places will be sold or taken by other people. They will belong to others. Your house will feel very empty and the room where you used to be will have a very vacant, very sad feeling.

Visualize your body at the graveyard or at the crematorium. While your body is there being burned, your fat melting down and your skull and all those other things turning black, your consciousness will have gone somewhere else completely. Just as a shadow follows the body, it will follow its karma. If you lived with attachment and clinging to this life, if nothing was purified before your death, if no practice of Dharma was done to change your attitude, you will definitely reincarnate in the lower realms after death.

Conclude with the thought that even if you cannot achieve enlightenment or liberation from samsara in this life before you die, you should try to actualize some realization of the path to enlightenment. Then, at the time of death, without difficulty you will be able to be reborn in a pure land, where you can practice Vajrayana and quickly achieve enlightenment. If that is not possible, then at the very least you should try to receive a perfect human rebirth.

The very essence of what makes life most beneficial is training the mind in the lamrim, the graduated path to enlightenment; year by year bringing your mind closer to lamrim realizations as much as possible. From now until your death, for as many days, hours, minutes, seconds there are, for as many breaths there are, on the basis of correctly devoting yourself to the virtuous friend, you should practice the lamrim, especially the heart practice of bodhichitta. You should live your life with the attitude of bodhichitta. Determine to do just this.

APPENDIX 2
HOW TO BENEFIT THE DYING AND THE DEAD[135]

How to Benefit the Dying and the Dead

During an illness the main thing is to take care of the dying person's mind. Many others can take care of the body, but few can take care of the mind. The most worthwhile thing to do is to inspire the person to think of others with loving-kindness and compassion, to wish others to be happy and free from suffering. If a person dies with the thought of benefiting others, their mind is naturally happy, and this makes their death meaningful.

You can teach the person tonglen—the taking-and-giving meditation—or loving-kindness meditation (*metta*), according to the capacity of his or her mind. If the person has a more compassionate nature, a "brave mind," they will be able to do tonglen, taking others' suffering and giving out happiness. If the person can do tonglen, it's the best way to die, as it means dying with bodhichitta. His Holiness the Dalai Lama calls this a "self-supporting death." For those who don't think others are more important than themselves, wishing others happiness and to be free of suffering is more difficult.

It's very important to know a person's mind. You can teach according to their capacity: with your own wisdom use the most appropriate method to help them. It would be best if you could give the dying person some idea of the death process according to tantra: the evolution of the dissolution of the elements, the senses, the consciousness, all the way to the subtle consciousness.

For a person who has lost their capacity to understand because of coma, dementia, and so forth, there is not much possibility for them to understand. We should aim to help them get at least a perfect human rebirth. This should be our aim: not that the person must necessarily believe in karma, for example, but that they die with a positive, happy mind, with loving-kindness and compassion; this is our precious gift. Our main aim in taking care of the physical body is so that we can take care of the mind, to transform their mind to be positive so that at least the person can die without anger, desire, etc.

You should learn various methods to benefit and calm the mind, and to benefit now and in the future. You should get an idea of what level of method to offer. If, for example, one visualizes Buddha in the mind or outside, or watches the conventional nature of mind, its clarity, other thoughts such as anger and attachment do not arise. If one is able to do this at the time of death, according to the person's mind you can talk about the "fully enlightened being" rather than the Sanskrit "Buddha." You can talk about God if that's more skillful: a compassionate God or a loving God, or an omniscient one. Explain to the person that the nature of their mind, their heart, is completely pure; that the fully enlightened one, God, is compassionate to everyone, including them. Help them to think that their loving heart is oneness with God, that the kingdom of God is within. This frees people from guilt and anger, from their negative thoughts.

Mantra, for example, helps one to eventually attain a higher rebirth after one's positive karma is used up. Even if a person doesn't want to hear some mantras, still it leaves a positive imprint on the mind, so that sooner or later that person will meet the path and have the ability to practice the teachings, to clear obscurations and attain enlightenment. Even if someone gets angry hearing mantras and dies with an angry mind, it's still better than not hearing any mantras at all and staying peaceful. In this way, step by step, a person's karma will bring them to the Mahayana path and to enlightenment. Mahayanists attain enlightenment, but arhats get stuck, even if the arhat starts off with the higher rebirth.

When the Person Is Dying

If you have studied the death process, you will be able to recognize the stages through which a person's consciousness is passing, what elements are being absorbed and so forth, when the person is actually dying.

It is better if the family members don't cry within hearing distance, as this creates clinging in the mind of the dying person. There are sounds to help the consciousness at the time of death, sounds that benefit, such as mantras and so on. Other than this, it is best to keep quiet and don't make any sounds. You should teach the family how to create this atmosphere.

It is okay to medicate pain in order to help the person be able to think. But medicating for mental anguish is not okay. Sedation before death prevents working out bad karma. Anguish becomes fruitful if the person can experience it. It is hard to tell the difference. Often families want the patient medicated, but it is more for their own comfort than the patient's.

At death, invite the sangha to chant mantras nicely, in an uplifting way. When they chant like this, the person feels that nothing is more important than Amitabha Buddha. They feel protected, supported, and guided.

Chanting the names of the Thirty-Five Confession Buddhas is extremely powerful; people can come there and chant together. Also, it is good to chant the very powerful mantras of the five deities normally used in jangwa puja that liberate both those dying and those already dead and that purify living ones and liberate those in the lower realms. The text *Giving Breath to the Wretched* has powerful mantras and is a text one can use to help.

You can place a stupa on the person's chest or let them hold it. Each time the stupa touches them it purifies negative karma. Even if the consciousness has already left the body, there is still benefit in touching the body with the stupa. This is also good to do with babies or with people who don't understand. Even to a non-Buddhist you can say that the stupa is for peace or healing or purification. The person can visualize light rays coming from the stupa.

It is also good to have a few stupas on hand for healing or to dispel spirit harms. Also, a sheet of paper with the ten great mantras written on it can be put on the dying person's body while reciting a dedication prayer.

When the Breath Has Stopped

The very first thing you can do after the breath has stopped is Medicine Buddha practice. This works for animals as well. As a group or individually, chant the names and the mantra. Medicine Buddha made a promise that if anyone chants his name and mantra, all their prayers and wishes will succeed. One of Medicine Buddha's ten powers is the power of prayer, so pray as if you are the Medicine Buddha's agent, on behalf of the being who has died.

Then you can do Amitabha powa (transference of consciousness to a pure land), followed by other practices. You can recite *Sang Chö: The Prayer of Good Deeds* (commonly known as *The King of Prayers*). At funerals it is also good for everyone attending to read it together. You can recite the Namgyalma (Ushnisha Vijaya) mantra twenty-one times, then blow on water, sesame seeds, or perfume or talcum powder, blessing it with the mantra, and then sprinkle that over the dead body.

The Namgyalma mantra is very powerful for purifying. It is best to recite the long mantra if possible, but the short mantra can also be recited. Also, if this mantra is written on cloth or paper and placed on a mountaintop or roof where the wind can blow it, whoever is touched by the wind receives blessings and their karma is purified. Circumambulating a stupa that contains the mantra purifies all the karma to be reborn in the hot hells.

When the breath stops, in Tibet you would not touch the body until a lama in the village did powa; this is important. Look for signs that the consciousness has left the body (such as after powa): the white drop, like pus or water from the nostril, or for a woman, blood and water from the lower part. First pull the hair in the center of the crown toward the back, so that the consciousness comes out through there.

Preparing for Death During Life

His Holiness the Dalai Lama says that it is more difficult to really meditate at the time of death than it was in life. If during your life you are unable meditate well, you won't be able to hold your concentration and meditate at death.

The essence, therefore, is to have accumulated merit and done purification in everyday life in your relationship with sentient beings; to have served others with a sincere heart, loving-kindness, and compassion; and to have done the hard work to benefit them. Also, to have made offerings to the guru and the Three Jewels.

Practicing the good heart, that is, bodhichitta, during your life purifies so much negative karma, even very heavy karma, and it stops you creating more. It is negative karma that makes death terrifying. And it is bodhichitta especially that stops the immeasurable suffering and the suffering rebirths that arise later from these negative actions. You should abide in morality, living in the precepts, taking them from a spiritual master or in front of holy objects.

It is very important to integrate the five powers into your life and to learn the five powers to be practiced at death. These are very special practices to achieve enlightenment quickly. They involve powa, transference of consciousness, at the time of death into a pure land. In the pure land you are able to receive teachings on the Vajrayana, which enables you to achieve enlightenment in one lifetime. The effectiveness of powa depends on how well you practice the five powers at death. And this depends on how well you do the general practices in life.

The lamrim explains the four ways to accumulate powerful, extensive merit. You should attempt this in everyday life while doing all the normal activities of eating, sleeping, walking, and so on, rather than doing every action with worldly desire and samsaric attachment.

Creating a Conducive Environment for the Dying[136]

[To the residents of Tara House] Make Tara House as beautiful as possible: a calm, peaceful, serene, holy environment is so important. There should be beautiful views, beautiful art, flowers, Tara images. Flowers give a very special spiritual feeling. The point is to make a positive imprint on the person's mind. Because of being there, each person's mind is elevated, and they are not afraid of dying. When their family comes, they will see it is a nice place, a place that makes one feel there's no need to be afraid of death, and they will want to come.

Because of His Holiness the Dalai Lama's wisdom and compassion, more and more people are feeling comfortable with Buddhism these days. We need to help people have an open mind to different methods. You can make it clear to people that Tara Home is Buddhist; then if they're okay with that, they can come.

The religious tradition of the residents depends on their prior practice in daily life. The advice you give them depends on what you have been doing yourself—the lamrim, thought transformation—what you have been practicing in daily life, beyond mere sitting meditation. In general, the Mahayana has much to offer to the dying, or to anyone with problems.

And highest yoga tantra is the only system that offers a real explanation of death. The precise instructions only exist in highest yoga tantra, not in other traditions. Other traditions give only general instructions; they do not provide explanations in terms of the subtle consciousness, winds, chakras, etc.

The robed sangha can live in Tara Home for several months at a time, to distinguish the level of practice that each patient can relate to, and to create a holy environment. The new people just joining, who haven't done this service before, need to learn from the people who have been doing service for a long time. Those who are experienced in how peoples' minds are should study different books, different teachings from different sources, and from their experience come to know the different states of mind of people who are dying.

You should meet together once or twice a month; everyone should read what has been compiled. People with more skill and wisdom can then edit this research, and it can become a book. There is no need to rush. In the long run, this book will become a guide for the organization, and to benefit other organizations.

The group should practice powa. Each year you should take powa teachings and do a powa retreat so that you can practice. It is very important to do powa retreat every year.

If one becomes accomplished at powa and receives the signs of accomplishment, then this can be the best public service—liberating others and helping them at the time of death.

It is okay to ask other lamas to do powa; one can ask any Tibetan lama who is a good practitioner. You can bring in high lamas to do powa and to do jangwa purification. If it is difficult to invite the lama to the hospice, then the lama can do powa wherever they are, from a distance. You will need to inform the lama which direction the head is facing.

In general, it would be good to do the elaborate Medicine Buddha puja once a week; it is very good for success for dying. Also, you can recite *The Medicine Buddha Sutra* once a month. The special text with one hundred thousand Buddha's names by Pabongka Rinpoche can also be recited at death. Ribur Rinpoche got the text recently from Lhasa; it is at Tushita Meditation Center in Delhi and Tibetan monks can read it. The text is very rare.

APPENDIX 3
THE DEATH PROCESS[137]

Chart 1: The First Cycyle of Simultaneous Dissolution

Factor dissolving	External sign	Internal sign
earth element	body becomes very thin, limbs loose; sense that body is sinking under the earth	appearance of mirages
aggregate of form	limbs become smaller, body becomes weak and powerless	
basic mirror-like wisdom (our ordinary consciousness that clearly perceives many objects simultaneously)	sight becomes unclear and dark	
eye sense	one cannot open or close eyes	
colors and shapes	luster of body diminishes; one's strength is consumed	

Chart 2: The Second Cycle of Simultaneous Dissolution

Factor dissolving	External sign	Internal sign
water element	saliva, sweat, urine, blood, and regenerative fluid dry greatly	appearance of smoke
aggregate of feelings (pleasure, pain, and neutrality)	body consciousness can no longer experience the three types of feelings that accompany sense consciousnesses	
basic wisdom of equality (one's ordinary consciousness mindful of pleasure, pain, and neutral feelings as feelings)	one is no longer mindful of the feelings accompanying the mental consciousness	
ear sense	one no longer hears external or internal sounds	
sounds	"ur" sound in ears no longer arises	

Chart 3: The Third Cycle of Simultaneous Dissolution

Factor dissolving	External sign	Internal sign
fire element	one cannot digest food or drink	appearance of fireflies or sparks within smoke
aggregate of discriminations	one is no longer mindful of affairs of close persons	
basic wisdom of analysis (one's ordinary consciousness mindful of the individual names, purposes, and so forth of close persons)	one can no longer remember the names of close persons	
nose sense	inhalation weak, exhalation strong and lengthy	
odors	one cannot smell	

Chart 4: The Fourth Cycle of Simultaneous Dissolution

Factor dissolving	External sign	Internal sign
wind element	the ten winds move to heart; inhalation and exhalation ceases	appearance of a sputtering butter lamp about to go out
aggregate of compositional factors	one cannot perform physical actions	
basic wisdom of achieving activities (one's ordinary consciousness mindful of external activities, purposes, etc.)	one is no longer mindful of external worldly activities, purposes and so forth	
tongue sense	tongue becomes thick and short; root of tongue becomes blue	
tastes	one cannot experience tastes	
body sense and tangible objects	one cannot experience smoothness or roughness	

Chart 5: Fifith to Eighth Cycles of Dissolution

Cycle	Factor dissolving	Cause of appearance	Internal sign
Fifth Cycle	eighty conceptions	winds in right and left at first, burning channels above heart enter central channel at butter-lamp; then, top of head	clear vacuity filled with white light
Sixth Cycle	mind of white appearance	winds in right and left channels below heart enter central channel at base of spine	very clear vacuity filled with red light
Seventh Cycle	mind of red increase	upper and lower winds gather at heart; then winds enter drop at heart	at first, vacuity filled with thick darkness; then, as if swooning unconsciously
Eighth Cycle	mind of black near-attainment	all winds dissolve into the very subtle life-bearing wind in the indestructible drop at the heart	very clear vacuity free of the white, red, and black appearances; then, the mind of clear light of death

GLOSSARY

aggregates (*skandha*). The psycho-physical constituents that make up a sentient being: form, feeling, discriminative awareness, compositional factors, and consciousness. Beings of the desire and form realms have all five, whereas beings in the formless realm no longer have the aggregate of form.

arhat (*drachompa*). Literally, "foe destroyer." A person who has destroyed his or her inner enemy, the delusions, and attained liberation from cyclic existence.

Aryadeva. Third-century Indian Buddhist philosopher and leading early proponent of Nagarjuna's Prasangika Madhyamaka philosophy. He is one of six great Indian scholars known as the Six Ornaments.

Asanga, Arya. The fourth-century Indian master who received directly from Maitreya Buddha the extensive, or method, lineage of Shakyamuni Buddha's teachings. Said to have founded the Chittamatra school of Buddhist philosophy. He is one of six great Indian scholars known as the Six Ornaments.

Atisha Dipamkara Shrijnana (982–1054). The renowned Indian master who went to Tibet in 1042 to help in the revival of Buddhism and established the Kadam tradition. His text *Lamp for the Path to Enlightenment* was the first lamrim text.

Avalokiteshvara. *See* Chenrezig.

bardo. *See* intermediate state.

Bodhgaya. The small town in the state of Bihar in North India where Shakyamuni Buddha became enlightened.

bodhichitta (*jangchup sem*). A principal consciousness that combines the two factors of wishing to free all beings from suffering and wishing to attain enlightenment in order to accomplish that.

bodhisattva (*jangchup sempa*). One who possesses bodhichitta.

buddha, a (*sangyé*). A fully enlightened being. One who has totally eliminated (*sang*) all obscurations veiling the mind and has fully developed (*gyé*) all good qualities to perfection. *See also* enlightenment.

Buddha, the. The historical Buddha. *See* Shakyamuni Buddha.

Buddhadharma. The teachings of the Buddha. *See also* Dharma.

buddhahood. See enlightenment.

Buxa Duar. A small town in West Bengal in eastern India, where most of the Tibetan monks who escaped to India in 1959 were accommodated.

capable being (lower, middle, or higher). See graduated path of the three capable beings.

causative phenomena. Things that come about in dependence upon causes and conditions; includes all objects experienced by the senses, as well as the mind itself; impermanent phenomena.

Chenrezig (*Avalokiteshvara*). Compassion Buddha. The meditational deity embodying the compassion of all the buddhas. The Dalai Lamas are said to be emanations of this deity.

chöd. A tantric practice aimed at destroying self-grasping, in which the practitioner visualizes dissecting and distributing the parts of the ordinary body to spirits and other beings as a feast offering.

clear light. Very subtle mind. This subtlest state of mind occurs naturally at death and through successful tantric practice and is used by practitioners to realize emptiness.

compassion (*karuna, nyingjé*). The wish that others be free from suffering.

completion stage (*dzokrim*). The second of the two stages of highest yoga tantra, during which control is gained over the vajra body through such practices as inner fire.

conventional truth (*samvritisatya, kunzop denpa*). As opposed to ultimate truth, which is the understanding of the ultimate nature of reality (emptiness), conventional truth is what is true to the valid conventional consciousness. It is also called *concealer truth* or *all-obscuring truth* because, although true on one level, it obscures the ultimate nature. Conventional and ultimate truth form the important subject in Buddhist philosophy called *the two truths. See also* ultimate truth.

cyclic existence. See samsara.

dakini (*khadroma*). Literally, "female sky-goer." A female being who helps arouse blissful energy in a qualified tantric practitioner.

Dalai Lama (b. 1935). Gyalwa Tenzin Gyatso. Revered spiritual leader of the Tibetan people and tireless worker for world peace; winner of the Nobel Peace Prize in 1989; a guru of Lama Zopa Rinpoche.

deity (*ishtadevata, yidam*). An emanation of the enlightened mind used as the object of meditation in tantric practices.

delusion (*klesha, nyönmong*). An obscuration covering the essentially pure nature of the mind, causing suffering and dissatisfaction; the main delusion is ignorance and all the others come from this. *See also* three poisons.

demigod (*asura, lhamayin*). A being in the god realms who enjoys greater comfort and pleasure than human beings but who suffers from jealousy and quarreling. *See also* six realms; samsara.

dependent origination. Also called *dependent arising*, this refers to the way that the self and phenomena exist conventionally as relative and interdependent. They come into existence in dependence upon (1) causes and conditions, (2) their parts, and most subtly, (3) the mind imputing, or labeling, them. *See also* twelve links of dependent origination.

Dharamsala. A village in the northwest of India, in Himachal Pradesh. The residence of His Holiness the Dalai Lama and the Tibetan government-in-exile.

Dharma (*chö*). The second refuge jewel. Literally, "that which holds or protects (us from suffering)" and hence brings happiness and leads us toward liberation and enlightenment. In Buddhism, absolute Dharma is the realizations attained along the path to liberation and enlightenment and conventional Dharma is seen as both the teachings of the Buddha and virtuous actions.

dharmakaya (*chöku*). The truth body of a buddha (the other "body" being the form body or rupakaya); the blissful omniscient mind of a buddha, the result of the wisdom side of the path. It can be divided into the wisdom body (*jnanakaya*, *yeshé nyiku*) and the nature body (*svabhavikakaya*, *ngowo nyiku*). *See also* rupakaya.

disturbing thoughts. *See* delusion.

eight freedoms. The eight states from which a perfect human rebirth is free: being born as a hell being, hungry ghost, animal, long-life god, or barbarian, or in a dark age when no buddha has descended; holding wrong views; being born with defective mental or physical faculties. *See also* ten richnesses.

eight worldly dharmas. The worldly concerns that generally motivate the actions of ordinary beings: being happy when given gifts and unhappy when not given them; wanting to be happy and not wanting to be unhappy; wanting praise and not wanting criticism; wanting a good reputation and not wanting a bad reputation.

emptiness (*shunyata*, *tongpanyi*). The absence, or lack, of true existence. Ultimately, every phenomenon is empty of existing truly, or from its own side, or independently.

enlightenment (*bodhi*, *jangchup*). Full awakening; buddhahood; omniscience. The ultimate goal of a Mahayana Buddhist, attained when all limitations have been removed from the mind and your positive potential has been completely and perfectly realized. It is a state characterized by infinite compassion, wisdom, and skill.

eon (*kalpa*). A world period, an inconceivably long period of time. The life span of the universe is divided into four great eons, which are themselves divided into twenty lesser eons.

faith. There are three kinds: *believing*, or pure-hearted; *lucid*, or understanding (that is, faith based on logical conviction); and *yearning*, or aspirational.

five aggregates. See aggregates.

five powers. The five forces to be practiced both in this life and at the time of death. They are the power of motivation, the power of acquaintance, the power of the white seed (developing positive qualities), the power of destruction (of self-cherishing), and the power of prayer.

formless realm (*arupyadhatu*, *sukmékyi kham*). The highest of samsara's three realms, with four classes of gods involved in formless meditations. The four levels are limitless sky, limitless consciousness, nothingness, and neither existence nor non-existence (also called *tip of samsara*).

four opponent powers (*nyenpo topshi*). The four practices used to purify nonvirtuous imprints on the mindstream. They are the *power of the object*, taking refuge in the Three Rare Sublime Ones and generating bodhichitta; the *power of regret*, feeling deep regret for the negativity committed; the *power of resolve*, determining not to repeat that negativity; and the *power of remedy*, a practice such as Vajrasattva that effectively acts as an antidote to the negativity.

generation stage (*kye rim*). The first of the two stages of highest yoga tantra, during which you cultivate the clear appearance and divine pride of your chosen meditational deity.

geshé. Literally, "spiritual friend." The title conferred on those who have completed extensive studies and examinations at Geluk monastic universities.

god (*deva*). A being dwelling in a state with much comfort and pleasure in the god realms of the desire, form, or formless realms.

graduated path. See lamrim.

graduated path of the three capable beings. Also known as the *three scopes* or *three levels of practice*, the three levels of the lower, middle, and higher capable being, based on the motivations of trying to attain a better future rebirth, liberation, or enlightenment respectively. *See also* higher capable being; middle capable being; lower capable being.

Great Treatise on the Stages of the Path to Enlightenment. See *Lamrim Chenmo*.

guru (*lama*). A spiritual guide or teacher. One who shows a disciple the path to liberation and enlightenment. Literally, "heavy"—heavy with knowledge of Dharma. In tantra, your teacher is seen as inseparable from the meditational deity and the Three Jewels of refuge.

guru devotion. The sutra or tantra practice of seeing the guru as a buddha then devoting oneself to him or her with thought and with action.

hell (narak). The samsaric realm with the greatest suffering. There are eight hot hells, eight cold hells, and four neighboring hells.

higher capable being. The highest of the three levels of practice or scopes, the higher capable being has the goal of full enlightenment. *See also* graduated path of the three capable beings; lower capable being; middle capable being.

highest yoga tantra (*anuttara yoga tantra*). The fourth and supreme division of tantric practice, sometimes called *maha-anuttara yoga tantra*. It consists of the generation and completion stages. Through this practice, you can attain full enlightenment within one lifetime.

hungry ghost (*preta*) The hungry ghost realm is one of the three lower realms of cyclic existence, where the main suffering is hunger and thirst.

ignorance (*avidya*, *marikpa*). Literally, "not seeing" that which exists, or the way in which things exist. There are basically two kinds: ignorance of karma and ignorance of ultimate truth. The fundamental delusion from which all others spring. The first of the twelve links of dependent origination.

illusory body. A subtle body generated through practice of the completion stage of highest yoga tantra; the cause of the rupakaya.

impermanence (*mitakpa*). The gross and subtle levels of the transience of phenomena, gross being the observable changes in things and events, and subtle being the moment-by-moment disintegration that happens the moment they come into existence.

imprint (*vasana*, *bakchak*). The seed, or potential, left on the mind by positive or negative actions of body, speech, and mind.

inherent (or *intrinsic*) *existence*. What phenomena are empty of; the object of negation, or refutation. To the ignorant, phenomena appear to exist independently, in and of themselves, to exist inherently. *See also* emptiness.

intermediate state (*bardo*). The state between death and rebirth.

kaka. Slang for feces.

karma (*lé*). Action; the working of cause and effect, whereby positive (virtuous) actions produce happiness and negative (nonvirtuous) actions produce suffering.

Karmapa. The head of the Kagyü lineage, one of the four Tibetan traditions. The tradition of the Karmapa was founded in 1110. His Holiness Gyalwa Karmapa Ogyen Trinley Dorje is the Seventeenth Karmapa.

Kopan Monastery. The monastery near Boudhanath in the Kathmandu valley, Nepal, founded by Lama Yeshe and Lama Zopa Rinpoche.

lama (*guru*). A spiritual guide or teacher. One who shows a disciple the path to liberation and enlightenment. Literally, "heavy"—heavy with knowledge of Dharma.

Lama Tsongkhapa. *See* Tsongkhapa, Lama Je.

Lama Yeshe. *See* Yeshe, Lama.

lamrim. The graduated path. A presentation of Shakyamuni Buddha's teachings in a form suitable for the step-by-step training of a disciple. *See also* Atisha; three principal aspects of the path.

Lamrim Chenmo. *The Great Treatise on the Stages of the Path to Enlightenment*. Lama Tsongkhapa's most important work, a commentary on Atisha's *Lamp for the Path to Enlightenment*, the fundamental lamrim text.

Lamp for the Path to Enlightenment (Bodhipathapradipa). The text that formed the basis for the lamrim, written by Atisha in the eleventh century.

liberation (*nirvana* or *moksha*, *nyang dé* or *tharpa*). The state of complete freedom from samsara; the goal of a practitioner seeking his or her own escape from suffering.

lojong. *See* thought transformation.

loving-kindness (maitri, yiong jampa). In the context of the seven points of cause and effect, the wish for all beings to have happiness and its causes, with the added dimension of *yiong* ("beautiful" or "affectionate"); often translated as "affectionate loving-kindness." Rinpoche suggests this is the "loving-kindness of seeing others in beauty."

lower capable being. The first of the three levels of practice or scopes, the lower capable being has the goal of a better future existence. *See also* graduated path of the three capable beings; higher capable being; middle capable being.

lower realms. The three realms of cyclic existence with the most suffering:

the hell being (*naraka*), hungry ghost (*preta*), and animal (*tiryanch*) realms. *See also* six realms; samsara.

Madhyamaka (*Umapa*). The Middle Way school of Buddhist philosophy; a system of analysis founded by Nagarjuna, based on the *Prajnaparamita*, or Perfection of Wisdom, sutras of Shakyamuni Buddha, and considered to be the supreme presentation of the wisdom of emptiness. This view holds that all phenomena are dependent originations and thereby avoids the mistaken extremes of self-existence and nonexistence, or eternalism and nihilism. It has two divisions, Svatantrika and Prasangika. Along with Chittamatra, one of the two Mahayana schools of philosophy.

Mahayana. Literally, "Great Vehicle." It is one of the two general divisions of Buddhism. Mahayana practitioners' motivation for following the Dharma path is principally their intense wish for all mother sentient beings to be liberated from conditioned existence, or samsara, and to attain the full enlightenment of buddhahood. The Mahayana has two divisions, Paramitayana (Sutrayana) and Vajrayana (a.k.a. Tantrayana or Mantrayana)

Maitreya (*Jampa*). The fifth of the thousand buddhas of this fortunate eon to descend to turn the wheel of Dharma, the first one after Shakyamuni Buddha. Presently residing in the pure land of Tushita (Ganden). Recipient of the method lineage of Shakyamuni Buddha's teachings, which, in a mystical transmission, he passed on to Asanga.

mala (*trengwa*). A rosary of beads for counting mantras.

mandala (*kyilkhor*). A circular diagram symbolic of the entire universe. The abode of a meditational deity.

mantra (*ngag*). Literally, "mind protection." Mantras are Sanskrit syllables, usually recited in conjunction with the practice of a particular meditational deity; they embody the qualities of the deity with which they are associated.

Marpa (1012–96). Founder of the Kagyü tradition of Tibetan Buddhism. He was a renowned tantric master and translator, a disciple of Naropa, and the guru of Milarepa.

meditation (*gom*). Familiarization of the mind with a virtuous object. There are two types: single-pointed (*jok gom*), also called *stabilizing*, *placement*, or *fixed*; and analytic or insight meditation (*ché gom*).

merit. Positive imprints left on the mind by virtuous, or Dharma, actions. The principal cause of happiness. The merit of virtue, when coupled with the merit of wisdom, eventually results in rupakaya.

method. All aspects of the path to enlightenment other than those related to emptiness, principally associated with the development of loving-kindness, compassion, and bodhichitta.

middle capable being. The second of the three levels of practice or scopes, the middle capable being has the goal of liberation from suffering. *See also* graduated path of the three capable beings; higher capable being; lower capable being.

Milarepa (1040–1123). Tibet's great yogi, who achieved enlightenment in his lifetime under the tutelage of his guru, Marpa, who was a contemporary of Atisha. One of the founding fathers of the Kagyü school.

mind (*citta*, *sem*). Synonymous with consciousness and sentience. Defined as that which is "clear and knowing"; a formless entity that has the ability to perceive objects. Mind is divided into six principal consciousnesses and fifty-one mental factors.

mind training (*lojong*). *See* thought transformation.

Nagarjuna. The great second-century Indian philosopher and tantric adept who propounded the Madhyamaka philosophy of emptiness. He is one of six great Indian scholars known as the Six Ornaments.

Naropa (1016–1100). The Indian mahasiddha, a disciple of Tilopa and guru of Marpa and Maitripa, who transmitted many tantric lineages, including that of the renowned six yogas of Naropa.

negative karma. *See* nonvirtue.

nirmanakaya (*tulku*). The emanation body of a buddha that manifests in a variety of forms for sentient beings. *See also* dharmakaya; rupakaya; sambhogakaya.

nirvana. *See* liberation.

nonvirtue. Negative karma; that which results in suffering.

nyungné. A two-day Thousand-Arm Chenrezig retreat that involves fasting, prostrations, and silence.

obscurations (*avarana*). Also known as obstructions; the negative imprints left on the mind by negative karma and delusions, which obscure the mind. The disturbing-thought obscurations (*nyongdrip*) obstruct attainment of liberation and the more subtle obscurations to knowledge (*shedrip*) obstruct the attainment of enlightenment.

Pabongka Dechen Nyingpo (1871–1941). An influential and charismatic lama of the Geluk order, Pabongka Rinpoche was the root guru of His Holiness the Dalai Lama's senior and junior tutors. He also gave the teachings compiled in *Liberation in the Palm of Your Hand*.

Padmasambhava. The eighth-century Indian tantric master who played a key role in establishing Buddhism in Tibet; he is revered by all Tibetans but especially followers of the Nyingma tradition, which he founded.

parinirvana. The final nirvana the Buddha attained when he passed away in Kushinagar.

perfect human rebirth. The rare human state, qualified by eight freedoms and ten richnesses, which is the ideal condition for practicing the Dharma and attaining enlightenment. The eight freedoms are being free from being born as a hell being, hungry ghost, animal, long-life god, or barbarian; or being born in a dark age when no buddha has descended; holding wrong views; and being born with mental or physical problems that preclude you from understanding the Dharma. The ten richnesses are being born as a human being, in a Dharma country, and with perfect mental and physical faculties; not having committed any of the five immediate negativities; having faith in the Buddha's teachings; being alive when a buddha has descended, the teachings have been revealed, the complete teachings still exist, and when there are still followers of the teachings; and having the necessary conditions to practice the Dharma, such as the kindness of others.

perfection (*paramita*). *See* six perfections.

pervasive compounding suffering. *See* three types of suffering.

powa. The practice whereby the consciousness is forcibly ejected from the body into a pure land just before the moment of death.

precepts. See vows.

prostrations. Paying respect to the guru-deity with body, speech, and mind; one of the tantric preliminaries.

puja. Literally, "offering"; a religious ceremony, usually used to describe an offering ceremony such as the *Offering to the Spiritual Master* (*Guru Puja*).

pure land. A pure land of a buddha is a place where there is no suffering. In some but not all pure lands, after taking birth, the practitioner receives teachings directly from the buddha of that pure land, actualizes the rest of the path, and then becomes enlightened.

purification. The eradication from the mind of negative imprints left by past nonvirtuous actions, which would otherwise ripen into suffering. The most effective methods of purification employ the four opponent powers: the powers of the object, of regret, of resolve and of the remedy.

refuge. The door to the Dharma path. Fearing the sufferings of samsara, Buddhists take refuge in the Three Rare Sublime Ones with the faith that Buddha, Dharma, and Sangha have the power to lead them to happiness, liberation, or enlightenment.

relics (*riksel*). Small, pearl-like pills that manifest spontaneously from holy objects such as statues, stupas, or the cremated bodies of great practitioners.

renunciation. The state of mind of not having the slightest attraction to samsaric pleasures for even a second and having the strong wish for liberation. The first of the three principal aspects of the path to enlightenment. *See also* bodhichitta; emptiness.

rinpoché. Literally, "precious one." Epithet for an incarnate lama, that is, one who has intentionally taken rebirth in a human form to benefit sentient beings on the path to enlightenment.

rupakaya (zukku). The form body of a fully enlightened being; the result of the complete and perfect accumulation of merit. It has two aspects: *sambhogakaya* (*longku*, enjoyment body), in which the enlightened mind appears to benefit highly realized bodhisattvas; and *nirmanakaya* (*tulku*, *emanation body*), in which the enlightened mind appears to benefit ordinary beings. *See also* dharmakaya.

sadhana. Method of accomplishment; the step-by-step instructions for practicing the meditations related to a particular meditational deity.

sambhogakaya (*longku*). The enjoyment body; the form in which the enlightened mind appears in order to benefit highly realized bodhisattvas. *See also* dharmakaya; nirmanakaya; rupakaya.

samsara (khorwa). Cyclic existence; the six realms of conditioned existence, made up of three lower realmshell being (*naraka*), hungry ghost (*preta*), and animal (*tiryanch*)—and three upper realms—human (*manushya*), demigod (*asura*), and god (*deva* or *sura*). The beginningless, recurring cycle of death and rebirth under the control of karma and delusions, fraught with suffering. Also refers to the contaminated aggregates of a sentient being

sangha (*gendun*). Spiritual community; the third of the Three Jewels of refuge. In Tibetan *gendun* literally means "intending (*dun*) to virtue (*gen*)."

self-cherishing. The self-centered attitude of considering your own happiness to be more important than that of others; the main obstacle to the realization of bodhichitta.

sentient being (semchän). An unenlightened being; any being whose mind is not completely free from gross and subtle obscurations.

Shakyamuni Buddha (563–483 BC). Fourth of the one thousand founding buddhas of this present world age. Born a prince of the Shakya clan in North India, he taught the sutra and tantra paths to liberation and enlightenment and is the founder of what came to be known as Buddhism. (From *buddha*, "fully awake.")

Shantideva (685–763). The Indian Buddhist philosopher and bodhisattva who wrote the quintessential Mahayana text *A Guide to the Bodhisattva's Way of Life* (*Bodhicharayavatara*).

six perfections (*paramita*). The practices of a bodhisattva. On the basis of bodhichitta, a bodhisattva practices the six perfections: generosity, morality, patience, perseverance, concentration, and wisdom.

six realms. The general way that Buddhism divides the whole of cyclic existence: three suffering realms (hell, hungry ghost, and animal) and three fortunate realms (human, demigod, and god). *See also* samsara.

Six Yogas of Naropa. Six advanced tantric practices devised by the great Indian scholar Naropa (1016–1100); they are the yoga of inner fire (*tummo*), of illusory body, of clear light, of the dream state, of the intermediate state (*bardo*), of the transference of consciousness (*powa*).

Solu Khumbu. The area in northeastern Nepal, bordering Tibet, where Lama Zopa Rinpoche was born; populated by the Sherpas.

stupa. Buddhist reliquary objects representing the enlightened mind, ranging in size from huge to a few inches in height.

suffering of change. See three types of suffering.

suffering of pain. See three types of suffering.

sutra (Pali: *sutta*). A discourse of the Buddha recognized as a canonical text.

taking and giving (*tonglen*). The meditation practice of generating bodhichitta by taking on the suffering of others and giving them your happiness.

tantra (*gyü*). The secret teachings of the Buddha; a scriptural text and the teachings and practices it contains. Also called Vajrayana or Mantrayana.

Tara (*Drölma*). A female meditational deity who embodies the enlightened activity of all the buddhas; often referred to as the mother of the buddhas of the past, present, and future. The *Praises to the Twenty-One Taras* prayer is the most popular prayer for lay and ordained Tibetans alike.

ten nonvirtuous actions. Three actions of body (killing, stealing, sexual misconduct); four actions of speech (lying, speaking harshly, slandering, and gossiping); and three actions of mind (covetousness, ill will, and wrong views). General actions to be avoided so as not to create negative karma.

ten richnesses. Along with the eight freedoms, the defining features of the perfect human rebirth: being born as a human being, in a Dharma country, and with perfect mental and physical faculties; not having committed any of the five immediate negativities; having faith in the Buddha's teachings; being born when a buddha has descended, when the teachings have been revealed, when the complete teachings still exist, and when there are still followers of the teachings; and having the necessary conditions to practice Dharma, such as the kindness of others.

thangka. Painted or appliquéd depictions of deities, usually set in a framework of colorful brocade.

thought transformation (*lojong*). Also known as *mind training* or *mind transformation*. A powerful approach to the development of bodhichitta, in which the mind is trained to use all situations, both happy and unhappy, as a means to destroy self-cherishing and self-grasping.

Three Jewels. See *Three Rare Sublime Ones.*

three poisons. Attachment, anger, and ignorance.

Three Rare Sublime Ones (*Triratna*; *Könchok Sum*). Also called the *Three Jewels* or the *Triple Gem*, these are objects of Buddhist refuge: the Buddha, Dharma, and Sangha. Lama Zopa Rinpoche prefers "Three Rare Sublime Ones" as a more direct translation of *Könchok Sum.*

three principal aspects of the path. The three main divisions of the lamrim: renunciation, bodhichitta, and the right view (of emptiness).

three types of suffering. (1) The suffering of pain: the commonly recognized suffering experiences of pain, discomfort, and unhappiness. (2) The suffering of change: what is normally regarded as pleasure, which because of its transitory nature sooner or later turns into suffering. (3) Pervasive compounding suffering: the most subtle of the three types of suffering, it refers to the nature of the five aggregates, which are contaminated by karma and delusions.

tonglen. See taking and giving.

true existence. The type of concrete, real existence from its own side that everything appears to possess, when, in fact, everything is empty of true existence.

tsatsa. A print of a buddha's image made in clay or plaster from a carved mold.

Tsongkhapa, Lama Je (1357–1417). Founder of the Geluk tradition of Tibetan Buddhism and revitalizer of many sutra and tantra lineages and the monastic tradition in Tibet.

Tushita (*Ganden*). The Joyous Land. The pure land of the thousand buddhas of this eon, where the future buddha, Maitreya, and Lama Tsongkhapa reside.

twelve links of dependent origination (*pratitya samutpada*; *tendrel chunyi*). Also called the *twelve dependent-related limbs* or *branches*, these are the twelve steps in the evolution of cyclic existence. They are ignorance, karmic formation, consciousness, name and form, sense bases, contact, feelings, craving, grasping, becoming, birth, and aging and death. This is Shakyamuni Buddha's explanation of how karma and delusions bind sentient beings to samsara, causing them to be reborn into suffering again and again; depicted pictorially in the Tibetan Wheel of Life.

ultimate truth (*paramarthasatya*; *döndam denpa*). One of the two truths, the other being conventional truth. It is the understanding of the ultimate nature of things and events, emptiness. *See also* conventional truth.

union of clear light and illusory body. The final stage of the completion stage of highest yoga tantra, where the practitioner is able to unite the clear-light mind called *the meaning clear light* (which is a direct realization of emptiness) with the pure illusory body, the experience of the winds entering the indestructible drop at the central channel.

Vajrasattva (*Dorjé Sempa*). Male meditational deity symbolizing the fundamental purity of all buddhas. A major tantric purification practice for removing obstacles created by negative karma and the breaking of vows.

Vajrayana. Another name for *tantra*; the Adamantine Vehicle; the second of the two Mahayana paths. It is also called Tantrayana or Mantrayana. This is the quickest vehicle of Buddhism as it allows certain practitioners to attain enlightenment within a single lifetime.

Vajrayogini (*Dorjé Naljorma*). Female meditational deity from the mother class of highest yoga tantra; sometimes a consort of Heruka.

virtue. Positive karma; that which results in happiness.

vows. Precepts taken on the basis of refuge at all levels of Buddhist practice. *Pratimoksha* precepts (vows of individual liberation) are the main vows in the Hinayana tradition and are taken by monks, nuns, and laypeople; they are the basis of all other vows. Bodhisattva and tantric precepts are the main vows in the Mahayana tradition.

Wheel of Life (*bhavachakra*). The depiction of cyclic existence, showing the six realms cycling around the hub of ignorance, greed, and hatred, symbolized by a pig, a rooster, and a snake, with the twelve links of dependent origination as the outer rim, all in the jaws and claws of Yama, the Lord of Death.

wisdom. Different levels of insight into the nature of reality. There are, for example, the three wisdoms of hearing, contemplation, and meditation. Ultimately, there is the wisdom realizing emptiness, which frees beings from cyclic existence and eventually brings them to enlightenment. The complete and perfect accumulation of wisdom results in dharmakaya.

wish-granting jewel. Also called *wish-fulfilling jewel.* A jewel that brings its possessor everything that they desire.

worldly concern. See eight worldly dharmas.

yama. A guardian of the hell realm.

Yama. The Lord of Death, seen on the Wheel of Life.

Yeshe, Lama (1935–1984). Born and educated in Tibet, he fled to India, where he met his chief disciple, Lama Zopa Rinpoche. They began teaching Westerners at Kopan Monastery in1969 and founded the Foundation for the Preservation of the Mahayana Tradition (FPMT) in 1975.

yoga. Literally, "to yoke." The spiritual discipline to which one yokes oneself in order to achieve enlightenment.

yogi. A highly realized meditator.

NOTES

1. Vajrayana (literally the "adamantine vehicle") is also called Tantrayana or Mantrayana. It is the second of the two Mahayana paths and is considered lightning quick because it allows practitioners under exceptional circumstances to become enlightened in one lifetime.
2. Atisha Dipamkara Shrijnana (982–1054) was the renowned Indian master who went to Tibet in 1042 to help in the revival of Buddhism. He established the Kadam tradition.
3. Shakyamuni (563–483 BCE), the historical Buddha, is the fourth of the thousand buddhas of this present world system. Born of the Shakya clan, for forty years after his enlightenment he taught the system of teachings that became known as Buddhism. Lama Zopa Rinpoche often adds "Guru" to remind us that the guru is the essence of all the buddhas.
4. Lama Jé Tsongkhapa (1357–1417) was founder of the Geluk tradition of Tibetan Buddhism and revitalizer of many sutra and tantra lineages and the monastic tradition in Tibetan Buddhism. Pabongka Dechen Nyingpo Rinpoche (1871–1941) was the root guru of His Holiness the Dalai Lama's senior and junior tutors. He also gave the teachings compiled in the seminal lamrim text *Liberation in the Palm of Your Hand*, which serves as the outline for this book.
5. The eight freedoms are freedom from being born (1) in the hells, (2) as a hungry ghost, (3) as an animal, (4) as a long-life god, (5) during a time when the Buddha has not descended, (6) as a barbarian in an irreligious country, (7) with impaired faculties such as being deaf or a fool, (8) as a heretic. The ten richnesses are (1) being born as a human being, (2) in the center of a religious country, (3) and with perfect organs; (4) being free of the five extreme negative actions (killing your mother, your father, or an arhat; wounding a buddha; or causing disunity among the Sangha); (5) having belief in the practice of Dharma; (6) being born when the Buddha has descended; (7) being alive when the teachings are alive and being followed; (8) the existence of experienced teachers; (9) being able to follow the path of the Buddha's teaching; (10) and receiving the kindness and compassion of others. See Zopa 2013, 21–76, and Pabongka 2006, 270–87.
6. The Abhidharma is the systemized philosophical and psychological analysis of existence, based on the Buddhist systems of tenets and mind training. It is one of the Three Baskets (Tripitaka) that the teachings of the Buddha are divided into, the others being Vinaya (monastic discipline and ethics) and Sutra (the other teachings of the Buddha).
7. Samsara (*khorwa*) is the beginningless cycle of death and rebirth caused by karma

and delusions. Nirvana (*nyang dé*) is liberation, the complete cessation of all suffering forever.

8. An unenlightened being with sentience, one whose mind is not free from gross and subtle delusions.
9. *Dhammapada* v. 183. FPMT 2020, 75–76.
10. There are two main strains of Buddhist teachings. The Hinayana (based on the early works written in the Pali language) emphasizes individual liberation. The Mahayana (Great Vehicle), based on the later Sanskrit canon emphasizes cultivating bodhichitta and attaining full enlightenment for the sake of all beings.
11. The *Abhidharmakosha* (*Treasury of Knowledge*) by Vasubandhu is one of the main philosophical texts studied in Tibetan monasteries.
12. Rangjung Neljorma Khadro Namsel Drönme, (b. 1976), known as Khadro-la, is a female oracle to His Holiness the Fourteenth Dalai Lama and a highly realized being, now teaching throughout the world.
13. Tibetan Buddhism explains that problems come from the disturbed mind, which is caused by the four elements within our body—earth (solidity), water (the fluid components), fire (heat), and air—becoming unbalanced. These internal imbalances, in turn, create negative effects in our external environment.
14. Quoted in Pabongka 2006, 281. This is commonly attributed to a quote in Prajnavarman's *Commentary to the Collection of Uplifting Sayings*, although this is not verified. See also *Liberation in Our Hands*, 1990, 11n21.
15. In Buddhism, merit—the positive imprints left on the mindstream by virtuous actions—is considered the principal cause of happiness.
16. Lamrim Chenmo Translation Committee 2000–2004, 1:145.
17. The eight worldly dharmas are the four sets of worldly concerns that generally preoccupy us: craving happiness and comfort and to be free from unhappiness and discomfort; craving possessions and wealth and to be free from poverty; craving a good reputation and to be free from a bad one; and craving praise and to be free from blame and criticism. See Rinpoche's book on the eight worldly dharmas, Zopa 2012.
18. The geshés of the Kadampa lineage are renowned for their practice of thought transformation.
19. A mala is a rosary, usually of 108 beads, used for counting mantra recitations. Thus, to recite "one mala" of a mantra is to recite it 108 times.
20. Padmasambhava was an eighth-century Indian tantric master and a central figure responsible for the establishment of Buddhism in Tibet; he is revered by all Tibetan Buddhists, especially the Nyingmapas.
21. Quoted in Pabongka 2006, 308.
22. *Heresy* (*lokta*), also called *mistaken wrong views*, is one of the five afflicted views that are part of the root afflictions. A deluded intelligence that rejects the existence of something that exists, such as karma, reincarnation, the Three Rare Sublime Ones, and so forth, and ascribes existence to that which is nonexistent, such as inherent existence. It is also the holding of incorrect views about the guru.
23. See Marcello 2003, 77.

24. Also called *wish-fulfilling jewel*: a jewel that brings its possessor everything that they desire.
25. Shantideva is the great eighth-century philosopher who propounded the Madhyamaka Prasangika view. He wrote the quintessential Mahayana text *A Guide to the Bodhisattva's Way of Life* (*Bodhicharyavatara*).
26. Ch. 1, v. 41; Gómez forthcoming.
27. Chöden Rinpoché (1933–2015) was an ascetic, learned lama who meditated in a small room in Lhasa for nineteen years after the Chinese occupation. He is a guru of Lama Zopa Rinpoche.
28. FPMT 2020, 261. Thupten Jinpa calls it *Songs of Spiritual Experience: Condensed Points of the Stages of the Path.*
29. Taken from Sopa 2004–17, 2:366.
30. Gyalwa Ensapa (1505–66) was a predecessor of the Panchen Lamas and a guru of Khedrup Sangyé Yeshé.
31. Here, *maras* refers to external interferences, such as those from spirits or devas. Specifically, the karmically created guardians of the hell and hungry ghost realms are referred to as maras. The term can also be used for internal interferences, such as those from karma and delusions.
32. Geshé Jampa Wangdu (d. 1984) was a close friend of Lama Yeshe and guru of Lama Zopa Rinpoche.
33. A town in the northwest of India in the Himalayas; the residence of His Holiness the Dalai Lama's government-in-exile.
34. Lama Atisha (982–1054) is the renowned Indian master who went to Tibet in 1042 to help in the revival of Buddhism and established the Kadam tradition. His text *Light for the Path to Enlightenment* was the first lamrim text. Dromtönpa (1005–64) was his heart disciple and propagator of the Kadam tradition.
35. Taken from Pabongka 2006, 127.
36. For extensive teachings on the lower realms see Pabongka 2006, 321–51, or Lamrim Chenmo Committee 2000–2004, 1:161–75.
37. Ch. 5, vv. 7–8; Gómez forthcoming.
38. The Three Rare Sublime Ones (Skt. *Triratna*; Tib. *Könchok Sum*), also called the Three Jewels or the Triple Gem, are the objects of Buddhist refuge: the Buddha, Dharma, and Sangha.
39. FPMT 2020, 260.
40. V. 55; Kangyur Rinpoché 2005, 49.
41. As a bodhisattva progresses on the Mahayana path to enlightenment, they pass through five paths: the path of merit, of preparation, of right seeing, of meditation, and of no more learning. From the path of right seeing onward they achieve the ten bhumis, or levels, progressively, the first seven bhumis being called *impure* and the last three *pure.*
42. Once attaining bodhichitta, a bodhisattva practices the six perfections: giving or charity, morality, patience, perseverance, concentration, and wisdom. The two merits they attain while on the path to enlightenment are the merit of wisdom, which principally means attaining a realization of emptiness, and the merit of virtue,

which refers to all the other non-wisdom aspects of the path, like compassion, forbearance, generosity, and so forth. The method side of the path leads to attaining the holy body of a buddha, the form body or rupakaya, and the wisdom side to the holy mind of a body, the truth body or dharmakaya.

43. Thokmé Sangpo (1295–1371), also known as Gyalsé Ngulchu Thokmé, was a great master of the Nyingma and Sakya traditions.
44. Sangpo v.4, Rinchen 2001.
45. A great yogi who lived at the time of Milarepa and taught in the Tingri region of Tibet.
46. Vv. 5 and 6. Taken from Dilgo Kyentse and Padampa Sangye 2006.
47. The three substances from the mother are skin, blood, and flesh; and three from the father are sperm, bone, and marrow.
48. Quoted in Pabongka 2006, 311.
49. Quoted in Sopa 2004, 1:324.
50. FPMT 2024, 111.
51. See Pabongka 2006, 303.
52. *Upasaka* (the feminine is *upasika*), literally "attendant," refers to a lay follower of the Buddha.
53. From *The Sayings of the Kadam Masters*, compiled by Chegom Sherap Dorjé. Taken from Jinpa 2008, 578. (My italics.)
54. Ch. 1, v. 12; Gómez forthcoming.
55. *Tulku* (*nirmanakaya*) is the Tibetan term generally used in Tibetan Buddhism for a reincarnated lama, but in the Geluk tradition, Lama Zopa's and the FPMT's tradition, the term used is "rinpoché" or precious one.
56. A set of completion-stage tantric practices: the yoga of inner fire (*tummo*), of illusory body, of clear light, of the dream state, of the intermediate state (*bardo*), and of the transference of consciousness (*powa*).
57. Tushita (*Ganden*), the Joyous Land, is the pure land of the thousand buddhas of this eon, where Maitreya and Lama Tsongkhapa reside.
58. See a brief explanation of powa in chapter 8. For more on powa see Lama Yeshe's *Powa: The Transference of Consciousness at the Time of Death*, https://www.lamayeshe.com/article/chapter/chapter-6-transference-consciousness (accessed August 30, 2022), or Lama Yeshe's *Life, Death and After Death* (Yeshe 2010).
59. An eleventh-century yogi and guru of Marpa, and author of *The Six Yogas of Naropa*.
60. The Karmapa is the head of the Kagyü lineage. The tradition of the Karmapa was founded in 1110. The current Karmapa, His Holiness Gyalwa Karmapa Ogyen Trinley Dorje, is the seventeenth incarnation.
61. Taken from Pabongka 2006, 304.
62. Quoted in Pabongka 2006, 301.
63. Translation from Lamrim Chenmo Committee 2000–2004, 1:147. The three realms are the desire realm, the form realm, and the formless realm. We live in the desire realm (*kamadhatu*; *döpai kham*), the realm dominated by the senses. By a very advanced level of concentration, meditators can be reborn in the form realm (*rupadhatu*; *sukkyi kham*), with seventeen levels of gods, or even the formless realm (*arupya-*

dhatu; sukmékyi kyi kham) where there is no form, only the four mental aggregates and ever-increasing levels of concentration, the most subtle being the "peak of samsara."

64. See the online glossary of LamaYeshe.com for a comprehensive list of the major marks.
65. See also Zopa and McDonald 2010, 52, and Pabongka 2006, 344, and a slightly different version of the quote in *Mahaparinibbana Sutta, The Buddha's Last Days*, in Walshe 1995, 270.
66. For a biography of Geshé Lama Konchog and an image of his relics, visit kopanmonastery.com/about-kopan/our-lineage/geshe-lama-konchok (accessed October 15, 2024). The 2008 documentary film *Unmistaken Child* provides an inspiring account of the search for Lama Konchog's reincarnation by his attendant Tenzin Zopa.
67. Although Marpa and Dagmema are often depicted in the stories as a married couple, acting "ordinary" in the way they lived, they were great practitioners and as his "secret wife" or consort, Dagmema was pivotal in Marpa achieving enlightenment.
68. Gomchen-la, Ngawang Norbu Gomchen Gampala, (1901–85), was a great meditator and the incarnation of the renowned fifteenth-century Tibetan lama Tangtong Gyälpo.
69. A small hand drum used in tantric practice.
70. Trijang Rinpoché (1901–1981), the late junior tutor of the Fourteenth Dalai Lama and root guru of Lama Yeshe and Lama Zopa Rinpoche. His Holiness also edited *Liberation in the Palm of Your Hand*.
71. A disciple of Atisha, Ben Gungyal was a robber before he renounced his life of crime and took monastic ordination.
72. Ch. 4, v. 48; Gómez forthcoming.
73. For the meditation, see appendix 1 and McDonald 1984, 69–79.
74. In *Friendly Letter*, verse 99, Nagarjuna described five signs thus:

    The color of his body becomes ugly,
    his throne no longer pleases him,
    his flower garlands wilt,
    his clothes become stained and smelly,
    and his body sweats for the first time.

    From Kangyur Rinpoché 2005, 67.
75. Pervasive compounding suffering is the most subtle of the three types of suffering, referring to the nature of the five aggregates, which are contaminated by karma and delusions.
76. Quoted in Sopa 2004–17, 2:346.
77. Snake-like beings of the animal realm who live in or near bodies of water; they are commonly associated with the fertility of the land but can also function as protectors of religion.
78. Quoted in Pabongka 2006, 305. A pratyekabuddha ("solitary realizer"; Tib., *rang sangyé*) is a Hinayana practitioner who strives for nirvana in solitude without relying

on a teacher, whereas a shravaka ("hearer"; Tib., *nyenthö*) is one who relies on a teacher.

79. Pabongka Rinpoche says instead that the people were hidden in a palace in the sun (Pabongka 2006, 306).
80. Ch. 2, v. 39; Gómez forthcoming.
81. Buxa Duar, in Northeast India, was a British fort and prison where Mahatma Gandhi and Jawaharlal Nehru were imprisoned. Starting in 1959, it served as a refuge camp for Tibetans—especially monks and nuns—fleeing the Chinese invasion. The Buxar Transit Camp soon became a temporary monastic center, where refugee lamas from many of Tibet's major monasteries established temporary monastic quarters and study centers.
82. Ch. 6, v. 72; Gómez forthcoming.
83. Vv. 73 and 74. Taken from Dilgo Khyentse 1992, 207.
84. Quoted in Lamrim Chenmo Committee 2000–2004, 1:153.
85. Quoted in Sopa 2004–17, 1:331. Rinpoche has Geshé Kamapa say this to a student, whereas Geshé Sopa has him saying it to himself.
86. Phabongkha 2023, 3–4. (Phabongkha is an alternate spelling for Pabongka.)
87. Phabongkha 2023, 4.
88. See chapter 8 for an explanation of the death process.
89. Phabongkha 2023, 5.
90. Phabongkha 2023, 9.
91. Phabongkha 2023, 10.
92. According to Vasubandhu's *Abhidharmakosha* (*Treasury of Knowledge*), in Buddhist cosmology there are four worlds or continents surrounding Mount Meru: The eastern continent, Purvavideha, whose sky is white rather than blue as ours is, a reflection of that side of the mountain, which is silver. We humans live in the southern continent, Jambudvipa; its sky is blue because it faces the south face of Mount Meru, which is made of lapis lazuli. The sky of the western continent, Aparagodaniya, is red due to Mount Meru's western face, which is made of rubies, and the northern continent, Uttarakuru, has a yellow sky and ocean, a reflection of the golden face of the mountain.
93. Quoted in Sopa 2004–17, 1:339. (An eon is an incredibly long period of time. The lifespan of the universe is four great eons, divided into twenty lesser eons.)
94. V. 317. Hopkins 1998, 136.
95. Ch. 2, vv. 34–36; Batchelor 2011.
96. Rinpoche is referring to Teresa Knowlton, the twenty-one-year-old from Seattle who was murdered by the notorious Charles Sobhraj in October 1975.
97. A tutor to the Eighth Dalai Lama, he lived from 1713 to 1793.
98. This is the biggest Shiva complex in the world, consisting of 518 temples.
99. The FPMT center in Delhi. At the time Rinpoche is speaking about, it was in Shantiniketan.
100. One of the first and largest of the FPMT centers, situated in the Lake District, in the north of England. It operated between 1976 and 1983.
101. See Zopa 2012, 169–92.

102. See chapter 8 on the death process, where the four elements are explained.
103. For most of Rinpoche's students, this paragraph will make tough reading, remembering that day in 2023 when the texts started arriving saying Rinpoche had died. "Suddenly departed to peace—what a great loss!" as His Holiness the Dalai Lama says in the swift return prayer he wrote for Rinpoche.
104. Ch. 2, vv. 59–60; Gómez forthcoming.
105. Strictly speaking, *reincarnation* refers to a soul or *atman*—something eternal—taking on a new body after death, and so *rebirth* is more exact for the process described here. In Tibetan Buddhism, *reincarnation* refers more specifically to bodhisattvas choosing to be reborn, but since it is the term generally used in the West to denote passing from one life to another and is very commonly used by Rinpoche in this context, I have kept it.
106. See Stevenson 2001.
107. Kyabjé Zong Rinpoché (1905–84) was a powerful Geluk lama renowned for his wrathful aspect and his great learning.
108. See appendix 3 for a chart of the death process. See also Lati Rinbochay and Hopkins 1985 for a detailed explanation.
109. In the tantric model there are five types of wind: the life-bearing wind, the upward-moving wind, the pervasive wind, the fire-dwelling wind, and the downward-voiding wind. See Lati Rinbochay and Hopkins 1985, 14.
110. Lati Rinbochay says, "A little blood and phlegm emerge from the nose and/or the sexual organ—these being the unrefined portions of the drops that have dissolved at the heart." See Lati Rinbochay and Hopkins 1985, 45–46.
111. A focal point of energy or energy wheel in the central psychic channel, where the various energy channels come together. There are five main ones in the body: at the crown, the throat, the heart, the navel, and the tip of the sexual organ.
112. This topic is also covered extensively in Zopa 2009. There is also a CD of mantra recitations by Lama Zopa.
113. A small statue of a buddha, usually made from a mold in clay or plaster.
114. Rinpoche has taught extensively on purification practices and on the four opponent powers. For instance, see *Purifying with the Four Powers* from the LYWA website: lamayeshe.com/article/purifying-four-powers (accessed September 8, 2022). Also see the four powers with a Vajrasattva practice in Zopa 2022, 115–34.
115. The eight Mahayana precepts are one-day vows to abandon killing; stealing; lying; sexual contact; intoxicants; high seats; eating at the wrong time; and singing, dancing, and wearing perfumes and jewelry. They are called Mahayana precepts because the ceremony comes from a lineage of *kriya* (action) tantra, not from the Pratimoksha or Vinaya lineage.
116. In some highest yoga tantra practices, a practitioner can regularly take a self-initiation—that is, re-initiate themselves into the practice of the deity—after completing a long retreat with a fire puja.
117. So called because they are so heavy they cause you to be born in hell "immediately"—in the very next life. The five immediate negativities are killing your mother, father,

or an arhat; causing disunity among the Sangha; and maliciously causing blood to flow from a buddha.

118. For more on the five powers see "Dying Happily with the Five Powers" in Zopa 2022, 6–16, and Zopa 2008a, 83–115, and Zopa and McDonald 2010, 58–61.
119. Ch 6, v. 93; Gómez forthcoming.
120. Lama Zopa Rinpoche has taught many times on how self-cherishing is the source of all problems. See particularly Zopa 2001 and Zopa 1994.
121. Ch. 6; v. 42; Gómez forthcoming.
122. For Rinpoche's teachings on tonglen see on the LYWA website teachings such as *The Wish-Fulfilling Golden Sun of Mahayana Thought Training*, lamayeshe.com /article/chapter/meditation-seven-seven-techniques-mahayana-cause-and-effect -part-iii-bodhisattvas (accessed October 16, 2024), and *The Preliminary Practice of Tong-len*, lamayeshe.com/article/preliminary-practice-tong-len (accessed August 9, 2022).
123. Rinpoche has taught extensively on helping dying people and many books of his teachings have been published. Of particular interest is *Heart Advice for Death and Dying* and *Heart Practices for Death and Dying*, collections of talks and practices issued by the FPMT and available either as a series of free downloads or to buy as a hardcopy set. We have included much of *Three Articles on How to Help the Dying and the Dead* as appendix 2, but also available are *The Bodhisattva's Confession of Moral Downfalls*, *The Method of Benefiting Sentient Beings at the Time of Death: Giving Breath to the Wretched*, *The Heart of the Perfection of Wisdom Sutra*, *The King of Prayers*, *Powerful Mantras for the Time of Death*, *Medicine Buddha Sadhana*, and *The Concise Essence Sutra Ritual of Bhagavan Medicine Buddha called The Wish-Fulfilling Jewel.* Also of importance is the *Liberation Box: Tools for a Fortunate Rebirth*, a collection of powerful mantras on cards and recitations to be said, which is available from the Foundation Store on the FPMT website: shop.fpmt.org/Liberation-Box-Tools-For -a-Fortunate-Rebirth--Digital-Edition_p_2416.html (accessed September 18, 2022). See the bibliography for other books on the subject.
124. Ch. 4, v. 17; Gómez forthcoming.
125. The ten great mantras are (1) the mantras of Chenrezig, (2) the Medicine Buddha mantra, (3) the Wish-Granting Wheel mantra, (4) the mantra of Mitukpa Buddha, (5) the mantras of Namgyalma, (6) Padmasambhava's mantra, (7) the mantra of Kunrik, (8) Milarepa's mantra, (9) the Zung of the Exalted Completely Pure Stainless Light, and (10) the mantras of Maitreya Buddha. See FPMT 2010, Zopa 2000b, or Zopa 2022, 209–16.
126. The *Bardo Thodröl*, literally *Liberation Through Hearing During the Intermediate State* but more commonly referred to as the *Tibetan Book of the Dead*, is a detailed description of the intermediate state, designed to be read aloud at the corpse of the dead person in order to help the intermediate-state being through the bardo experience.
127. The four seals, the basic tenets that define Buddhism, are that (1) all compositional phenomena are impermanent, (2) all contaminated phenomena are by nature suffering, (3) all phenomena are empty of self-existence, (4) and nirvana is true peace.

128. Gampopa Sonam Rinchen (1079–1153), the "sun-like" disciple of Milarepa, guru of the First Karmapa and author of *The Jewel Ornament of Liberation*, was also called Dagpo Lahje (the physician from Dagpo).
129. Taken from Zopa 1984, 51. Also available as Khenpo Konchog Gyaltsen Rinpoche 1998.
130. FPMT 2024, 79.
131. Of the four philosophical schools within Mahayana Buddhism, the Middle Way (Madhyamaka) school is said to hold the most subtle views on emptiness, and of the two subschools within the Middle Way, the Consequentialist (Prasangika) school is said to be subtler than even the Autonomist (Svatantrika) school.
132. Taken from FPMT 2024, 112.
133. Taken from Zopa and McDonald 2010, 51.
134. Woodville Rockhill 1975, 4.
135. These two articles are from a booklet entitled *Three Articles on How to Help the Dying and the Dead* by Lama Zopa Rinpoche (the third is essentially the nine-point death meditation), available from FPMT 2010. This advice from Lama Zopa Rinpoche was compiled from various occasions of advice and teachings on the subject.
136. Advice Rinpoche gave to the staff of Tara Home, an FPMT hospice established in Soquel, California, USA. Extracted from *How to Benefit the Dying and Dead*: www.lamayeshe.com/article/how-benefit-dying-and-dead (accessed October 24, 2004).
137. Taken from *Death, Intermediate State and Rebirth in Tibetan Buddhism*, Lati Rinbochay and Hopkins 1985, 16–18

BIBLIOGRAPHY

Sutras (Listed by English Title)

Collection of Verses from the Buddhist Canon (*Udanavarga*). Available in Woodville Rockhill, 1975.

The Heart Sutra (*Prajnaparamitahridayasutra*; *Sherab kyi pharöl tu chinpai nyingpö do*). Available in several languages at FPMT n.d.

The Play in Full. Available at 84000: Translating the Words of the Buddha 2013.

Indian and Tibetan Texts

Aryadeva. *Four Hundred Stanzas* (*Catuhshataka shastranamakarika*; *Tenchö shi gyapa shejawai tsik leur jepa*). Available as Rinchen 2008.

Gampopa. *The Jewel Ornament of Liberation* (*Damchö yizhin norbu tharpa rinpoché gyen*). Available as Khenpo Konchog Gyaltsen Rinpoche 1998.

Nagarjuna. *Precious Garland* (*Ratnavali*; *Rinchen Trengwa*). Available as Hopkins, 2007.

———. *Friendly Letter* (*Suhrllekha*; *Bshes pa'i spring yig*). Available as Kangyur Rinpoche 2005.

Padmasambhava. *The Tibetan Book of the Dead (Bardo Thödröl).* Available as Gyurme Dorje 2006.

Shantideva. *A Guide to the Bodhisattva's Way of Life* (*Bodhisattvacharyavatara*; *Jangchup sempai jöpala jukpa*). Available as Gómez forthcoming; Batchelor 2011; Wallace 1997; Padmakara Translation Group 2006.

Tsongkhapa. *The Great Treatise on the Stages of the Path to Enlighten-*

ment (*Lamrim Chenmo*). Available as Lamrim Chenmo Translation Committee 2000–2004.

———. *A Hymn of Experience* (*Lamrim nyamgur*). Available in FMPT 2020, 258–66.

English-Language Texts

84000: Translating the Words of the Buddha. 2013. *The Play in Full: Lalitavistara*. Accessed September 16, 2024. https://84000.co/translation/toh95.

Batchelor, Stephen. 2011. *Guide to the Bodhisattva's Way of Life*. Dharamsala, India: Library of Tibetan Works and Archives.

Capra, Fritjof. 1988. *Uncommon Wisdom: Conversations with Remarkable People*. New York: HarperCollins Publishing.

Dilgo Khyentse Rinpoche. 1992. *The Heart Treasures of the Enlightened Ones: The Practice of View, Meditation, and Action*. Boston: Shambala Publications.

Dilgo Khyentse Rinpoche and Padampa Sangye. 2006. *Hundred Verses of Advice: Tibetan Buddhist Teachings on What Matters Most*. Boston: Shambala Publications.

FPMT. N.d. "Sutras and Dharanis." Accessed September 16, 2024. https://fpmt.org/education/prayers-and-practice-materials/sutras/#heart-sutra.

———. 2020. *FPMT Retreat Prayer Book*. Portland OR: FPMT.

———. 2024. *FPMT Essential Prayer Book*. Portland OR: FPMT.

Gómez, Luis O., trans. Forthcoming. *Guide to the Bodhisattva's Way of Life*. Boston: Wisdom Publications.

Gyurme Dorje, trans. 2006. *The Tibetan Book of the Dead: The Great Liberation by Hearing in the Intermediate States*. Edited by Graham Coleman and Thupten Jinpa. London: Viking.

Hopkins, Jeffrey, trans. and ed. 2007. *Nagarjuna's Precious Garland*. Ithaca, NY: Snow Lion Publications.

Jinpa, Thupten, trans. 2006. *Mind Training: The Great Collection*. Boston: Wisdom Publications.

Kangyur Rinpoche. 2005. *Nagarjuna's Letter to a Friend.* Translated by Padmakara Translation Group. Ithaca, NY: Snow Lion Publications.

Konchog Gyaltsen Rinpoche, Khenpo, trans. 1998. *The Jewel Ornament of Liberation: The Wish-Fulfilling Gem of the Noble Teachings.* Ithaca, NY: Snow Lion Publications.

Lamrim Chenmo Translation Committee. 2000–2004. *The Great Treatise on the Stages of the Path to Enlightenment (Lamrim Chenmo).* 3 vols. Ithaca, NY: Snow Lion Publications.

Lati Rinbochay and Jeffery Hopkins. 1985. *Death, Intermediate State and Rebirth in Tibetan Buddhism.* Ithaca, NY: Snow Lion Publications.

Marcello, Patricia M. 2003. *The Dalai Lama, a Biography.* Westport, CT: Greenwood Press.

Pabongka Rinpoche. 2006. *Liberation in the Palm of Your Hand* (*Namdröl lakchangs*). Translated by Michael Richards. Boston: Wisdom Publications. Also published as *Liberation in Our Hands* (three parts). 1990–2001. Translated by Geshé Lobsang Tharchin and Artemus B. Engle. Howell: Mahayana Sutra and Tantra Press.

Padmakara Translation Group, trans. 2006. *The Way of the Bodhisattva.* Ithaca, NY: Shambhala Publications.

Phabongkha Rinpoche. 2023. *The Heart's Utmost Need: Urging Myself and Others to Remember Impermanence.* Portland, OR: FPMT.

Rabten, Geshe. 1984. *The Essential Nectar: Meditations on the Buddhist Path.* London: Wisdom Publications.

Rinchen, Geshé Sonam. 2001. *The Thirty-Seven Practices of the Bodhisattvas.* Translated by Ruth Sonam. Ithaca, NY: Snow Lion Publications.

———. 2008. *Aryadeva's Four Hundred Stanzas on the Middle Way.* Translated by Ruth Sonam. Ithaca, NY: Snow Lion Publications.

Sopa, Geshe Lhundub. 2004–17. *Steps on the Path to Enlightenment.* 5 vols. Boston: Wisdom Publications.

Wallace, Alan and Vesna. 1997. *Guide to the Bodhisattva's Way of Life.* Ithaca, NY: Snow Lion Publications.

Walshe, Maurice, trans. 1995. *The Long Discourses of the Buddha: Digha Nikaya.* Somerville, MA: Wisdom Publications.

Woodville Rockhill, William. 1975. *Udanavarga: A Collection of Verses from the Buddhist Canon Compiled by Dharmatrata*. Amsterdam: Oriental Press.

Zopa Rinpoche, Lama. 1976. *The Wish-Fulfilling Golden Sun*. Boston: Lama Yeshe Wisdom Archive. See lamayeshe.com/article/wish-fulfilling-golden-sun-mahayana-thought-training. Accessed October 16, 2024.

———. 1994. *The Door to Satisfaction: The Heart Advice of a Tibetan Buddhist Master*. Boston: Wisdom Publications.

———. 2001. *Transforming Problems into Happiness.* Boston: Wisdom Publications.

———. 2008a. *Heart Advice for Death and Dying*. Portland: FPMT.

———. 2008b. *Heart Practices for Death and Dying*. Portland: FPMT.

———. 2009. *Liberating Animals from the Danger of Death*. Portland: FPMT.

———. 2012. *How to Practice Dharma: Teachings on the Eight Worldly Dharmas.* Boston: Lama Yeshe Wisdom Archive.

———. 2013. *The Perfect Human Rebirth: Freedom and Richness on the Path to Enlightenment*. Boston: Lama Yeshe Wisdom Archive.

———. 2022. *The Power of Mantra: Vital Practices for Transformation.* Somerville, MA: Wisdom Publications.

Zopa Rinpoche, Lama and Kathleen McDonald. 2010. *Wholesome Fear: Transforming Your Anxiety about Impermanence and Death.* Boston: Wisdom Publications.

Suggested Further Reading

Bokar Rinpoche. 1993. *Death and the Art of Dying in Tibetan Buddhism.* San Francisco: ClearPoint Press.

Buckman, Robert. 1989. *I Don't Know What to Say: How to Help and Support Someone Who Is Dying*. Boston: LittleBrown.

Callanan, Maggie and Patricia Kelley. 1992. *Final Gifts: Understanding the Special Needs and Communications of the Dying.* New York: Poseidon.

Carr, Christopher. 1993. "Death and Near Death: A Comparison of

Tibetan and Euro-American Experiences," *Journal of Transpersonal Psychology* 25, no. 1:59–110.

Didion, Joan. 2007. *The Year of Magical Thinking*. New York: Knopf.

Gyatso, Tenzin, the Fourteenth Dalai Lama. 2005. *The Universe in a Single Atom*. New York: Morgan Road Books.

Gyatso, Tenzin, the Fourteenth Dalai Lama, and Jeffrey Hopkins. 2002. *Mind of Clear Light: Advice on Living Well and Dying Consciously*. New York: Atria Books.

Kapleau, Philip, ed. 1989. *The Wheel of Life and Death*. New York: Doubleday.

Kübler-Ross, Elisabeth. 1969. *On Death and Dying*. New York: Macmillan.

———. *To Live Until We Say Goodbye*. 1978. Englewood Cliffs, NJ: Prentice Hall.

Levine, Stephen. 1982. *Who Dies? An Investigation into Conscious Living and Conscious Dying*. Garden City, NY: Doubleday.

———. 1987. *Healing into Life and Death*. Garden City, NY: Doubleday.

Lodo, Lama. 1985. *Bardo Teachings*. Ithaca, NY: Snow Lion Publications.

Longaker, Christine. 1997. *Facing Death and Finding Hope*. New York: Doubleday.

Mackenzie, Vicki. 1988. *Reincarnation: The Boy Lama*. London: Bloomsbury Publications.

———. 1995. *Reborn in the West: The Reincarnation Masters*. London: Bloomsbury Publications.

McDonald, Kathleen. 1984. *How to Meditate: A Practical Guide*. Boston: Wisdom Publications.

Sogyal Rinpoche. 2002. *The Tibetan Book of the Living and Dying*. San Francisco: HarperCollins.

Mullin, Glenn. 1986. *Death and Dying: The Tibetan Tradition*. London: Arkana.

Stevenson, Ian. 2001. *Children Who Remember Previous Lives: A Question of Reincarnation*. Jefferson, NC: McFarland.

Stoddard, Sandol. 1991. *The Hospice Movement: A Better Way to Care for the Dying*. New York: Random House.

Visuddhacara. 1993. *Loving and Dying.* Penang: Malaysian Buddhist Meditation Centre.

Yeshe, Lama Thubten. 2010. *Life, Death and After Death.* Boston: Lama Yeshe Wisdom Archive.

Zopa Rinpoche, Lama. 2020. *How to Face Death without Fear.* Somerville, MA: Wisdom Publications.

———. 2022. *Helping Yourself and Others Die Happily: Instructions and Practices for the Time of Death.* Portland, OR: FPMT.

INDEX

K

L

ABOUT THE AUTHOR

Lama Zopa Rinpoche (1945–2023) is one of the most internationally renowned masters of Tibetan Buddhism, who worked and taught ceaselessly on almost every continent for fifty years. He was the spiritual director and cofounder of the Foundation for the Preservation of the Mahayana Tradition (FPMT), an international network of Buddhist projects, including monasteries in six countries and meditation centers in over thirty; health and nutrition clinics, and clinics specializing in the treatment of leprosy and polio; as well as hospices, schools, publishing activities, and prison outreach projects worldwide. Lama Zopa Rinpoche is the author of numerous books, including *Patience*, *The Six Perfections*, *Bodhichitta*, *The Four Noble Truths*, *Transforming Problems into Happiness*, *How to Enjoy Death*, *Ultimate Healing*, *The Door to Satisfaction*, *How to Be Happy*, *Wholesome Fear*, *Wisdom Energy*, and *Dear Lama Zopa*, all from Wisdom Publications.

About the Editor

Gordon McDougall was director of Cham Tse Ling, the FPMT's Hong Kong center, for two years in the 1980s and worked for Jamyang Buddhist Centre in London from 2000 to 2007. He helped develop the Foundation of Buddhist Thought study program and administered it for seven years. Since 2008 he has been editing Lama Zopa Rinpoche's teachings for Lama Yeshe Wisdom Archive and Wisdom Publications.

WHAT TO READ NEXT FROM WISDOM PUBLICATIONS

Patience
A Guide to Shantideva's Sixth Chapter
Lama Zopa Rinpoche

"Often in the West we think that patience is passive aggression: waiting for that horrible thing to go away. Lama Zopa Rinpoche shows us in great detail how to cultivate actual patience, the practice of the bodhisattva: wholeheartedly welcoming the problems. Rinpoche's powerfully experiential teachings give us the confidence to know that we can do it, too."
—Ven. Robina Courtin

The Six Perfections
The Practice of the Bodhisattvas
Lama Zopa Rinpoche

"A jewel of a book, containing much practical advice on how we can start working on these six precious practices, even if we are not yet bodhisattvas."
—Sangye Khadro (Kathleen McDonald), author of *How to Meditate*

Bodhichitta
Practice for a Meaningful Life
Lama Zopa Rinpoche

An accessible, inspiring book on one of the most important topics in Tibetan Buddhism, written by one of its renowned masters.

The Four Noble Truths
A Guide to Everyday Life
Lama Zopa Rinpoche

The Buddha's profound teachings on the four noble truths are illuminated by a Tibetan master simply and directly, so that readers gain an immediate and personal understanding of the causes and conditions that give rise to suffering as well as the spiritual life as the path to liberation.

How to Be Happy
Lama Zopa Rinpoche

"Rinpoche works with determination and great sincerity in the service of Buddha's teachings and sentient beings."
—His Holiness the Dalai Lama

Transforming Problems into Happiness
Foreword by His Holiness the Dalai Lama
Lama Zopa Rinpoche

"A masterfully brief statement of Buddhist teachings on the nature of humanity and human suffering. . . . This book should be read as the words of a wise, loving parent."
—*Utne Reader*

How to Face Death without Fear
A Handbook by Lama Zopa Rinpoche

"The reality of death is an important opportunity for spiritual transformation. Kyabje Lama Zopa Rinpoche's combined teachings and practices lead the reader to an understanding of this reality and help the person who is dying to achieve a better future life. Rinpoche's clarity and blessings will be tremendously beneficial."
—Yangsi Rinpoche, president, Maitripa College

Ultimate Healing
The Power of Compassion
Lama Zopa Rinpoche

"This truly is an awesome book."
—Lillian Too

Bliss of Inner Fire
Heart Practice of the Six Yogas of Naropa
Lama Thubten Yeshe
Foreword by Lama Zopa Rinpoche

"An impressive contribution to the growing body of Buddhist literature for an English-reading audience."
—*The Midwest Book Review*

How to Meditate
A Practical Guide
Kathleen McDonald

"Jewels of wisdom and practical experience to inspire you."
—Richard Gere

The Power of Mantra
Vital Practices for Transformation
Lama Zopa Rinpoche
Compiled and edited by Gordon McDougall

Beloved teacher Lama Zopa Rinpoche guides us through the most popular mantras in Tibetan Buddhism: Shakyamuni Buddha, Chenrezig, Manjushri, Tara, Medicine Buddha, Vajrasattva, and more.

The Power of Meditation
A Complete Guide to Transforming Your Mind
Lama Zopa Rinpoche

In *The Power of Meditation*, Lama Zopa Rinpoche, beloved teacher and co-founder of the Foundation for the Preservation of the Mahayana Tradition, offers clear explanations and instructions for the life-changing practice of meditation.

Wisdom

About Wisdom Publications

Wisdom Publications is the leading publisher of classic and contemporary Buddhist books and practical works on mindfulness. To learn more about us or to explore our other books, please visit our website at wisdom.org or contact us at the address below.

Wisdom Publications
132 Perry Street
New York, NY 10014 USA

We are a 501(c)(3) organization, and donations in support of our mission are tax deductible.

Wisdom Publications is affiliated with the Foundation for the Preservation of the Mahayana Tradition (FPMT).